HIGH TIMES

An Unofficial and
Unauthorised Guide
to *Roswell*

By the same author:

SLAYER: THE REVISED AND UPDATED UNOFFICIAL GUIDE TO *BUFFY THE VAMPIRE SLAYER*

HOLLYWOOD VAMPIRE: THE UNOFFICIAL GUIDE TO *ANGEL*

By the same author with Paul Cornell and Martin Day:

THE NEW TREK PROGRAMME GUIDE

X-TREME POSSIBILITIES

THE AVENGERS DOSSIER

By the same author with Martin Day:

SHUT IT! A FAN'S GUIDE TO 70S COPS ON THE BOX

HIGH TIMES
An Unofficial and Unauthorised Guide to *Roswell*

Keith Topping

First published in Great Britain in 2001 by
Virgin Books Ltd
Thames Wharf Studios
Rainville Road
London
W6 9HA

A catalogue record for this book is available from the British
Library.

ISBN 0 7535 0630 0

Typeset by TW Typeseting, Plymouth, Devon
Printed and bound in Great Britain by
Mackays of Chatham PLC

High Times is for
Suzie Campagna.
God only knows what I'd be without you.

And Diana Dougherty
my 'voodoo sister'.

And Alyson and Zack Topping.

Acknowledgements

I would like to thank the following friends and colleagues for their help and inspiration during this project: Ian Abrahams, Becki Ablett, Greg Bakun, Rebecca Barber, Wendy and Paul Comeau (and Laura), Martin Day, Rob Francis, Robert Franks, the *Godlike Genius* of Jeff Hart, Mike Lee, Liz Mortenson, Ingrid Oliansky, Trina Short, Dan Smiczek, Jim Smith, Jim Swallow, Lily Topping, Jason Tucker and Mark Wyman. I cannot fail to mention Colin, Maureen, Graeme, Terry and Gudi *again*. So I won't. Also, school bullies everywhere – especially those in their thirties.

In particular, my gratitude to Joanne Brooks my former editor at Virgin, who had so much faith in this project (and many others), and Kirstie Addis who finished the job. To all at *www.crashdown.com* for their invaluable assistance (see 'Roswell and the Internet'). Paul Simpson and Kathy Sullivan, again, provided research materials and sanity way above-and-beyond the call of duty. And Susannah Tiller, who once again found the time in her busy life to proofread my work. You're a *star*.

Suggested soundtrack for this book: PJ Harvey, Delerium, the Chemical Brothers, Oasis, Beth Orton, James, R.E.M., the Smiths, Kraftwerk and Dido (inevitably). *High Times* was written on location in Newcastle-upon-Tyne, North Hollywood and Van Nuys.

Enough of the self-indulgence . . .

Contents

1947 And All That . . .

A bit of *necessary* background . . .

North of the border, down New Mexico-way, Roswell is a one-horse town in the empty expanse of the American South West, midway between Tuscon and Waco. A place that could have, literally, been dragged from the frames of a John Ford western. Population 50,000, nothing remarkable *ever* happened in Roswell. Until 1947 that is, when *something* remarkable is *alleged* to have happened close to it. And from that moment on the very name of the town itself has become synonymous with what has been described as 'a cosmic Watergate'.

In the summer of 1947, Roswell was home to the US Air Force's 509 bombardment group, which carried America's first-strike nuclear warheads. It was a tight-knit community of military personnel and civilians in the heartland of rural America. On 3 July, Mac Brazel, a foreman at the Foster Ranch 75 miles north of the town, found some scattered debris that seemed metallic. Brazel drove into Roswell and showed what he had found to Chaves County sheriff George Wilcox. Wilcox called Roswell Airfield and talked to Major Jesse Marcel, the base's intelligence officer. Marcel inspected the wreckage then reported to his commanding officer, Colonel William Blanchard, who ordered Marcel to gather as much of the material as possible. Soon after this, military personnel arrived at the sheriff's office to collect the items Brazel had left, which were then flown to Air Force headquarters in Fort Worth. Meanwhile, Blanchard authorised Lieutenant Walter Haut, an information officer, to issue a press release claiming that the Air Force had found the remains of a crashed 'flying saucer'. Haut delivered the release to Frank Joyce at radio station KGFL, along with Roswell's other radio station and the town's two newspapers. Joyce sent the story on the

Western Union wire to the United Press bureau and, by 8
July, the story had appeared in newspapers all around the
world, even making the pages of the *Daily Telegraph*,
which described the object as a 'flimsy construction almost
like a box-kite'. However, on the afternoon of 8 July,
General Roger Ramey held a press conference, with
Marcel, in Fort Worth, at which he announced that what
had crashed was actually a weather balloon. And *that*
(despite much local tradition of military interference and
suspicious goings-on) was the end of the matter as far as
the rest of the planet was concerned.

Until 1978 that is, when a now-retired Marcel told his
story in public for the first time on US TV's *Eyewitness
News*. Suddenly, Roswell was back in the limelight and a
series of sensationalist books appeared. Many witnesses
emerged claiming to know fragments of what had gone on
during those five days. About how an alien craft (or two)
had crashed in the desert. How a number of small
dome-headed alien corpses were found and brought to a
local hospital for autopsy. And how the military went to
great lengths to protect these secrets, threatening those
with knowledge of the events, if they revealed what they
knew. By the early 90s, the Pentagon had reinvestigated the
incident and issued a report which suggested that the
weather balloon fiasco was in reality a cover story, and
that the debris was actually part of a highly-classified
operation called Project Mogul, concerning radiation de-
tection. Other theories abounded: that the craft was
actually an early US rocket, designed by Werner Von
Braun's team at White Sands, and that the 'alien creatures'
onboard were chimpanzees, like those publicly sent into
space a decade later. In 1995, video footage of what was
claimed to be the autopsy of one of the aliens was released
by a British company to much debate (and in most
quarters, derision). Genuine article or elaborate hoax?
Truth or humbug? (as *The X-Files* episode 'Jose Chung's
From Outer Space' memorably parodied it.) As author and
TV writer Jim Swallow notes in the article 'The Spoof is
Out There: The Roswell Incident and Other Fairy Stories':

'The fog of claim, counterclaim and theory-upon-theory about the event has helped to muddy the waters so much that it is likely we'll never know what happened . . . Even the few remaining people who were there probably aren't sure any more.'

The rumours, however, were just the inspiration that earth-based alien encounter SF needed. It is, perhaps, no coincidence that at almost the exact moment that the Roswell incident became public property, in 1978, *Close Encounters of the Third Kind* was taking the idea of aliens away from the 'blond men in silver jumpsuits from *Star Trek*' image, and moving it towards grey creatures with domed heads and large black eyes.

Science fiction fans had a new icon to play with.

Based on the book *UFO Crash at Roswell*, a 1994 TV Movie, *Roswell*, told the story of Jesse Marcel (played by Kyle MacLachlan) and his thirty-year search for the truth behind the government's web of secrecy. The incident also provided a basis for the TV series *Dark Skies*, which pitted its hero, John Loengard, against the dark forces of the mysterious Majestic-12 group, set up by President Truman in response to the Roswell incident. Even more importantly, Roswell was a key conceptual element in the investigations of FBI Agents Mulder and Scully in *The X-Files*, a series that mixed SF's often wide-eyed innocence, and gentle aliens from utopian planets, with a hard-edged paranoia and post-Watergate mistrust of officialdom. And, more importantly, one that got a decent-sized audience.

It was inevitable that, sooner or later, a TV series would take on Roswell the town, rather than just its most famous event. A popular series of teenage novels by Melinda Metz had already put an interesting twist on the Roswell legend, by wondering what would have happened if the aliens had stayed and had children as part of the small-town American dream. *Roswell* is the story of how hyper-intelligent teenager Liz Parker (Shiri Appleby) and her friends Maria (Majandra Delfino) and Alex (Colin Hanks), become involved with three other (rather mysterious) students, Max Evans (Jason Behr), his sister Isabel

(Katherine Heigl) and their friend Michael (Brendan Fehr). And how these six odd bedfellows have their lives changed by a series of earth-shattering incidents, and must then keep their newly discovered secrets from town sheriff Jim Valenti (William Sadler) and his son, Liz's (soon-to-be-ex) boyfriend, Kyle (Nick Wechsler), their own parents and new school counsellor, the sinister Ms Topolsky (Julie Benz).

With an experienced crew, *Roswell* was an immediate cult hit on WB Network in the US, fitting in nicely alongside other shows aimed at the teenage years like *Dawson's Creek*, *Felicity* and *Popular*. But the series it most closely resembles, for obvious reasons, is the WB's jewel in the crown, *Buffy the Vampire Slayer*. And, whilst *Roswell* could be said to lack some of the quick-fire humour of Sunnydale's finest, it does possess its own quietly confident wit and amusing characters. If you can imagine a slightly more moody and paranoid version of *Buffy* with elements of *The X-Files* and *Twin Peaks* mixed-in, then you'll have a pretty good idea of what to expect from *Roswell High*.[1]

'One of the exciting things about the premise is that the three alien characters don't have a history,' series creator Jason Katims told Candace Havens. 'From a writing point of view it's exciting because, as they discover their back-story, the audience is discovering it with them. We have a way of doing it that will be personal and, hopefully, very emotional.' And, of course, at the heart of *Roswell* is a love story, Katims noting that he always wanted to write a *Romeo and Juliet*-type scenario. 'If you want to do a contemporary story about young people, it's hard to find a real obstacle,' he notes. 'I think that the fact they are

---

[1] A note of explanation about the title for season one to avoid confusion: The series is called *Roswell* in the US, but *Roswell High* for most overseas broadcasts (including the UK). The reason for this, seemingly, is that the producers were unsure whether anyone outside of the US would know what 'Roswell' was and, by adding 'High', at least assured potential viewers that the series concerned a school. The series is also called just *Roswell* in Canada and New Zealand.

different life-forms gives you a *real* obstacle. As teenagers we are *all* aliens.'

Background

Roswell is easily the most interesting of the very attractive breed of *Buffy*-alike TV series to have emerged from the US over the last half-decade. And, as the success of both *Buffy* and its spin-off show *Angel* has ably demonstrated, such series as these usually very quickly acquire a knowledgeable and vocal young fanbase. Mostly with Internet access, these viewers appreciate well-written, intelligent and humorous TV on subjects that are both fantastical and yet also (often by metaphor) deal with issues that have a direct relevance to their own lives. As Tony Atherton of the *Ottawa Citizen* notes: 'In the 1990s, full-blown fantasy series – *Buffy*, *Charmed*, *Angel*, *Xena: Warrior Princess* and *Roswell* – have proved themselves capable of commanding a loyal cult following, while attracting more than their share of media attention. These are important attributes in a TV environment where the viewing choices are so numerous, it's easy for a program to get lost. When conventional dramas are embroidered with elements of fantasy, they are also trying to set themselves apart, to brand themselves.'

Roswell proved such an instant critical hit in the US that it was rapidly acquired in Britain by the satellite/digital broadcaster Sky (who began showing it whilst *Roswell*'s first season was still running in America – something that they hadn't done with a new US series since *The X-Files* six years previously). The BBC bought the terrestrial rights in 2000 and the series has slipped nicely into an early Thursday evening time slot. Along with series such as *Buffy*, *Xena* and *The X-Files*, *Roswell* has also brought an interesting new audience to mainstream Telefantasy, covering a wide demographic and gender range that the genre had always struggled to acquire. Put simply, 'normal' people seem to like these shows.

Hence, this book. A handy, but fun, episode guide to the first two seasons of *Roswell*, together with interview extracts, cast and crew biographies, a look at the novels that spawned the series and a study of *Roswell* fandom on the Internet.

Roswell is, at its best, as good as just about anything on television at the moment. True, its occasional (ambitious, let it be said) attempts to straddle two vastly different genres can lead to gross miscalculations (such as the series' worst episode, **14**, 'Blind Date', for instance). *Roswell*'s aloofness in form and subject matter can often be its salvation, though sometimes the feeling of grim certainty in what it is doing renders it a touch gauche next to, for example, *The X-Files*' groundbreaking and urbane recontextualisation, and completely anaemic compared to the sophisticated metaphors of *Buffy the Vampire Slayer*. Nevertheless, there is much to admire here. The following categories will help to explain why.

Headings

'Dear Diary . . .': The world, as recorded in Liz Parker's journal.

Roswell Iconography: Aspects of Roswellian-lore, SF clichés and traditional conspiracy theory voiced or subverted by the series.

High School Life: A necessary look at what's going on in the classroom.

Dudes and Babes: A meditation on the pretty girls and boys that flit across our screens.

'You Might Remember Me from Such Films and TV Series As . . .': A category that hopefully answers all of those annoying 'where have I seen his/her face before?' questions.

References: Generation X, pop-culture or plain esoteric. All of the references that make the average viewer go 'huh?'

Teen-Speak: For those who, like, *totally* don't understand what's being said. *You know*?

Sex and Drugs and Rock'n'Roll: For a television series about sixteen-year-old schoolkids, there's an awful lot of references to all three.

Logic, Let Me Introduce You to This Window: Goofs, gaffs and the bits of the episodes that require far too much thinking about.

Quote/Unquote: Dialogue that's worth rewinding the video for.
Other categories will appear occasionally, most should be self-explanatory. Each episode concludes with a review and copious notes on continuity and other general trivia. So, get out a bottle of Tabasco sauce to go with your popcorn and enter the world of West Roswell high school.

Remember, *they're here*.

Keith Topping
His Gaff
Planet Earth
June 2001

List of Episodes

First season

1. Pilot
2. The Morning After
3. Monsters
4. Leaving Normal
5. Missing
6. 285 South
7. River Dog
8. Blood Brother
9. Heatwave
10. The Balance
11. The Toy House
12. Into the Woods
13. The Convention
14. Blind Date
15. Independence Day
16. Sexual Healing
17. Crazy
18. 'Tess, Lies & Videotape'
19. Four Square
20. Max to the Max
21. The White Room
22. Destiny

Second Season

23. Skin and Bones
24. Ask Not
25. Surprise
26. Summer of '47
27. The End of the World
28. The Harvest
29. Wipe-Out!
30. Meet the Dupes
31. Max in the City
32. The Miracle [AKA: 'A Roswell Christmas Carol']
33. To Protect and Serve
34. We Are Family
35. Disturbing Behavior
36. How the Other Half Lives
37. Viva Las Vegas
38. Heart of Mine
39. Cry Your Name
40. It's Too Late, And It's Too Bad
41. Baby, It's You
42. Off the Menu
43. The Departure

'There is truth to every rumour'

Roswell – Season One (1999–2000)

**Jason Katims Productions/Regency Television/
20th Century Fox**
Developed by Jason Katims
Producers: Phillip M Goldfarb (1), Barry Pullman (2–13),
Carol Dunn Trussell (2–22)
Co-Producers: Tracey D'Arcy (2–22), Emily Whitesell
(2–13), Gordon Wolf (16–22)
Consulting Producers: Jon Harmon Feldman (2–22),
Toni Graphia (13–22)
Co-Executive Producer: Thania St John (2–22)
Executive Producers: Jonathan Frakes, Lisa J Olin,
Kevin Kelly Brown, David Nutter (2–15), Jason Katims

Regular Cast:
Shiri Appleby (Liz Parker)
Jason Behr (Max Evans)
Brendan Fehr (Michael Guerin)
Katherine Heigl (Isabel Evans)
Majandra Delfino (Maria DeLuca)
Colin Hanks (Alex Whitman, 1–3, 5, 8–14, 16–22)
William Sadler (Sheriff Jim Valenti, 1–4, 6–7, 9, 11–13,
15, 17–22)
Nick Wechsler (Kyle Valenti, 1–9, 11–12, 14, 18–19, 22)
John Doe (Jeffrey Parker, 1, 4, 9, 12, 16)

Michael Horse (Deputy Owen Blackwood, 1–2, 6–7)
Jason Peck (Deputy Hanson, 1–2, 9, 12–13, 20)
Wendle Josepher (Jennifer Kattler, 1, 13)
Kevin Weisman (Larry Trilling, 1, 13)
Richard Schiff (Special Agent John Stevens, 1[2], 2, 7)
Yolander Lloyd Delgado (Ms Hardy, 1, 3, 9)
Jonathan Frakes (Himself, 1[3], 13[4])
Channing Carson (Young Liz, 1[5], 16)
Zoe K Nutter (Young Isabel, 1[6], 10–11, 19)
Daniel Hansen (Young Max, 1[7], 10–11, 19)
Joe Camareno (Paramedic, 1, 8)
Julie Benz (Agent Kathleen Topolsky, 2–8, 17)
Mary Ellen Trainor (Diane Evans, 2, 3[8], 7–8, 11, 15–16, 18)
Robert F Lyon (Hank Whitmore, 2, 12, 15)
Ebonie Smith (Genoveve, 2–3)
Steve Hytner (Milton Ross, 3, 5–7, 10, 12–13)
Zack Aaron (Heavy Metal Kid, 3, 8)
Jo Anderson (Nancy Parker, 4–5, 16)
Richard Anthony Crenna (Agent Baxter, 5–8[9])
Robert Neary (Moss, 5, 8)
Ned Romero (River Dog, 7, 10, 12)
Tod Thawley (Eddie, 7, 10)
Diane Farr (Amy DeLuca, 9, 13, 15)
Dan Martin (Principal, 9, 16)
Nicholas Stratton (Young Michael, 10, 17[10], 19)
Garrett M Brown (Philip Evans[11], 12, 15–16)
Ted Rooney (Mr Whitman, 12)
John Cullum (James Valenti Snr, 12–13)

---

[2] Uncredited in **1**, 'Pilot'.

[3] Uncredited in **1**, 'Pilot'.

[4] Uncredited in **13**, 'The Convention'.

[5] Credited in **1**, 'Pilot' as 'Liz at 7 Years'.

[6] Credited in **1**, 'Pilot' as 'Isabel at 7 Years'.

[7] Credited in **1**, 'Pilot' as 'Max at 7 Years'.

[8] Uncredited in **3**, 'Monsters'.

[9] Credited as 'Baxter' in **5**, 'Missing' and **7**, 'River Dog'.

[10] Uncredited in **17**, 'Crazy' (this is a 'flashback'-scene drawn from **10**, 'The Balance').

[11] The character of Philip Evans was played by a different actor, Michael O'Neill, in **2**, 'The Morning After'.

Robert Katims (Judge Lewis, 15)
Fernando Negrette (Hispanic Man/Nasedo, 15–16)
Michael Chieffo (Mr Seligman, 16, 18)
Kevin Cooney (Doctor Malcolm Margolin, 17–18)
Emilie de Ravin (Tess Harding, 17–22)
David Conrad (Agent Daniel Pierce, 17[12], 20–22)
Jim Ortlieb (Ed Harding/Nasedo, 18–22)
Stephen O'Mahoney (Agent Morris, 20–21)
Jacob Bruce (Agent Samuels, 20[13], 21–22)
Gunnar Clancey (Agent Bello, 21[14], 22)

1
Pilot

US Transmission Date: 6 October 1999
UK Transmission Date: 10 January 2000 (Sky One),
7 September 2000 (BBC2)

Writer: Jason Katims
Director: David Nutter
Cast: Vance Valencia (Mayor Sandler)
French title: *Révélations*

Liz Parker is a highly intelligent sixteen-year-old schoolgirl
from UFO mecca Roswell, working part-time as a waitress
at her parents' diner, The CrashDown, with her feisty
friend Maria. One evening, she is shot during an argument
involving two customers. As Liz lies, dying, on the floor
her life is saved by a mysterious 'laying-on-of-hands' by
brooding teenage loner, Max Evans. Liz keeps Max's gift
a secret from everyone else but, when she confronts him
later, he is forced to reveal that he, his sister Isabel, and

---

[12] Uncredited and in voice-over only in **17**, 'Crazy'.
[13] Credited as 'Man in Suit' in **20**, 'Max to the Max'.
[14] The role of Agent Bello in **21**, 'The White Room' was also played
during the scenes in which Nasedo assumes Bello's form by Bo Clancey
(Gunnar Clancey's twin brother).

their friend Michael Guerin are not from 'around here'. They are from ... 'Up there'. Abandoned on Earth after crashing in an alien spaceship, they are living as everyday teenagers. In order to lead normal lives, this unlikely alliance must band together to keep the affair secret. To do so, they must outwit their adoptive families, friends and a local sheriff intent on exposing the truth about them. With Liz and Maria's help, Max, Isabel and Michael lay a trap to throw Valenti off their trail.

'Dear Diary ...': 'September 23rd. Journal entry one. I'm Liz Parker and five days ago I died. After that, things got really weird ...' As a framing device for the episode, the use of entries into Liz's journal in voice-over works quite well, although within a couple of episodes it was obvious that its limitations outweighed its strengths (see **5**, 'Missing').

'I've Got the Power': Max: 'You use your powers all the time.' Isabel: '*Recreationally*!'
   Liz asks Max what powers he has, to which he replies: 'We can manipulate molecular structures.' When Max touches Liz, he experiences a connection, a flashback to her in kindergarten wearing a dress with cupcakes on it that her mom made (it was the single supreme embarrassment of Liz's life). Liz later confirms that she didn't meet Max until they were in third grade. Max says 'I don't read minds. When I healed you, I made this connection and I got this rush of images ...' With the connection established, when they touch again, Liz experiences similar flashes from Max's psyche, seeing herself through his eyes. Isabel can listen to a CD without using a machine to play it and heat food with her hand (see **4**, 'Leaving Normal', and **24**, 'Ask Not').

Roswell Iconography: Liz's opening line at The CrashDown is: 'I've got one Sigourney Weaver and one Will Smith. Can I get you anything else? Green Martian Shake? Blood-of-Alien Smoothie?' The tenth annual Crash Festival in Roswell is taking place in a town that seems quite happy to play-up the alien angle for tourist purposes (see **13**, 'The Convention'). There is a $500 prize for Best Costume. Liz has an obviously fake 'alien photograph' that she occasionally shows to the foolish or the unwary in The CrashDown, in this case Jen and Larry. Liz tells them that her grandmother 'took this picture at the crash site right before the government cleaned it up' (see **4**, 'Leaving Normal').

Max tells Liz that when the ship crashed in 1947, he wasn't born ('all I know is it wasn't a weather balloon that fell that night'). Max, Isabel and Michael were in 'some kind of incubation pods' (see **6**, '285 South', **19**, 'Four Square', **26**, 'Summer of '47'). Michael confirms that they don't come from 'this solar system'. Isabel thinks: 'It's only a matter of time before they find us and turn us over to some government agency where they're gonna test us and *prod* us and exterminate us.'

In one of the pilot's most pointed scenes, the festival is crawling with people in alien costumes who watch a mock spaceship crash on the ground. Max, Michael and Isabel watch this, made outsiders in the crowd by the fact that they are seeing a tawdry representation of their own violent arrival on Earth. Excellent.

The Conspiracy Starts at Home Time: Agent Stevens tells Valenti: 'I have a flying saucer sighting in Phoenix. An accountant in Barstow who thinks he's Jesus. Both cases are more solid than this.' Valenti has clearly been in contact with the agency before, since he knows that if he sees anything strange he should call them. His father was nicknamed 'Sergeant Martian' by Stevens's people. Valenti notes: 'I was eight years old when my father discovered that corpse. My whole life I thought he was as crazy as everyone else did. Crazy to believe. Now I'm not so sure.' Valenti shows Liz a photo of the corpse his father found on or around 16 November 1959, with the same silver handprint on the chest that Max's laying-on-of-hands caused on Liz's stomach (see **13**, 'The Convention').

High School Life: West Roswell High's motto is 'Pathway to Excellence and Integrity'. The school football and/or basketball team is called The Roswell Comets (in US high schools it is quite common for all school sports teams to have the same name). In Biology, the class have spent the last week talking about genus and phylum. Liz is also taking a US Government class. Pupils need a pass to go to the bathroom, which seems a touch unconstitutional.

Dudes and Babes: You can, literally, hear the sound of every female in the vicinity swooning each time Max or Michael is on-screen. What is it about monosyllabic, hunky, brooding teenagers that make them so attractive? And whatever it is, can the rest of us have some?

'You Might Remember Me from Such Films, TV Series and Pop Music Videos As . . .': Minnesota-born Jason Behr appeared in a star-making role as Buffy Summers' exboyfriend Billy Fordham in *Buffy the Vampire Slayer*, played Chris Wolfe in *Dawson's Creek* and Tyler Baker in *Sherman Oaks*. Other guest roles include TV series as diverse as *JAG*, *Profiler* and *Push*. Jason was also in the movies *Rites of Passage*, *Pleasantville* and *The Shipping News*. Shiri Appleby first appeared on TV as a four-year-old in a Cheerios commercial. Her CV includes episodes of *7th Heaven*, *ER*, *Xena: Warrior Princess* (as Tara), *thirtysomething* and *Doogie Howser, MD* and films such as *Perfect Family*, *The Thirteenth Floor* (as Bridget) and *I Love You to Death* (as Millie). She also appeared in Bon Jovi's video for 'It's My Life'.

Canadian Brendan Fehr's debut came on *Breaker High*, whilst his other TV credits include *Millennium*, *Every Mother's Worst Fear*, *Perfect Little Angels* and *The New Addams Family*. He also featured in movies such as *Disturbing Behavior*, *The Forsaken*, *Christina's House* and *Final Destination*. Daughter of a Venezuelan father and Cuban mother, Majandra Delfino was a pre-teen star with the Miami Ballet and, at eleven, joined an all-girls singing quartet named China Doll. Her acting debut came in the movie *Zeus and Roxanne*, and she also appeared in *Shriek If You Know What I Did Last Friday the 13th*, *Traffic*, *The Secret Life of Girls* (as Natalie Sanford) and *The Learning Curve*.

Katherine Heigl made her acting debut as a twelve-year-old in *That Night* (alongside Juliette Lewis and *Buffy*'s Eliza Dushku) and went on to appear opposite Gérard Depardieu as Nicole in *My Father the Hero*, *Bride of Chucky* (as Jade), *King of the Hill*, *Wish Upon a Star* (as Alexia Wheaton), *Under Siege 2*, *Valentine* (as Shelley Fisher) and *Prince Valiant*. On TV, Heigl starred as Miranda alongside Peter Fonda in *The Tempest*. Colin Hanks has previously appeared in a small role in *that thing you do!*, directed by and starring his Oscar-winning father, Tom. Colin's other movies include *Whatever it Takes* (as Cosmo), *Get Over It* and *Orange County*. Nick Wechsler can be seen in *Team Knight Rider* (as 'Trek'), *The Lazarus Man* and the film *Chicks, Man*.

In a thirty-year acting career William Sadler has played an extraordinary range of roles. Classically trained on the New York stage (where he won numerous awards for his performance as Sergeant Toomey in *Biloxi Blues*), his movie work includes memorable roles as the villainous Colonel Stuart in *Die Hard 2*, Heywood in *The Shawshank Redemption* and the Grim Reaper in *Bill and Ted's Bogus Journey*. He's also in *Disturbing Behavior* (as Dorian Newberry), *Trespass*, *Rocket Man*, *Rush*, *The Green Mile* (as Klaus Detterick), *Skippy*, *Freaked*, *K-9* and *Witness Protection* and appeared on TV in *Roseanne*, *Murphy Brown*, *St Elsewhere*, *The Outer Limits*, *Tales from the Crypt* and as Sloan in *Star Trek: Deep Space Nine*. Michael Horse shot to fame as 'Hawk' in *Twin Peaks*. He's also been in *The X-Files* and movies such as *Navajo Blues*, *House of Cards*, *Passenger 57* and *Deadly Weapon*.

John Doe was in *Forces of Nature*, *Black Cat Run*, the San Fernando Valley comedy *Boogie Nights*, *Scorpion Spring*, *Great Balls of Fire!*, *Slam Dance* and *Salvador*. Before becoming an actor Doe was bassist, singer and songwriter with legendary Los Angeles punk band X. Jason Peck played Benji in *George Lucas in Love*. Wendle Josepher was in *Edtv*, *Twister* and *Last Action Hero* and, on TV, the US version of *Men Behaving Badly*, *Mad About You* and *Ellen*. Kevin Weisman's movies include *Robbers*, *Gone in Sixty Seconds* and *Man of the Century*, whilst he can also be seen in *Felicity, Buffy, Frasier* and *Just Shoot Me* on TV. Vance Valencia's movie work includes *Die Hard 2, Contact, Reform School Girls, I, Madman* and *I Know My First Name is Steven*. Richard Schiff (who appears in the pilot uncredited) is a veteran of numerous films including *Stop! Or My Mom Will Shoot, Se7en, Speed, Hoffa, Malcolm X, Heaven, Doctor Dolittle* and *The Lost World: Jurassic Park* (as Eddie Carr). On TV, he's been in *NYPD Blue, Ally McBeal* and *LA Law*. Readers will probably know him best for his Emmy award-winning performance as Toby Ziegler in *The West Wing*.

Behind the Camera: Creator and producer Jason Katims has previously worked as story editor on *My So-Called Life* and producer of *The Pallbearer*. 'Ed Zwick, who was producer of *My So-Called Life*, read one of my plays and called me and said, "Do you want to write for television?" ' Katims told an online interview. 'I got on a plane, and I've been in LA ever since.' Director David Nutter's work includes the movie *Disturbing Behavior* and, on TV, episodes of *Millennium, Space: Above and Beyond, The X-Files, Dark Angel* and *21 Jump Street*.

Executive Producer Jonathan Frakes, who appears briefly on-screen as himself (see **13**, 'The Convention') is probably the most famous name associated with *Roswell*, instantly recognisable as Commander Will Riker on *Star Trek: The Next Generation* and various spin-offs (several of which, including the movies *Star Trek: First Contact* and *Star Trek: Insurrection*, he directed). He was also Ben Frye in *Brothers of the Frontier*, Stan Hazard in *North and South* and appeared in TV series as diverse as *3rd Rock from the Sun, Gargoyles, Married . . . with Children, Matlock, Highway to Heaven, Remington Steele, Quincy, Hill Street Blues, The Dukes of Hazzard, The Waltons, Hart to Hart* and *Fantasy Island*, together with a lucrative sideline as the host of the numerous 'factual' TV documentaries like *Beyond Belief: Fact or Fiction?, The Alien Autopsy* and *The Paranormal Borderline*. He directed the movie *Clockstoppers* and episodes of *Diagnosis Murder*.

Roswell's original music is variously provided by Joseph Stanley Williams and WG Snuffy Walden. Williams is also an actor, appearing in movies such as *Poison Ivy II*, *Snitch* and *Phat Beach*, providing the voice for the adult Simba in *The Lion King* and he was the musical arranger on *Return of the Jedi*. An Emmy-nominated composer on series such as *Early Edition*, *My So-Called Life*, *thirtysomething*, *The West Wing* and *Felicity*, Walden was also guitarist/musical director for acts as diverse as Chaka Khan, Laura Brannigan, Donna Summer and former Animals singer/songwriter Eric Burdon.

References: Name-checks for SF-icons Sigourney Weaver (*Aliens*) and Will Smith (*Men in Black*, *Independence Day*), *Beavis and Butt-head* and Roger Corman's *Not Of This Earth*. Liz dresses as a Klingon at the Crash festival. *Romeo and Juliet* allusions abound, from the premise of galaxy-crossed lovers to Michael's Mercutio-like character, plus the scene where Max calls to Liz and she looks down from the roof.

Teen-Speak: Maria: 'You are *so* bad, girl. Max Evans is staring at you again.' Liz: '*No way*. That is *so* in your imagination.'
 Ms Hardy: 'High maintenance today, aren't we?'
 Liz: 'Maria is a *total* drama queen.'

Fashion Victims: The CrashDown waitress uniforms qualify easily, as does Jen's goth-style black lipstick, Alex's checky shirt and Maria's horrible Technicolor blue top.

Sex and Drugs and Rock'n'Roll: Maria sniffs Cypress oil which, she says, reduces stress. Kyle plays the drums, rather ineptly.

Logic, Let Me Introduce You to This Window: Do the aliens need Tabasco sauce to live, or do they simply *like* spicy food? And, if so, is *that* why the ship landed (specifically) in New Mexico? It's probable that the government removed the crashed spaceship in 1947; if that were the case, how did the pods containing Max, Isabel and Michael survive unnoticed? (A question finally answered in **26**, 'Summer of '47'). Isabel's hair changes style between scenes on more than one occasion. The voice-over in the teaser identifies Liz's diary as 'entry number one'. Didn't she think her life before this point was interesting enough to chronicle? Alex reads the *Roswell Daily Record*, the headline of which is SHOOTOUT AT THE SHAKE DOWN. It should, of course, be CrashDown. Isn't it odd that both the Crash Festival here and the UFO convention seen in **13**, 'The Convention', are the tenth annual events. As though Roswell only realised that there was money in the UFOs in or around 1990? As the excellent Greystone Communications/History Channel documentary *UFO: Then and Now?* (2000) pointed out, Space Craft and Flying Saucer conventions have been popular in the US since the mid-50s (one in June 1954, in Giant Rock, attracting 5,000 attendees). During the gunfight, one of the protagonists drops his cap but it's back on his head a moment later. A bottle of Tabasco sauce mysteriously appears in Michael's hands at The CrashDown when Max had it a split second earlier. Liz's necklace keeps appearing and disappearing. Max's healing of Liz also seems to remove the blood from her bra! Liz tells Kyle that she has a mid-term exam, although it's obviously a lie. Kyle must be really stupid to be taken in by it, as who has mid-terms in September? Jason Behr seems to make Katherine Heigl laugh during one dialogue scene but she manages to carry on with the next line. Max uses his left hand to heal Liz, and in doing so leaves his silver handprint. But when she goes home and takes off the uniform, the handprint is from a right hand, with the thumb pointing down. They must serve horrid lukewarm coffee at The CrashDown as Maria holds the coffee pot with her hand supporting the bottom. The specimens that Liz looks at are not what you would usually prepare in a high school science lab. The first, especially, is a complex tissue sample of cells, not of just the few shed in the cheek that can be sampled with a toothpick.

Quote/Unquote: Maria: 'The guy with the gun was kind-of like a muscular Beavis. The other one was like a beefy Butt-head.' Deputy Owen: 'I'm gonna need a better description than that. I'm assuming they weren't *actually* cartoons.'

Maria: 'What happened to you? You were on this whole like, valedictorian path. You were on your way to be this world-renowned scientist and I was gonna be your wacky friend. I can't be a wacky friend to someone who's already wacky. It'd be, like, repetitious . . .'

Alex, on Isabel's revealing costume: 'Nice cones.'

Notes: 'It's September 24th, I'm Liz Parker and five days ago I died. But then the really amazing thing happened. I came to life.' A very effective pilot that sets up the characters nicely and displays a keen sense of (often very dry) humour. Excellent performances by all of the young cast (especially Delfino, who quickly gained a cult following for her hippychick-role, and the quietly impressive Hanks). And a sinister yet also haunted turn from the great Bill Sadler. A very promising beginning, albeit with a rather pat *Scooby Doo*-style ending. Best bit: Liz asking Maria not to flip out as she prepares to tell her about the aliens and the following reaction shot of Maria running (screaming) out of the diner.

The Parker family have lived in Roswell for four generations (see **26**, 'Summer of '47'). Liz is currently dating Valenti's son Kyle (though the implication is that *he* is more committed to the relationship than she is. See **2**, 'The Morning After'). She admits to Maria that she hates an (unseen) girl called Pam Troy. Michael indicates that Mr and Mrs Evans found Max and Isabel 'on the side of the road', which is contradicted in later episodes (see **11**, 'The Toy House'). Michael's stepfather, he says, 'just keeps me around for the monthly cheque' (see **15**, 'Independence Day'). In New Mexico, a person can have a driving licence at the age of fifteen, so there's no incongruity in the fact that Maria can drive and uses her mother's Jetta. Max, Isabel and Michael drive around in Max's Jeep.

Subsequent episodes reveal that Michael can drive and that both Kyle and Alex have their own cars. Max's driving licence number is 1111Z1409 and it expires on 15 February 2001. His address is in Newton Avenue, Roswell (see **21**, 'The White Room'). The Parkers live at house number 152.

Premiering on 6 October 1999, *Roswell* enjoyed a phenomenally strong opening night. Surpassing its lead-in show, *Dawson's Creek*, *Roswell* attracted 6.72 million viewers. The figure was the second highest audience ever for a WB show, behind the 7.7 million who watched the 1998 pilot of *Charmed*. The episode took twelve days to shoot, though some scenes were subsequently edited out of the aired pilot, including a lengthy chase scene. These were put to good use in both the title sequence and in several promotional trailers for the show. It was anything but love at first sight for Majandra Delfino and Brendan Fehr. During the filming of the pilot sparks, literally, flew between them. 'I hated Brendan [at first]. He was like "Girls have cooties . . .".' Majandra even asked Jason Katims not to put them in any scenes together!

Soundtrack: The series' wonderfully moody theme song is 'Here With Me' by British singer Dido Armstrong, though it isn't actually used until episode two. Sarah McLachlan's 'Fear', Dave Matthews Band's 'Crash Into Me', Eagle Eye Cherry's 'Save Tonight', 'Hey Man, Nice Shot' by Filter, 'I Think I'm Paranoid' by Garbage and 'Boys on the Radio' by Hole.

Cast and Crew Comments: Although Jason Katims originally intended that Sheriff Valenti should serve as the nemesis to the show's teenage protagonists, producer David Nutter was quick to note: 'Our goal is not to make William Sadler the "black hat". Our goal is to give him another dimension and a sense of purpose that he needs to find out,' he told *DreamWatch*. 'I think that journey can be an exciting and compelling, fulfilling one for him as well.' Katims added: 'Finally we'll see some sort of sea-change in his attitude. He's very single-minded and determined to get to the bottom of this mystery at the beginning, because of his father's being chastised for believing in aliens.'

Critique: TV critic Tim Goodman enjoyed the pilot, with reservations: 'This is a fine year for television and if a show has a weakness, a structural fault, it'll be exposed pretty quickly. *Roswell* is a quirky little show that works hard to defy the pigeon-holing tendencies of critics, but it's clear that someone thought fusing *The X-Files* with *Dawson's Creek* was a great idea. In fact, it *is* a great idea . . . *Roswell* succeeds in making you care about what might happen to these teens. What it doesn't do so well is make that point with an exclamation mark. You *want* to care. There's much to like. Max and Liz clearly are going to be soul mates, even though he doesn't technically have a soul. Still, who can resist romance? There's the whole panic-inducing cover-up, the relentless sheriff and a good dose of subtle alien humour. But the pilot has more potential than pop. And in the current TV landscape, no show can afford to let viewers slide.'

Miami Herald's Terry Jackson was more positive: 'Three seasons ago, it was *Buffy*. Two seasons ago, it was *Dawson's Creek*. Last season, it was *Felicity*. Can the WB make it a four-peat this fall and score another hit show that uniquely captures teen-angst and action? Bet on it. Specifically, bet on *Roswell*, a charmingly-odd hourlong drama that ties two very popular TV genres: alien conspiracies and teen romance. It's just strange enough to work.'

Did You Know?: When filming started the actors insisted they could handle eating Tabasco sauce. But it soon became apparent that they couldn't. 'We used the real stuff and tried to be men about it,' Jason Behr told *Dolly* magazine. 'First take our eyes started to water. By the end of the scene we were sweating and shaking. That's why we don't use real Tabasco sauce any more.' The 'sauce' used is, in reality, V8 juice.

2
The Morning After

US Transmission Date: 13 October 1999
UK Transmission Date: 17 January 2000 (Sky One),
14 September 2000 (BBC2)

Writer: Jason Katims
Director: David Nutter
Cast: Michael O'Neill (Philip Evans),
Reggie Hayes (Agent Hart),
Christopher Holloway (Paul Aronson),
Marc Brandon Daniel (Boy in Class),
Paul Goebel (Heavy Set Customer),
Debra Connolly (Customer)
French title: *Soupçons*

Liz tries to continue her relationship with Kyle, but finds it difficult as she becomes more interested in Max. Several newcomers appear in town, including the alluring yet sinister Kate Topolsky, a Geometry substitute who lacks any great maths skill, but sports a photographic memory, and who seems very interested in Michael. Michael himself is obsessed with a recurring (and disturbing) vision, and he goes to dangerous lengths to find out what it might mean. Meanwhile, Valenti is frustrated when the FBI interferes in his investigation.

'Dear Diary . . .': 'September 27th. I'm Liz Parker and I will never look at the stars in the sky the same way again.' Liz wonders what Max means when he says, 'I'll see you in school?' 'Was it "I won't be able to breathe until we meet again" or was it just something someone says to, like, fill space?' She questions if he is also obsessed, tortured, 'going through one sleepless night to the next, wondering what's going to happen between us?'

'I've Got the Power': Michael possesses the ability to disable the jail's security system, whilst Max later fuses shut the metal bars on Valenti's window.

Roswell Iconography: Liz is confused. 'If you crash-landed in 1947, are you really sixteen or are you fifty-two in a sixteen-year-old's body? Or do you guys just age different-ly? Is one alien year equal to three human years?' she asks Max, who replies: 'You've thought about this a lot, haven't you? We know we came out of the pods in 1989. We just don't know how long we were there. When we came out we looked like six-year-olds.'

The Conspiracy Starts at Home Time: Agent Stevens tells Valenti that amongst the substances found on Liz's dress were: 'tomatoes, salt, water, sugar, vinegar. Ketchup, sheriff, no blood. We've wasted enough taxpayer dollars to try to find something that isn't out there. I've been given the authority by the governor to search the premises to remove any information pertaining to UFOs, alien sight-ings and other alleged paranormal occurrences in this county.' Valenti doesn't believe him, reasoning that unless blood *had* been found on the dress, Stevens wouldn't be removing his files and wasting *more* taxpayer dollars.

High School Life: Mr Singer is the Geometry teacher and Miss Topolsky says that she is substituting for him. But she doesn't know the difference between the number of degrees in a circle and a triangle. *Come on!* Ten-year-olds know *that* . . . She later claims to be the new Guidance Counsellor (another lie, see **6**, '285 South').

Dudes and Babes: Kate Topolsky. *Foxy! Lady!*

'You Might Remember Me from Such Films and TV Series As . . .': Mary Ellen Trainor appeared in all four *Lethal Weapon* movies (as Stephanie Woods), *Anywhere But Here*, *Executive Decision*, *Congo*, *Forrest Gump*, *Death Becomes Her*, *Die Hard*, *Romancing the Stone*, *Ghostbusters II* and *Kuffs*. She played Mrs Lewis in one of this author's favourite US series, the seminal 90s high school comedy *Parker Lewis Can't Lose*, and also guested on *Remington Steele*, *Crazy Like a Fox* and *Cheers*.

Former ice-skater Julie Benz (once rated twelfth in the US) unsuccessfully auditioned for the role of Buffy

Summers in 1996, but was rewarded with the semi-regular part of Darla, Angel's vampire sire, on both *Buffy* and *Angel*. She also appeared in movies like *Satan's School for Girls*, *Jawbreaker* and *A Fate Totally Worse Than Death*.

Michael O'Neill was Father Jansen in *Days of Our Lives* and was also in *The Mod Squad*, *Sea of Love*, *The West Wing* and *Ghost Story*. Reggie Hayes appeared in *Being John Malkovich*. Ebonie Smith was Carrie Murtaugh in the *Lethal Weapon* movies, played La Toya Jackson in *The Jacksons: An American Dream* and Susie Matthews in *General Hospital*. Marc Brandon Daniel was 'Sharkey' Alvarez in *Hypernauts*. Paul Goebel played Johnny Bosco in *Hey Anthony* and Fat Joey in *The Deal*.

Behind the Camera: Stunt coordinator Steve M Davison has worked as a stunt man on a stunning variety of movies including *Gone in Sixty Seconds*, *End of Days*, *The X-Files* movie, *Jackie Brown*, *Mulholland Falls*, *Waterworld*, *True Lies*, *La Bamba*, *Beverly Hills Cop*, *Scarface* and *Smokey and the Bandit II*. He was second unit director on *Serial Mom* and has acted in *TJ Hooker* and *Grease 2* (as the Cycle Lord). His stunt colleague, and brother, Tim Davison, has a movie CV that is equally impressive: *The Green Mile*, *The Astronaut's Wife*, *Volcano*, *From Dusk Till Dawn*, *Patriot Games*, *Die Hard 2*, *To Live and Die in LA* and *Rumble Fish*. He also had a small acting role in *Kuffs*.

References: Maria alludes to Samantha's powers in *Bewitched* ('How do we know they can't just, like, wiggle their noses and *poof* us into oblivion?'), namechecks Madonna and she thinks that Alex isn't exactly James Bond. Isabel refers to physicist Albert Einstein (1879–1955). She tells Valenti that she is Max's 'sister, not his keeper', a misquote from the biblical story of Cain and Abel (Genesis 4:9) and claims to have seen singer Ricky Martin 'in the shower'. Liz's locker contains a sticker for teenage pop stars B*witched. Topolsky says 'if Mohammed doesn't come to the mountain . . .'

Teen-Speak: Girl: 'Okay, that is *totally* not Mr Singer.'
   Liz, to Max: 'You're such a jerk.'

Michael: 'The fact that my life basically *sucks* is a good thing.'

Fashion Victims: Check out Liz's silly astronomy trousers. Isabel's orange T-shirt would be the best thing on display but for her later leopardskin top and extremely tight black skirt.

Sex and Drugs and Rock'n'Roll: Maria claims the reason that she and Liz continually change the subject whilst Alex is around is that they have cramps. And he definitely doesn't want to hear such graphic details whilst he's eating. Maria says that the second floor eraser room, at school, is where Greg Coleman gave Marlene Garcia 'that hickey the size of a softball' and where Ritchie Roher and Amanda Lourdes 'consummated everything' ... The eraser room, she continues, does two things: 'Cleans erasers and *takes our innocence* ... The eraser room has taken some of the best of us.' This suggests she has had previous sexual experience (which is flatly contradicted in **15**, 'Independence Day') . Liz claims never to have been in the eraser room before (see **16**, 'Sexual Healing').

When Liz drops her ring to the floor of Max's Jeep and goes looking for it, Kyle seems to assume that she's performing oral sex on Max.

Logic, Let Me Introduce You to This Window: Liz wears different coloured jeans in her first and second school scenes, which seems to indicate a full day has passed. However, her later conversation with Michael suggests otherwise. Why hasn't Michael assumed his foster father's surname, Whitmore? Indeed, where did he get the name Guerin from? Liz's locker contains a sticker for *West* Roswell High and subsequent episodes (e.g. **4**, 'Leaving Normal') confirm that that is, indeed, what their school is called. So, why is the series called *Roswell High* when sold outside the US? When Topolsky is taking the register she reaches Guerin, finds he isn't present, and then immediately starts taking the class without completing the rest of the attendance record. How doesn't Valenti hear Michael and

Max jumping into the dumpster beneath his window. When Liz drops her ring, the soundtrack features her saying 'my ring!' but her lips don't move. Liz tells Maria to 'sniff some Cedar oil'. It should be Cypress oil.

Quote/Unquote: Liz stops Maria from saying 'aliens' in public. Maria: 'The point is that we don't know anything about these *Czechoslovakians*. Are they *good* Czechoslovakians? *Bad* Czechoslovakians? We don't know. Are they just *random* Czechoslovakians? For all we know, they don't have their *passports*!'

Max, on Michael's visit to the police station: 'What was your cover story?' Michael: 'I was selling candies for charity?' Max: 'And they bought it?' Michael: 'No, they all seemed to be on a diet.'

Customer: 'Excuse me, I've been waiting for my hot fudge blast-off for twenty minutes.' Maria: 'Yeah, like *you* need eighty grams of fat.'

Notes: 'The thing about Czechoslovakians that you sorta have to factor in, is they have these incredibly soulful eyes.' A meditation on secrets in which Liz describes herself as 'the smallest of small-town girls' and discovers that everybody has *something* to hide. Events take a sinister turn with the arrival of Topolsky (a truly disturbing performance by the wonderful Julie Benz) and the soap-opera nature of the series clicks nicely into gear. Worthwhile for Maria's rant about the masses demanding 'alien-themed greasy food'.

Liz feels her life is claustrophobic and bemoans her inability to be more invisible in a small town like Roswell. Max says he has the opposite problem. He keeps a baseball bat by his bed. Michael sometimes sleeps on Max's bedroom floor if he and his foster father have been arguing (see **5**, 'Missing'). One of Kyle's friends is called Tommy Hilligan (see **4**, 'Leaving Normal'). Kyle has recently been voted 'Student Athlete of the Month'. His football shirt number is 32. Valenti keeps the 1959 aliens file in his 'N-X' drawer. In the back of the file is the mysterious key (see **7**, 'River Dog') which he hides in his Thermos flask and that

Michael subsequently steals. Topolsky claims to have a photographic memory (Liz notes she has never met anyone with this ability before). Alex says that Czechoslovakia is a country 'that hasn't existed for ten years'. He claims to be double-jointed and can do amazing things with his wrists! Watch out for a poster on the school wall that says 'Live with care, life has no spare.'

This is the first episode to feature the series' impressive title sequence, including the famous 8 July 1947 edition of the *Roswell Daily Record* and its headline RAAF CAPTURES FLYING SAUCER ON RANCH IN ROSWELL REGION.

Soundtrack: 'Honestly OK', by Dido, 'Blank Page', by Smashing Pumpkins, the Cardigans' enormous hit 'My Favourite Game', 'Ladyshave' by Gus Gus and Loni Rose's 'I Never Thought You'd Come'.

Critique: An impressed David Kronke in the *Los Angeles Daily News* noted: 'When a network devotes a quarter of its entire original prime-time schedule to paranormal youth programs, it's either seeking an insanely specific demographic or simply crazy like a network of a different name. In the WB's case, these quirky genre items are among its best shows. *Roswell* is an estimable companion to *Buffy the Vampire Slayer* and *Angel*, more innocent (save a mildly blue sight gag in episode two) and less action-packed but equally concerned with abstruse romantic convolutions. It takes the metaphor of the high-school outsider to literal extremes – some of these kids don't feel like they fit in with their peers because, well, they're a whole other species.'

Did You Know?: The town used for many of the Roswell town exterior locations is West Covina, around twenty miles east of Los Angeles (a popular spot with many films and TV series). 'It's a beautiful little town, a really nice feel to it,' notes Julie Benz. However, 'it's just so far away – it's out in the middle of nowhere. But when you get there [you realise] why they picked this location. It's definitely worth it.' The school used for the West Roswell High scenes is Millikan High School in Long Beach, which is also the location for *Roswell*'s WB stablemate *Popular* and the dryly scatological teen-comedy *American Pie*.

3
Monsters

US Transmission Date: 20 October 1999
UK Transmission Date: 24 January 2000 (Sky One),
21 September 2000 (BBC2)

Writer: Thania St John
Director: David Semel
Cast: Amy Lyndon (Arlene), Daryl Sabara (Corey),
Maria Bembenek (Waitress),
Adam Weisman (Preteen Boy Tourist), Donna
May (Woman Tourist), Christos (Mechanic)
French title: *Le Temps d'un Rêve*

Maria gives Isabel, whose car has broken down on the highway, a lift and they make an unsuccessful attempt at bonding. Then they crash into the back of the sheriff's car. When Maria apologises because her mother makes tacky tourist 'alien' key rings, Isabel replies that 'my mother does stupid things, too'. Later, she reveals another of her powers when she visits Maria in her dreams, in an attempt to find out whether Maria can be trusted. Meanwhile, Topolsky interviews students to find out their career choices. This, she says, will help her get to know them better.

'I've Got the Power': Isabel 'improves' the air conditioning and the sound system in Maria's car, much to Maria's chagrin.

Dreaming is Free: Isabel has the ability to walk into people's dreams. Max indicates that she once did this to her mother and that Mrs Evans didn't go back to sleep for a week. Touching a yearbook picture of Maria, Isabel finds herself in a dream-version of The CrashDown, where she and Max are represented as green-haired aliens. Michael, meanwhile, is in a tuxedo, which Isabel finds 'interesting', before he turns into a monster and wraps a tentacle around Maria's neck. Isabel tells Maria that she is an interloper and cannot change her dreams, merely observe them.

Roswell Iconography: Maria's mother makes hokey plastic alien keychains for the tourists. There's something called the 'Heavenly-Hash Special' on the menu at The Crash-Down.

At the UFO Center, Milton gives the audience an overview of the alleged events in Roswell, stating that the evidence suggests the aliens had been studying humans for some time. On that night in July 1947 'something went terribly wrong, and one, though some say more than one, of the alien crafts crashed onto our planet, starting what was to become one of the most elaborate cover-ups mankind has ever known.' He mentions both eyewitness accounts from people still in Roswell of strange metal debris inscribed with purple hieroglyphs and 'those who on their deathbeds spoke of being present at alien autopsies, and of the threats made . . . if they ever spoke of what they saw.'

Milton later shows Max a photograph of himself as a boy outside an ice cream parlour 'next to that alien shadow'. He says that the UFO Center is 'a tourist-trap cash-cow, but every penny I make goes to my research. Everything you've ever wanted to know about extraterrestrials since 1947', is held in 'the most complete collection of UFO facts and findings ever compiled'. He offers Max a job at the UFO Center (for a 'minimum wage and long hard hours').

The Conspiracy Starts at Home Time: Maria asks Isabel if Mrs Evans knows that she and Max are different. 'You mean horrible disgusting creatures from outer space who sneak into your room at night and perform excruciating experiments?' Max implies to Topolsky that he doesn't remember anything from before he was adopted (though this isn't strictly true, see **10**, 'The Balance', and **11**, 'The

Toy House'). Topolsky tells Max that when she was at college she barely left her dorm for three years. As with much she says, it's probably a lie.

High School Life: Liz tells Topolsky that the first time she walked into a chemistry lab and smelled sulphur, she knew she 'was home'. She says that the world is a mysterious place and science is a way 'of figuring it out. With science, there are answers to everything.'

In Biology, Ms Hardy comments that outside forces are very powerful and that nothing in the universe is immune to them. 'If no man is an island, then no molecule lives in a vacuum. Heat makes them expand, and cold forces them together.'

Dudes and Babes: Isabel thinks that Maria is irrational and Michael agrees that she is 'kinda weird'. Judging from her conversation with Topolsky and her designing of a colour-coordinated shift pattern chart, Liz seems to be something of a control freak.

'You Might Remember Me from Such Films and TV Series As . . .': Stephen Hytner's face will be very familiar from movies like *Love Stinks*, *Face/Off*, *In the Line of Fire* and *The Prophecy* (as Joseph). On TV, he was Bania in *Seinfeld*, Roger Harris in *Herman's Head* and he has also appeared in *Friends*. Amy Lyndon was Lydia in *Slaves of Hollywood*, Miss Hatter in *$40,000* and Ann Spinelli in *Odessa*, a movie she also directed. Daryl Sabara played Roger in *Love & Money* and can be seen in *Spy Kids*. Maria Bembenek appeared in *Shameful Secrets*. As well as being an actress, Donna May was also costume designer on *Cupid*.

Behind the Camera: Thania St John was a writer/producer on *Strange World*, *Crisis Center* and *VR.5*. She co-wrote (with Jane Espenson) the *Buffy* classic 'Gingerbread'. David Semel was a producer on *Dawson's Creek* and *Beverly Hills 90210*, and has directed episodes of, amongst others, *Chicago Hope*, *Malibu Shores*, *7th Heaven*, *Buffy the Vampire Slayer*, *Judging Amy* and *Angel*.

References: When Miss Topolsky asks the class what they think the future will bring for them, Maria tells Liz 'let me just make it easy for her' and, pointing to various classmates, refers to Tasty Freeze, diner chain Denny's, Gas World and prison. Also mentioned, actor Brad Pitt (*Se7en*, *Kalifornia*, *Interview with the Vampire*, *Twelve Monkeys*, *Meet Joe Black*, *Fight Club*), the US gold reserve at Fort Knox and thrash metal band Metallica. Maria calls Isabel Queen Amidala (from *Star Wars Episode 1: The Phantom Menace*). 'No man is an island' is a quote from *Devotions* by poet John Donne (1572–1631). 'Oh ... My ... God' (said exactly like that), is a regular catchphrase on *Friends*. 'Whatever', as a dismissive phrase, was first popularised in the movie *Clueless*.

On the list of students in Topolsky's office is the name John Feldman, probably a reference to Consulting Producer Jon Harmon Feldman. Topolsky owns an Apple Mac. The office has a YOU ARE NOW ENTERING THE LEARNING ZONE poster. Watch out, also, for posters advertising a forthcoming ALIEN CREATURE DOUBLE FEATURE.

Teen-Speak: Liz: 'So you rear-ended Sheriff Valenti, are you okay?' Maria: 'I'm telling you, it was a total fender-bender, minor damage ... It probably would've never happened if Miss Isabel hadn't been playing with my head.'

Isabel: '*Whatever*.'

Fashion Victims: Check out Isabel's red spotty dress. It's certainly much easier on the eye than Alex's nasty brown shirt. Maria's catholic schoolgirl outfit is disturbingly sexy (see **Logic, Let Me Introduce You to This Window**).

Dreams *Can* Come True (But they Usually Don't): When Topolsky asks her students for their dream jobs amongst the answers she gets are: 'Brad Pitt's love slave' (Genoveve); 'Houston Astro's left field' (Kyle); 'lead guitar for Metallica' (Heavy Metal Kid); 'that's an interesting question. Do you always ask it first?' (typical smart-Alex); 'Supermodel' (Isabel); 'Molecular biologist. Or a dream,

dream, dream job would be head of molecular biology research at Harvard' (Liz). Topolsky then asks for the job they *actually* think they'll be doing in ten years. Kyle, Liz and Isabel give the same replies (Isabel: 'I usually get what I want'); Maria says they could all be *dead* in ten years; Alex turns on more of the greasy charm ('excellent follow-up question') whilst Genoveve's reply is 'Cheese factory, I guess', and the Heavy Metal Kid says, confidently 'Video store. No, wait . . . Cheese factory'.

The results of the computer profiles suggest the following careers: Genoveve, writer ('Cool. How hard could *that* be?'); Kyle, law enforcement; Alex, psychologist; Heavy Metal Kid, video store clerk ('My dream!').

Logic, Let Me Introduce You to This Window: When Maria goes to Valenti's office, she is wearing a very striking schoolgirl outfit (white blouse, grey skirt, black tie and socks). After leaving she meets Isabel and gives her a lift. Next time we see them, arriving back at school, Isabel is wearing the same clothes as she was when Maria picked her up, but Maria is now wearing the same white blouse, but with a thin jacket and a pair of trousers. Where did she get them from? Also, Valenti arranged to meet Maria 'about this time' tomorrow. Since this conversation took place whilst Maria was at The CrashDown, it would seem likely that this would be in the evening. However, after leaving Valenti, Maria and Isabel return to school and arrive just seconds after the bell has gone for the end of the school day. How did they get out of class? Come to that, what are Liz, Max and Michael doing hanging around in the school corridor during final period? Haven't they got classes to go to either?

In real life there are two UFO museums in Roswell.

Quote/Unquote: Max: 'People see movies with aliens. Aliens killing humans. Evil aliens. Green aliens. If you keep acting this way with Maria, she's going to think that's what we are.' Isabel: 'Exactly. This *evil alien thing* could work for us. The way to deal with her is to make her sweat . . . Make her afraid of my shadow. Of *her* shadow. Of

Michael's shadow.' Michael: 'Or, we could just *kill* her? Kidding.'

Topolsky: 'How well do you think you know yourself? You might be a little surprised by your computer profile. You said in our first meeting that you wanted to be a supermodel.' Isabel: 'You work with what you're given.' Topolsky: 'That's quite a jet set career for someone who puts family first, craves stability and security and leans towards care/giving fields.' Isabel: 'I never trusted computers.'

Notes: 'You remind me of myself as a confused, dazed adolescent. I've spent my entire life searching for aliens. And I swear on my mother's grave that, one day, I'll stand face-to-face with one of these creatures. And say "*I told you so*"!' The best episode so far, as unlikely alliances are formed and the nature of the threat to Max, Isabel and Michael becomes clearer. Much more of a character-building exercise than was probably necessary at this point (an attempt to soften the haughtiness of Isabel, for instance), but it all works wonderfully well. Best bit: Maria asking a stranded Isabel 'going home?' and then spotting a dreadfully fake alien spacecraft behind her. Isabel's non-verbal reply alone justifies the episode's existence.

Max is a non-smoker. A guitar case and a skateboard can be seen in his bedroom. Maria's (mom's) Jetta is a '92, and it's never been towed, even if the air conditioning is poor and Isabel thinks the sound system is pathetic. Valenti tells Maria about his father, whom he says he never got to know very well: 'He was the sheriff around here about forty years ago ... Strong man. Strong hands. And he had this theory about aliens. That they were real ... He was a very stubborn man and he wouldn't let it go. He believed, and he lost his job over it. And he lost his family over it.' (See **13**, 'The Convention', **26**, 'Summer of '47', **33**, 'To Protect and Serve'.) There's a dartboard in the staff room at The CrashDown.

Soundtrack: Christina Aguilera's 'Genie In A Bottle', 'Head' by Tin Star, Third Eye Blind's 'The Background',

'Drip' by Other Star People, 'My Ritual' by The Folk
Implosion and, at the end, 'Made To Last' by Semisonic.

Critique: Devin O'Leary in *Weekly Wire* commented:
'High school is that magical time when you can wear your
alienation on your sleeve like a badge of honour. What
teenager worth his or her salt doesn't feel freakish and
outcast and utterly lacking in self-understanding? The most
clever thing about the WB's new sci-fi series *Roswell*, then,
is that it has cast actual extraterrestrials in the roles of
alienated teens. Set in modern-day Roswell High, [it]
introduces us to a trio of teenage space aliens stranded on
Earth ... The show is also dipped in a shiny coating of
humour. Liz and her pal Maria, for example, come up with
the codeword "Czechoslovakians" when discussing
"aliens" in public. *Roswell* has all the necessary elements
to spell "hit" on the teen-oriented WB. Which isn't to say
the show won't become a guilty pleasure among older
viewers bored by TV's tidal wave of dour adult dramas.'

Did You Know?: The aquamarine and silver waitress
costumes at The CrashDown were designed by the costume
designer, Laura Goldsmith, who was given the task of
making them look 'kitschy'.

4
Leaving Normal

US Transmission Date: 27 October 1999
UK Transmission Date: 31 January 2000 (Sky One),
28 September 2000 (BBC2)

Writer: Jason Katims
Director: Chris Long
Cast: Carroll Baker (Claudia Parker),
David Smigelski (Tommy), Troy Robinson (Paulie),
Marisa Ramirez (Vanessa), Sarah Laine (Elana),
Eve Sigall (Agnes), Paul Hayes (Ortho #1),
Kent Kasper (Ortho #2), Floyd Vanbuskirk (Customer),

Michael Hernandez (Jose),
Octavia L Spencer(Nurse),
Harry Johnson (Doctor Sanchez),
Bonnie Brennan (Paramedic), Charles Martiniz (Janitor)
French title: *Suis ton Cœur*

There's a sense of excitement in Roswell. Not only is there
an orthodontists' convention in town (and the dentists are
massively impressed with Liz's seismic overbite), but Liz is
also expecting a visit from her beloved grandma. However,
Max pays the price for stealing Kyle Valenti's girl from
him, as he is beaten to a bloody pulp by Kyle's bonehead
friends, who tell him to stay away from Liz. Max decides
that it's in everyone's interests to comply with this request,
but if there's one thing guaranteed to make Michael mad,
it's seeing his friend bullied by Neanderthals without the
powers that he has.

'Dear Diary . . .': 'It's October 19th. I'm Liz Parker and
this is what I've been thinking. Can life ever go back to
normal?'

'I've Got the Power': Michael uses his power for a bit of
justified revenge on Kyle and his friends, melting the lock
on Kyle's locker, causing one of the jocks some severe
itching (see **13**, 'The Convention') and changing all of the
multi-choice answers on another's test paper. Isabel heats
an underdone burger with her hand and returns it to a
startled customer ('it looks well done to me'). She later
repeats the trick on a cup of lukewarm coffee.

Max seems to be able to create an out-of-body experience for Claudia at the end, although it's a very confusing
scene and it raises a number of issues about *Roswell*'s
position on the concept of the soul, life after death and half
a dozen other spiritual matters.

Roswell Iconography: On the menu at The CrashDown:
Venus Meatloaf Platter, a *Trekkie* Special, the Will Smith
Burger (see **1**, 'Pilot'), the Tommy Lee Jones Bacon Basket,
the legendary Alien Blast and Space Fries.

High School Life: Max has PE during fourth period, but he claims to be going to an English mid-term exam instead to avoid Liz.

Dudes and Babes: Cheerleader overload.

'You Might Remember Me from Such Films and TV Series As . . .': Carroll Baker made her movie debut in 1953's *Easy to Love* and, in a career stretching over almost 50 years, has appeared in such diverse films as *Giant*, *Something Wild*, *Cheyenne Autumn*, *The Big Country*, *How The West Was Won*, *Andy Warhol's Bad*, *Paranoia*, *The Watcher in the Woods*, *Kindergarten Cop* and *Rag and Bone*, though her place in cinema history was made as the eponymous *Baby Doll* (1956). She also played Rae Morrison in *LA Law*. Jo Anderson can be seen in *From the Earth to the Moon*, *JFK* and *Prime Target*. She was Diana Bennett in *Beauty and the Beast*, and her other TV appearances include *Northern Exposure*, *She-Wolf of London* and *Miami Vice*. Troy Robinson was in *John Carpenter's Vampires*, though he is chiefly known as a stunt man on *Blue Streak*, *The Patriot* and *Escape from LA* and as George Clooney's stunt-double on *Batman and Robin*. Marisa Ramirez played Gia Campbell in *General Hospital*. Eve Sigall was in *End of Days*. Charles Martiniz has appeared in *8 Heads in a Duffel Bag*, *Dark Goddess* and *Fire! Trapped on the 37th Floor*. David Smigelski was Brad Thompson in *Bloody Murder*. Octavia Spencer played Cynthia in *Never Been Kissed* and also featured in *What Planet Are You From?*, *American Virgin* and *Being John Malkovich*. Prior to this, she was a staffing assistant on *A Time to Kill*.

Behind the Camera: Chris Long's CV includes directing series as diverse as *Dark Angel*, *Timecop*, *Hercules: The Legendary Journeys* and *Lois & Clark: The New Adventures of Superman* (which he also produced). Special Effects guru Shawn Roberts also worked on *Fight Club* and *The Parent Trap*.

References: The title is from a 1992 film directed by Edward Zwick. Interestingly, Snuffy Walden also did that movie's music. Maria mentions Meg Ryan (*When Harry Met Sally*, *The Doors*, *Sleepless in Seattle*, *You've Got Mail*) and, obliquely, Rosie O'Donnell's chat show. Michael refers to Indian political and spiritual leader Mahatma Gandhi (1869-1948). Also Will Smith (*Enemy of the State*, *Wild Wild West*) and Tommy Lee Jones (*The Executioner's Song*, *JFK*, *The Fugitive*) the stars of *Men in Black* (see **1**, 'Pilot'). Kyle's sarcastic comment on Liz's film suggestion, 'Wings of Boringness' could refer to *Wings of the Dove* (1997) or *Wings of Courage* (1995). Kyle has a 'Yahoo!' sticker on his locker and a US flag on the inside of the door. Isabel's 'I can't handle the truth' is a misquote from *A Few Good Men*.

Teen-Speak: Max: 'Got to feed the monkey.'
  Isabel: 'Chill out.'

Fashion Victims: Isabel *really* suits that waitress dress. One of her friends wears a pair of *hot* leather trousers.

Logic, Let Me Introduce You to This Window: Maria believes that Liz shouldn't be at school but, 'at home, bingeing on junk food and *Rosie*'. Unless she taped an episode of the chat show (which broadcasts in the late afternoon), that would be impossible. And what, exactly, is Michael *doing* in the toilet cubicle when Max comes in and punches the wall? He seems to be just sitting there, with his trousers *up*.

Quote/Unquote: Liz: 'I can't believe you actually rented this. Looks like the worst movie in history.' Kyle: 'For your information, *Massacre at Sunset Village* is a modern-day classic. And the serial killer homes in on this retirement community so it's got something for your grandmother!'
  Isabel, to Maria: 'I thought we agreed that you would never address me until we'd established complete privacy.' And: 'To put this as succinctly as possible, I'm not really a service-oriented person.'

Notes: 'Sometimes your heart takes you to places that can never lead to a happy ending.' A disappointing dip in quality, in which mawkish and sentimental auto-pilot scripting replaces the witty situations of the previous episodes. It could still have worked if the Max/Kyle subplot had been anything other than shallow posturing. The first *Roswell* episode not to live up to its potential and to spectacularly fail to surprise the audience.

This episode confirms that the name of the school is *West* Roswell High. Liz's grandmother, Claudia, is an author. She was writing a book last time Liz saw her though we never find out if she's finished it or not. Her most recent piece 'Lost Treasures', an article on the first findings of the Navajo Indians in hundreds of years, was published in the *American Journal of Archaeology*. She once made a citizen's arrest on three hunters who were shooting deer in Yosemite National Park. Judging by Kyle asking his father how things were 'with you and mom, back when things were good if you can remember that far back', it appears that Valenti's marriage ended in divorce (see **29**, 'Wipe-Out!'). Two CrashDown waitresses are unavailable for extra shifts, Stephanie is on vacation and Karen's pregnant. That only leaves (the seemingly workshy) Agnes with Maria. So she asks Isabel for help. With *hilarious* consequences.

The episode was a victim of network constraints. Grandma Claudia was introduced and then struck down with illness after the first half hour. Originally this was intended to unfold over three or four episodes. Two variations on the final scene were shot. 'There was an orthodontists' convention in one episode,' noted Brendan Fehr in an online interview. 'There was a standup alien with a toothbrush and braces. I stole that and have it in my house!'

Soundtrack: Jeff Parker croons along to The Band's 1969 standard 'The Weight' ('still listening to *them*?' Claudia asks. 'You're dating yourself'). Also, Mandy Moore's 'Candy', Smash Mouth's 'Then the Morning Comes', 'Mistaken' by Save Ferris, 'Someday' by Sugar Ray and Sarah McLachlan's 'I Love You' (accompanying Liz hugging Max).

Cast and Crew Comments: When John Doe's X played the LA club scene in the late 1970s, he often found himself surrounded by troubled youth. Now, as Jeff Parker, owner of The CrashDown diner, he's once again amid alienated teens. Quite literally. 'I'm loving it,' Doe told Janet Weeks. 'Jeff is an understanding dad without being weak or a Milquetoast-y, bland guy.' In *Roswell*, Jeff is an ageing hippie doing his best with a teenage daughter. 'It gives me a little practice [in parenting] without wrecking my own kids' lives,' he notes. Making the transition from punk star to a modern day Howard Cunningham wasn't easy, however. 'Two years ago, I was Claire Danes's dad in *Brokedown Palace* and it was a little weird. I was thinking, "She's so smart and cool and pretty." Then I thought, "I really *could* be her dad"!' Doe's new band, the John Doe Thing, recently released a fine CD *Freedom Is . . .* But he doesn't intend to break out in song on *Roswell*. 'That would be a little too Ricky Nelson.'

Did You Know?: The CrashDown toilets are a little more unisex than shown, because the Men's restroom doubles as the Women's between shots. They just change the sign outside.

5
Missing

US Transmission Date: 3 November 1999
UK Transmission Date: 7 February 2000 (Sky One),
5 October 2000 (BBC2)

Writer: Jon Harmon Feldman
Director: David Semel
Cast: Robert Clendenin (Mr Cowan)
French title: *Le Journal Intime*

Liz is thrown into a panic when her diary goes missing. Because it contains detailed information about Max and the others, Liz feels compelled to tell Max. She also tells Maria, creating even more problems. The plot thickens as suspicion and false accusations develop. Meanwhile, thanks to an art class, Michael's recurring vision becomes more clear. He begins to believe that the mysterious dome he sees may hold the answer to everything.

'Dear Diary . . .': 'October 28th. I've missed a few days. But in my absence I've been thinking about life before Max Evans saved me, of how I used to pray for something to happen, something to just break the routine of school and work. Something that would make a small town feel bigger.' The diary itself is the focus of the episode after Liz gets careless with it at The CrashDown. Liz appears to keep her journal in her knickers' drawer.

'I've Got the Power': By touching the CD in Liz's room, Max can tell that Kyle has handled it ('when things get intense, heightened, sometimes we feel things. See things'). He also causes the school snack machine to vibrate and spill its load. Michael can sharpen a pencil with his hand. Isabel can speed-read. She flicks through James Atherton's *Among Us* in seconds, declaring it 'boring'.

Roswell Iconography: A season pass to the UFO Center costs nineteen dollars and includes a guided tour and a box lunch.

The Conspiracy Starts at Home Time: Discussing some of the books that he gives Max, Milton notes: 'Szcerbiak's theory that the military cover-up of the 1947 landing was financed by an international consortium lacks credible evidence to support it. Still, it debunks several fallacies that have long troubled me.' Another writer, Walton, he describes as 'garbage'. He does, however, recommend *Among Us*. 'A bit on the alternative side. Atherton had an underground following. Never truly embraced by the mainstream, such as it is. But it may be of some interest to a true believer like yourself.' Max subsequently discovers that the writer didn't believe that aliens would possess the lung or brain capacity for more than short-term survival on Earth.

High School Life: History class are doing an oral report on 'McCarthy'; probably Senator Joseph (1908–57), the notorious anti-Communist, but possibly Democrat Senator and Presidential Candidate Eugene (b.1916) or novelist and critic Mary Therese (1912–89). Meanwhile, in the gym, Alex plays that most notorious of US 'sports', dodge ball.

Mr Cowan says that Michael's work is the best thing to come out of the class all year. Michael wasn't aware that he had any artistic talent.

Dudes and Babes: When Alex tells Topolsky that he doesn't have a girlfriend, she says this doesn't surprise her: 'Teenage girls can never spot the good ones. Look at Liz Parker dating Kyle Valenti. He's a little *obvious*, don't you think?'

'You Might Remember Me from Such Films and TV Series As . . .': Robert Clendenin played Godfrey in *Popular* and David Rogers in *The Practice* and has appeared in *Star Trek: Voyager*, *That '70s Show*, *LA Confidential*, *The Thirteenth Floor*, *8MM* and *Dude, Where's My Car?*. Richard Anthony Crenna was in *Critical Mass* and *Predator 2* whilst Robert Neary featured in *Torch Song Trilogy*, *Teen Wolf Too* and *Suddenly Susan*.

Behind the Camera: Jon Harmon Feldman was producer on *Dawson's Creek* and *The Wonder Years* and the writer/director of *Lovelife*. Grip Chris Trillo's previous work included *Dora was Dysfunctional* (as best boy), *The Mask* (as rigging gaffer) and *The Celluloid Closet* (as key grip).

References: The title was a worldwide hit for Hull-based pop-duo Everything But the Girl. Also, the state of REM sleep, Marvin Gaye's 'What's Goin' On?', *The Wild Ones* ('what have you got?'), *Friends* and an oblique reference to David Bowie's 'Hello Spaceboy'. Topolsky reports to a man called 'Control', a possible allusion to John le Carré's espionage classic *Tinker, Tailor, Solider, Spy*. A BAKE SALE poster is briefly glimpsed. Amongst the items in the snack machine are Dorritos and Oreo biscuits. The CD Kyle leaves for Liz is Moby's 'Play' (Kyle might be a git, but you can't fault his musical taste). There's a poster for Power Sports Network in Kyle's bedroom and the door contains a NO TRESPASSING. VIOLATORS WILL BE PROSECUTED sign.

Teen-Speak: Michael: 'Hey man, what's going on?'

Fashion Victims: Mr Cowan describes a geodesic dome to Michael as 'a type of house, architecturally postmodern'. There are some sharp clothes on display, including Maria's tight blue top and Liz's even tighter red skirt.

Logic, Let Me Introduce You to This Window: We see Maria at school wearing a long blue dress. Next scene, it's changed to a brown dress.

Quote/Unquote: Max, to Michael: 'I appreciate that I'm the one you chose to wake at three in the morning to tell that you've been dreaming about semicircles.'

Topolsky: 'This is not just a diary, agent. This is potential proof of alien contact. Not from a crackpot farmer or a drunk somewhere, but from a *Straight A student*. Treasurer of the Roswell science club.'

Notes: 'Liz loses her diary and, the next thing I know, Inspector DeLuca tells me that they have me pinned as the main suspect.' A much more (literal) down-to-earth episode, though with a few very witty moments (the art teacher's little pop at Michael, for instance). The episode has a strange, lopsided structure, running out of steam a good ten minutes from the end, but it's mostly fun.

Michael keeps a bottle of Tabasco sauce by his bed. Topolsky's code reference number is 73290. According to Nick Wechsler, during the scene where Liz confronts Kyle at the basketball court, a fly hovered around Shiri Appleby's face, causing countless retakes.

Soundtrack: 'Pick a Part that's New' by Stereophonics, Filter's 'Take a Picture', Beck's 'Novacane' (accompanying Michael drawing his vision), Creed's 'Torn' and 'Colorblind' by Counting Crows.

Critique: 'Jason Katims inspires adequate, if not comprehensive, suspension of disbelief,' wrote Kendall Hamilton in *Newsweek*. 'The adolescent struggles here – alienation, rebellion, first love – are presented metaphorically, which takes the edge off the angst and saves *Roswell* from becoming a *Dawson's Creek* clone. It is, however, a neat show.'

Cast and Crew Comments: 'Originally they hired somebody else, and then fired them,' Julie Benz told Paul Simpson and Ruth Thomas. 'I was shooting a movie at the time and I had just got back into town when I got a call saying, you need to go in tomorrow. I had auditioned for David Nutter when he did *Disturbing Behavior*. I didn't get the part in the movie, but I really made an impression, to the point when he called me at home about my audition, which was nice. I was still playing teenagers up to that point, but the character was written to be thirty-two, and I was like, "no way can I play thirty-two, and an FBI agent and a teacher. Forget it!" I almost blew it off. But that's the clever thing about writers, they just made it that I was a clever little girl. I was closer to the kids' age than the adults'. I went in and read for Jason Katims, and he really liked me. I think that was a Friday, and we were starting on Monday, so I had to have wardrobe fittings all over the weekend. I was only originally hired for two episodes. Then it became much more than that.'

Did You Know?: According to an interview in the *New York Post*, Katherine Heigl used to do kickboxing three times a week, 'but I burned out. Now I do less extreme sports like walking, hiking.' Katherine notes that she is a huge fan of Abercrombie & Fitch wear. 'I like their comfort and style and how they make me feel sporty', though her friends tease her about it. Her biggest fashion *faux pas*, however, was 'when I was sixteen, I wore this really beautiful Victor Alfaro leopard dress on *The Jon Stewart Show* and it was a little too revealing.'

6
285 South

US Transmission Date: 10 November 1999
UK Transmission Date: 14 February 2000 (Sky One),
12 October 2000 (BBC2)

Writers: William Sind and Thania St John
Director: Arvin Brown
Cast: Daniel Hagen (Steve Somers),
Michael Garvey (Highway Patrolman),
Frankie Ray (Biker), Marilyn Sue Perry (Secretary)
French title: *Le Mystère du Dôme*

In an exercise that Maria describes as 'cruel and unusual
education', Mr Somers (under Topolsky's instruction)
pairs off students with a test to find out as much as they
can about a chosen partner. As Michael's visions continue,
he becomes convinced that he may have discovered the
location of the mysterious domed building. Determined to
find it, he does what any rational alien would in the
circumstances – steals Maria's car (with Maria still inside)
and heads south. Soon Liz, Max and Isabel are in hot
pursuit.

'I've Got the Power': Isabel uses her power to remove the
coffee stains from Liz's sweater. Michael reveals that he
isn't very good at the powers he possesses (his attempts to
repair Maria's car results in the engine blowing up). Both
Isabel and Max display the ability to open locked doors.

Roswell Iconography: Milton has a ROSWELL CRASH –
BELIEVE! sticker on his PC.

The Conspiracy Starts at Home Time: James P Atherton
was born in East Pohawnee, Tennessee in 1911. World
War I and the Depression tore his family apart. He gained
a scholarship to the local Technical Institute astronomy
department. His curiosity was pricked by the infamous
1927 'Buffalo Visitation' and he became interested in

extraterrestrials. His modernist domed home (featured on the cover of *Among Us*, see **5**, 'Missing') is in Marathon, Texas. There are references to successive US Air Force UFO investigations Project Sign (1948), Project Grudge (1949) and Project Blue Book (1952).

High School Life: For homework, Somers pairs students together. The pairings are: Daskal with Hausman, Kalinowski with Nell, Trussell with Wolf, Papis with Cooney and, more relevantly, Liz with Isabel, Max with Kyle, and Maria with Michael.

Revelations: Questions on the biographical questionnaire include: Favourite ice cream flavour (vanilla for Liz, pistachio for Michael); favourite relative; favourite TV show (Max claims not to watch TV, Kyle's is *America's Most Wanted*, which he views with his father, Michael's is *Win Ben Stein's Money*) and favourite book. 'What's the best thing that ever happened to you?' provokes Max to venture 'getting adopted', whilst for Kyle it was 'winning the statewide junior rifle competition'. Question 8 is 'Have you ever been in love?' ('No,' says Max, flatly). 'Who do you envy?' is question 12. 'What are you afraid of?' is number 16.

Maria asks Michael: 'If you're so smart, how come you fail every class in school?'

'You Might Remember Me from Such Films and TV Series As . . .': Daniel Hagen can be seen in *The Deep End of the Ocean*, *Wilder Napalm*, *Bonfire of the Vanities*, *Friends* and *Mad About You*. Marilyn Sue Perry played Robin in *Head Games*.

Behind the Camera: Arvin Brown's previous work has included *Popular*, *Snoops*, *Ally McBeal*, *Party of Five* and *The Inspector General*.

References: Maria mentions the Geneva Convention. Michael claims to watch *The View*, a TV talk-show once memorably described as 'a bunch of chicks sitting around a table drinking coffee and daring each other to go a day without wearing make up' (Michael claims it 'keeps me in touch with my feminine side'). Liz calls Isabel 'the Elle McPherson of the sophomore class', referring to the Australian supermodel. Also, the 1932 movie *Trouble in Paradise*, 60s TV classics *Bewitched* and *I Dream of Jeannie* ('Wiggle your nose, blink your eyes, do the Samantha-Jeannie alien-thing'), *Aladdin*, Big Gulp – a soda drink sold mainly at petrol stations – game show *Win Ben Stein's Money*, and Irish author James Joyce's *Ulysses* (Michael quotes autobiographically from it: 'What incensed him the most was the blatant jokes of the ones who pass it all off as a jest, pretending to understand everything and in reality not knowing their own minds'). The students Trussell and Wolf are named after producer Carol Dunn Trussell and production supervisor Gordon Wolf. There's an 'In Your Face' poster in Kyle's bedroom. A briefly glimpsed poster on the service station wall advertises a rodeo in Rocksprings, Texas between 27 and 29 July.

Teen-Speak: Milton: 'What do you want, you two-bit punk?'
   Michael: 'Your car sucks.' And: 'Jackpot, Maximilian!'
   Maria: 'That is, like, so unreal.'

Fashion Victims: Isabel's scarlet coat, Liz's outrageously figure-hugging sweater.

Sex and Drugs and Rock'n'Roll: Lovely innuendo in the sequence where Michael accidentally inflates one of Mrs DeLuca's blow-up aliens. Maria thinks their motel room at the Sultan's Hideaway is like 'the porno version of *Aladdin*'. She asks Michael what other human urges he feels, to which he replies: 'Not if you're the last woman on Earth.'

Logic, Let Me Introduce You to This Window: Somers says he wants the class to write an 'oral history report for tomorrow'. The whole point about an oral report, surely, is that is *isn't* written? The time-scale of the episode is up the spout. Max gets the call to go to the sheriff's office whilst he's in school, yet when he gets there the clock outside the building says 7:55. During the exchange of cash for goods at the gas station, Maria has a fist full of money and runs after the hijacked car with cash still in hand. Next shot, the money has vanished. When Liz tells her mother that she is staying at Maria's in the initial shot her phone is on the left side, but in the next shot it's on the opposite side. When Michael and Maria are stopped by the cop and Maria explains to him she's 'got to pee', her seatbelt is buckled. When she turns to look out of the window it's unbuckled.

Quote/Unquote: Isabel: 'The perfect Liz Parker lying to her mother?' Liz: 'At least she knows what species I am.'

Maria: 'You kidnap me and you blow up my car and you expect me to spend the night in here with you?' Michael: 'Not exactly my fantasy evening either.'

Notes: 'Sometimes you end up with the most revealing details just by putting the right people together.' A terrifically well-structured episode, with a bunch of clever peaks in the action that keep the viewer guessing the climax right to the wire, and then leaves them with a stupendous cliff-hanger. The theme of the episode is that unusual pairings of characters produces surprising results, and that's certainly true of Maria and Michael, one of the oddest (yet most watchable) couples on TV this side of Xander Harris and Cordelia Chase, or Chandler Bing and Monica Gellar. Love Max's awkwardness when he's in Liz's bedroom.

Michael uses the excuse that he has a bad back to get out of helping Maria carry a heavy box. Amongst the laws he violates at one time or another are kidnapping, car theft, driving across a state line with a minor and vandalism of personal property (Maria's cell phone). 'I just *knew* you had criminal tendencies,' she notes. 'You even drive erratically.' Maria claims to have a weak bladder condition. When Maria was a child she used to make up stories about her father (whom, she says, she never knew – which is flatly contradicted in **16**, 'Sexual Healing'). They all ended the same way – he would come in a limo and pick up Maria and her mother and take them to some exotic place where they would live like royalty. As Michael notes, if you were to substitute a spaceship for a limo, his dream would be the same.

Topolsky claims to have done her graduate thesis on the importance of oral history in psychology (given the evidence here, this may well be true). The message she writes on her computer is: 'Special Investigation Unit. Code Name: West Roswell High. Tension in the Ranks. Waiting for them to slip up. Will happen soon.' This episode confirms the Christian names of Max and Isabel's parents (Philip and Diane) and Maria's (as yet unseen) mom (Amy, see **9**, 'Heatwave'). Donnie Jenkins is a radio announcer for station KZTX 97. There are geographical references to Pecos on 285 South and Crown Gulch.

Colin Hanks doesn't appear in this episode or the next as he was filming his part in *Whatever it Takes* at this time.

Soundtrack: Stroke 9's 'Little Black Backpack', Euphoria's 'Wait For You' and 'Delerium', Laura Webb's 'On Any Given Day' and 'Safe' by Grassy Knoll.

Did You Know?: When he was growing up in Orchard Park, William Sadler lived on a farm and, with his best friend, would sit in a chicken coop and pretend they were in a spaceship. 'We would play *Star Trek*,' Bill told *Starlog*. 'We were Spock and Kirk, and we would trade off playing the characters. Every time we stepped outside, we were on a different planet. In a way, I feel like I've always been rehearsing for all the genre projects I've done since I was about eight years old. So, it really doesn't surprise me that I'm comfortable in the genre.'

7
River Dog

US Transmission Date: 17 November 1999
UK Transmission Date: 21 February 2000 (Sky One),
19 October 2000 (BBC2)

Writer: Cheryl Cain
Director: Jonathan Frakes
Cast: Toochis Morin (Native American Woman)
French title: *Vers la Lumière*

Max and Isabel's home is broken into and the papers they found at the dome are stolen. All that is left is a mysterious necklace with a symbol that they all recognise. In an effort to find out what the symbol means, Liz and Max head to the Mesaliko Indian Reservation, where an elderly man named River Dog gives them information on the alien that disappeared in 1959. Meanwhile, Maria and Michael continue their awkward flirtation.

'Dear Diary ...': Brilliant opening voice-over rant from Liz: 'It's November 11th. All logic is gone. Here were my plans last night; finish my shift, dinner with the parents, half-hour of talking to Maria on the phone, then dive into this issue I've been having with geometry and hopefully finish in time to watch this A&E biography on Madame Curie. Instead, I took off in an open-air vehicle that probably shouldn't be allowed on the road ... Broke into a house, essentially stole things from it, and engaged in general bonding with aliens. Welcome to my world.'

Roswell Iconography: Milton says that metal allegedly found at the 1947 crash-site 'matches none of the 92 trace elements known on the planet, defies the properties of all metals known to man. When bent, it bends back on its own.' He tells Valenti that James Atherton was one of the first authors to publish on the '47 crash. *Among Us* (one of several books he wrote on the events) was published in 1955. Atherton vanished in 1959. 'Supposedly he was on to some amazing discoveries right before his disappearance. Direct contact. That sort of thing. Legend has it that he was abducted by aliens.'

There is a 'Redskin Basket' on the menu at The CrashDown. Liz is embarrassed by such racism (un-redeemed by any saving irony, anyway) and says she's been trying to get it removed for months. Isabel finally explains

the Tabasco sauce fetish: 'We all like things extremely
sweet mixed with extremely spicy. It's our little dietary
quirk.' River Dog tells Max about 'someone like you. He
stayed pretty much to himself.' Besides River Dog, the
only man this mysterious stranger trusted was Atherton,
who he eventually killed in November 1959. The mysterious stranger subsequently turns out to be Nasedo (see **10**,
'The Balance').

The Conspiracy Starts at Home Time: Topolsky's assignment is the covert observation of the subjects [Max, Isabel
and Michael] and to 'determine whether or not the theories
about them are substantiated'. She reports directly to
Stevens (is *he* 'Control'? see **5**, 'Missing'), who orders her
to use 'whatever means necessary' to recover what was
taken from the dome. The break-in at the Evans' is made
to look like a real robbery by the stealing of the TV and
the stereo.

Valenti has been following Topolsky for 'a while' and
notes that she 'seems like the healthy type', working out at
the gym and buying health food. He also knows that she
is an FBI agent.

High School Life: Max claims he and Isabel spent the
previous evening 'cramming for the Maths mid-term'.

Dudes and Babes: Maria's opinion of Michael changes and
she realises that underneath the 'weird, poorly bathed
exterior' there is a 'deeply wounded, vulnerable guy'. She
tells Liz that there can never be anything between them.
'There's a number of obstacles. His hair, his personality,
the fact that he was hatched.' But she does say that she
finds him interesting.

**'You Might Remember Me from Such Films and TV Series
As . . .':** Born in 1925, Ned Romero has a TV career
stretching back to the 1950s with appearances on shows
like *Star Trek*, *The Incredible Hulk*, *The Munsters*, *The
High Chaparral*, *Harry O*, *The Six Million Dollar Man*,
MacGyver, *Star Trek: The Next Generation* and *Walker,
Texas Ranger*. He played Sergeant Joe Rivera in *Dan*

August and his movies have included the Clint Eastwood classic *Hang 'em High*, *House IV* and *Children of the Corn II: The Final Sacrifice*. Tod Thawley can be seen in *Buffy the Vampire Slayer*, *Baywatch* and the movie *Terminal Justice*.

Behind the Camera: Cheryl Cain was assistant production coordinator on the 90s cult classic *Pulp Fiction*, along with movies like *12:01* and *Flight of Black Angel*.

References: The group engages in subterfuge to lose Topolsky outside a theatre showing the Alfred Hitchcock movies *The Lady Vanishes* (1938) and *The Secret Agent* (1936). Also, the A&E (arts and entertainment) TV channel and Polish physicist and chemist Marie Curie (1867–1934).

Teen-Speak: Maria: 'All this time that I've known you, I've just always thought of you as, like, this weird guy from the other side of the tracks going nowhere in life, which, of course, you know, you *still are* . . .'

Liz: 'I have to go talk to Kyle.' Maria: 'The stalker? Good luck with that.'

Michael: 'The plan sucks a big one, all right? They're out there on my vision quest, and I'm sitting here in the kitchen with two girls yakking.' And: '*Cool your jets.*'

Fashion Victims: Liz's silly woollen hat takes all the awards here. A nice juxtaposition, however, is provided by Isabel's black leather pants. *Damn!*

Sex and Drugs and Rock'n'Roll: Kyle wonders which of the following Liz is involved in. 'Just gimme a hint. Is it drugs? You part of some cult, or is it just about sex?' Kyle and Liz's first kiss was on the last day of school last year in the janitor's closet. Maria notes that 'what Michael and I share, it's nonverbal. Michael is the type of person my mom likes to refer to as a vibrator.' Topolosky seems to be drinking Southern Comfort when she and Valenti talk in the bar.

Logic, Let Me Introduce You to This Window: More timing issues: Michael says in **6**, '285 South' that Marathon is three hours' drive from Roswell. It is daylight when the gang are at Atherton's house. They spend time hiding from Valenti and Topolsky and then have to get back to the motel, fix Maria's car and drive back to Roswell. Yet Max and Isabel are *still* home in time for breakfast. Additionally, the scenes of Michael and Maria driving back to Roswell look suspiciously like they were filmed in the early evening instead of the morning.

Quote/Unquote: Topolsky: 'I've been acting covertly.' Stevens: 'Drop-kicking the sheriff? You call *that* covertly?'

Milton: 'As a concerned citizen and as an extraterrestrialist, I'm compelled to ask. What's this all about?'

Notes: 'Miss Topolsky, you are a walking, talking, moving violation!' A far better dabbling in Native American culture and mythology than *The X-Files* usually manages. A very complicated episode with a really clever chase sequence in the middle. Frakes's fluid direction is worthy of attention on its own.

During their youth Max and Isabel went on holiday to Florida with their parents. Isabel had sunstroke throughout August and Max sprained his ankle on the shuffleboard court. On the beach one day, they drew 'this thing in the sand', a symbol exactly the same as that on the necklace they find in Atherton's home. There's a horseshoe above the door in Max's bedroom. Deputy Owen grew up on the Mesaliko reservation outside of town, where Max meets Eddie and River Dog. Maria is late picking up Liz and Max because her mother's acupuncturist appointment ran late. Miss Topolsky performs t'ai chi exercises.

Soundtrack: Bachelor Girl's 'Blown Away', 'Get You in the Morning' by Crash Test Dummies, Finger Eleven's 'Quicksand' and Bramhall's 'Snakecharmer' (in the bar as Valenti and Topolsky flirt with each other).

Cast and Crew Comments: Nick Wechsler auditioned for four or five different roles before being cast as Kyle. 'The closer I got, the more I thought, "They're not going to cast me." How could I possibly get a part? A kid from New Mexico!' Moving to California to become an actor can be challenging. Wechsler notes that 'I told myself if I haven't found anything within a year I'd move back. Luckily, I got something.' As someone accustomed to seeing desert landscapes, Wechsler says he was awestruck when he saw the Pacific. 'It's amazing, I love the ocean. It's not so much California's beaches, it's just seeing this huge volume of water.' However, Nick isn't a great fan of LA's popular food trends like sushi and Thai cuisine. He mostly cooks at home, but he admits that he misses New Mexico's green chili.

Did You Know?: In an interview with *Playboy*, Majandra Delfino was asked if she receives scary mail from fans. 'Not too much,' she replied. 'I get lots of letters from girls who love the show and my character, but then there *are* the ones that come from boys telling me what they'd do to me in bed. I had one guy send me a condom with a note that said, "Save this because it's for us when we meet." I also get gifts, usually really sweet stuff. But for security reasons I try not to get too personal. We're advised not to disclose much info.'

Majandra did, however, reveal a love for Tim Burton's movies ('they're so cool, dark, quirky. I love all of them. Maybe that has something to do with Johnny Depp!') and some secrets behind her performance in the legendary-before-it-was-released horror-spoof *Shriek If You Know What I Did Last Friday the 13th* ('When I read the script I thought it was so funny. But after we shot it we had to take out a lot of jokes for legal reasons. I play the Jennifer Love Hewitt/Neve Campbell role. There were scenes with lesbian insinuations which will probably get cut'). She also confessed that her school nickname was 'Fish Lips', that she has a phobia about public toilets ('I can't put my ass on a seat that thousands of others have sat on') and that her publicists advised her to always keep her shirt on at photo shoots. That's got to be a first for *Playboy*?

8
Blood Brother

US Transmission Date: 24 November 1999
UK Transmission Date: 28 February 2000 (Sky One),
2 November 2000 (BBC2)

Teleplay: Barry Pullman
From a Story By: Breen Frazier and Barry Pullman
Director: David Nutter
Cast: Jonathan Nichols (Doctor),
Hilary Shepard-Turner (Nurse Susan),
Victor Campos (Mr Bruckner), Eric Jungmann (Lester),
Paul 'PJ' Palmer (Paramedic #2), Kevin Calisher (Bob)
French title: *Sang pour Sang*

During a blissful drive along a twisting country road, Max swerves his Jeep to avoid a wild horse and he and Liz are injured in the resulting crash. At the hospital, a sample of Max's blood is taken, evidence that will expose him as an alien. Although Michael recovers the sample, Isabel says that they will need a replacement and asks Liz to provide a suitable male volunteer.

'Dear Diary . . .': Liz's voice-over begins the episode: 'Have you ever had a moment when you're with the one person in the world you want to be with and the wind is blowing through your hair and the song that just describes your entire soul happens to come on, and then the person that you want to be with happens to love the same song . . . And that no matter how crazy your life has gotten there's this one moment.'

'I've Got the Power': When Liz asks Isabel what happens when aliens get sick, Isabel replies: 'We *don't*.' Michael shares his friends' ability to open locks (see **6**, '285 South').

Roswell Iconography: On the menu at The CrashDown is a $3.99 meal containing Blue Moon Burger, Saturn Rings and a Mercury Milkshake, whilst the marvellous sounding

Beam-Me-Up Burger sells for the same price (also seen in the next episode). The UFO Center appears to sell the blowup alien dolls that Maria's mom makes (see **6**, '285 South'). Certainly a whole bunch of visitors to the centre are carrying them.

Top marks for the clever idea of having Topolsky drinking from a 'UFO' coffee mug!

The Conspiracy Starts at Home Time: It's confirmed that Topolsky, Moss and their colleagues work for a section of the FBI.

High School Life: Max has Trigonometry at the same time as Liz's English class. Topolsky has put together an AP tutorial in computer languages for next semester for Alex.

Dudes and Babes: Topolsky tries to interest Alex by telling him that she too used to peel the marshmallow off so she could get to the cupcake inside. On discovering her secret, Maria calls Topolsky an 'all-American guidance counsellor and big, fat liar'. 'Never trust a blonde,' adds Michael helpfully.

This episode reveals that Jason Behr hasn't got a hairy chest in the slightest, poor lad. Check out a couple of great shots of members of the West Roswell cheerleading team.

'You Might Remember Me from Such Films and TV Series As . . .': Jonathan Nichols appeared in *The President's Man*, *Becker* and *NYPD Blue* and was a voice coach on *The Last Marshal*. Kevin Calisher played Billy in *Voodoo Academy*. Hilary Shepard-Turner can be seen in *Addams Family Reunion*, *Scanner Cop*, *Avalanche*, *Star Trek: Deep Space Nine* and *Murphy Brown*. Veteran actor Victor Campos played Detective Gomez in *Kojak* and has appeared in numerous TV series including *The FBI*, *Cannon*, *The A-Team* and *Kolchak: The Night Stalker*. His movies have included *Black Sunday*, *Scarface* and *Human Desires*. Eric Jungmann appears in *The Faculty*, *Varsity Blues* and *The Boy With the X-Ray Eyes*.

References: The title is a stage play by Liverpool-writer Willy Russell. Michael mentions *Mr Ed*, the 50s TV series about a talking horse. There's an oblique reference to *The A-Team*, plus a more obvious one about Sherlock Holmes. Visual references include *JFK* and *Zabriskie Point*.

Teen-Speak: Maria, to Michael: 'Toiletries say a lot about a man which, by the way, you should take note of.'

Topolsky: 'The school keeps me in the loop about these things.'

Kyle describes Alex as 'the B-team'.

Alex: 'If I had a therapist, he'd say talking to you is detrimental to my mental health.'

Jock: 'Tough game of dodge ball, Whitman?' Alex: 'Yeah, sure. Why not? *Loser*.'

Fashion Victims: Max's denim jacket (several episodes carry the credit 'Wardrobe Provided by Levi Jeans'), Liz's red vest, Maria and Isabel's Ray-Bans when tailing Agent Moss, and Isabel's obscenely tight greeny-white top. On the downside, Alex's grey baggy jeans.

Sex and Drugs and Rock'n'Roll: Alex tells his nerdy friends that there are no garage bands in Roswell. 'Which makes for a potential genius situation. We could start an entire music scene.' His friend, Lester, who is described as 'tone deaf', is told that drums would be a suitable instrument for him. Maria arrives and asks for Alex's help. Alex notes: 'The point here is, *musicians get the ladies*', and he grabs Maria's butt to much nodding of heads. Alex's bass is a rather fine electric-blue Fender percussion.

When Alex's blood is swapped for Max's, Alex suspects that the reason is 'drugs? You and Max go out for a drive. He gets wasted, almost kills you both. You can't use Michael's blood because he's just as high.' Trapped into lying, Liz confirms this.

Michael's chatting up of Nurse Susan (to obtain Max's blood) is curiously erotic: 'Age doesn't matter ... I've always been more mature than most people I know. Girls my age, they just don't do it for me, you know?'

Logic, Let Me Introduce You to This Window: Where did Isabel, Liz, Maria and Michael obtain an identical (typewritten) label to put on the replacement for Max's blood sample? Max has a poster of the Earth from space on his bedroom wall. Isn't that a touch *obvious* for an alien? What exactly is it that Topolsky slips into Alex's drink to make his nose bleed? Isn't Alex tapping into the Secret-FBI *website* just the most ludicrous plot-device imaginable? When Topolsky first asks Alex to write down everything he knows about Max and Liz she is wearing a grey dress and Alex has on a blood-red shirt. Afterwards Alex visits Liz at The CrashDown, where she's in uniform, so the implication is that this takes place in the evening. However, the following scene has Alex visiting Topolsky, presumably the next day, but they're both wearing the same clothes.

Max's date of birth is mentioned in this episode whilst we discover Isabel's in **25**, 'Surprise'. It is never made clear whether these are supposed to refer to the date on which they began incubating, when they emerged from the pods (both unlikely), the time of their discovery, or merely an approximation of how old they *should* be. Given that Max and Isabel were found together (and adopted together as brother and sister), a seven-month gap between their birthdays seems rather arbitrary and unlikely. When Alex is talking to Liz in the halls, he has books in one of his hands. Suddenly his nose starts to bleed and he dabs at it with both hands, as though he's not holding any-thing. Entering the bathroom, he's holding books again. However, when he re-emerges after cleaning up, they've vanished.

Quote/Unquote: Liz: 'I need you to do me a huge favour.' Alex: 'Of course. Anything.' Liz: 'I need your blood.'

Maria: 'This is the second time you've dragged me to some cheap motel.' Michael: 'Don't spread it around. You'll ruin my reputation.'

Max, on Alex: 'Liz told him we were into drugs to get him to stop asking questions.' Isabel: 'That'll be a lot easier to explain to mom and dad.'

Notes: 'Can any one of us really be safe with Max Evans around? If you think you've just helped yourselves, you're wrong.' Such a simple idea and such an obvious one (an alien posing as a human is never able to be ill or injured in case the medical treatment designed to cure them discovers what they really are). Once again, the characterisation is magnificent, with a really meaty role this time for Colin Hanks, and a couple of amusing cameo bits as Michael uses his teenage charm on Nurse Susan to gain access to Max's blood.

The road that Max drives Liz down is 'the old highway'. Mr Evans used to take this route when driving the family to Albuquerque. Max's date of birth seems to be 15 May 1983, judging by the date given on his blood sample. Liz says she did some volunteer work at the hospital last summer and saw blood being taken many times. She finally meets Mrs Evans in this episode. Alex has been Liz's friend since 'Ms Elmer's class in fifth grade', although they actually met a year earlier but she didn't notice him at first.

Miss Hardy (see **1**, 'Pilot', **3**, 'Monsters') is mentioned; she's sick with stomach flu. Ms Topolsky's telephone number in Roswell is 555-4378 (see **17**, 'Crazy'). Maria has experience as a babysitter.

Soundtrack: 'Learn To Fly' by Foo Fighters, Jeremy Toback's 'You Make Me Feel', Citizen King's 'Long Walk Home', 'Alien' by Pennywise, 'America' by Bree Sharp, 'If You Want Me To', by Ginny Owens. Walden and Williams' incidental music is some of the best of the season, including a particularly hot sub-*Shaft* burst of funky guitar early in the episode.

Cast and Crew Comments: According to Brendan Fehr, *Roswell* is 'intelligently written. It doesn't play down to the characters or to the audience. You have aliens as teens trying to hide the fact that they're aliens. I didn't have to make a leap of faith. If you tell good stories and people like the characters and want to go through an experience with them, it doesn't really matter what the story is.'

Did You Know?: Katherine Heigl swears that her perceived sex appeal completely escapes her. 'I don't walk around in halter tops and mini skirts,' she told *TV Guide*'s Shawna Malcolm. 'I'm more a jeans, T-shirt and baseball cap kind of chick.'

9
Heatwave

US Transmission Date: 1 December 1999
UK Transmission Date: 6 March 2000 (Sky One),
9 November 2000 (BBC2)

Writer: Jason Katims
Director: Patrick Norris
Cast: Meghan Gallagher (Vicky Delaney),
Trevor Lissauer (Octave), Eamon Behrens (Metal),
Fred Estrada (Juan), Jodi Taffel (Secretary)
French title: *Vague de Chaleur*

It's yet another white-hot day in the 'bizarre December heatwave' currently making New Mexico sweat. Maria and Michael indulge in some passion at The CrashDown and Liz, with Max still distant from her, feels left out of whatever madness it is that's taken hold of the town. Ms Topolsky is missing, and even Kyle has a new girlfriend, Vicky, who invites Liz to an illegal party at the abandoned soap factory. Liz is still worried about Alex, however, and confides to Max that she doesn't know what he will tell the authorities.

'Dear Diary . . .': 'It's December 2nd, 1999. I'm Liz Parker, and this heatwave has made everyone crazy.' We briefly glimpse the diary as Liz is making a later entry in it, and Max climbs up the fire escape to see her.

'I've Got the Power': Isabel changes the colour of Liz's nail varnish to match her sandals.

Having told Liz that she will 'look into' what Alex is thinking, Isabel invades his dreams and finds Alex waiting for a date with a dream version of Isabel, herself. A flustered Isabel later tells Max that Alex is 'a complex individual with a lot of complexities'.

Roswell Iconography: Liz gives Alex a little potted history of what she has learned about the aliens so far: They think they were in the 1947 crash; they were in incubation pods for a long time; they came out in the form of humans and both Topolsky and Valenti suspect them.

There's an 'out of this world' 'Solar Special' at The CrashDown. Amy DeLuca's tacky homemade alien novelties include cocktail stirrers that glow in the dark (which she sells to local traders like Jeff Parker). As well as making such merchandise, Amy also owns a shop.

The Conspiracy Starts at Home Time: Topolsky has disappeared after her cover was blown by Alex and Liz in **8**, 'Blood Brother' (see **17**, 'Crazy').

Sarcasm is the Lowest Form of Wit: Alex, to Liz: 'What do you want from me? More blood? A urine sample? How about my kidney?'

There's a wonderful twist on Max's *'we're from up there'* bit in **1**, 'Pilot' as Liz tells Alex that Max, Michael and Isabel are not from around here and then points upwards, as Max did to her. 'What? Like, Wyoming?' asks a less than impressed Alex, before his horrifying suspicions are confirmed. They're *Canadians*!

Dudes and Babes: Liz asks Isabel about guys. She wonders why, when Isabel has practically every single guy in school interested in her, 'you kinda tend to keep pretty platonic'. 'Are you afraid to let someone in? To let someone see who you really are?' Isabel asks. Liz says that she is, and Isabel replies: 'Multiply that by about a million.' Is it just me, or is there something disturbingly erotic about Liz eating that doughnut in the opening scene?

'You Might Remember Me from Such Films and TV Series As . . .': A former co-host of the game show *Loveline*, Diane Farr played Tracy in *The Drew Carey Show* and appeared in *The David Cassidy Story* and *Silk Stalkings*.

She's also a writer, her book *The Girl Code* being published in 2001. Dan Martin's CV includes *Rush Hour*, *Heat*, *The Stand*, *Nowhere Man*, *Katts and Dog*, *Friends* and *Hangin' with Mr Cooper*. Trevor Lissauer plays Miles Goodman in *Sabrina, The Teenage Witch*. Eamon Behrens featured in *Sliders* and *Chicken Soup for the Soul*.

Behind the Camera: Patrick Norris has directed episodes of *Jack & Jill*, *Cupid*, *The Net*, *Malibu Shores*, *Xena: Warrior Princess* and *My So-Called Life*. Previously he was costume supervisor on *Sunset*, *The Milagro Beanfield War* and *Blood & Orchids*.

References: The title is a classic Motown song by Martha Reeves and the Vandellas. Liz quotes, possibly unconsciously, from the Beatles' 'I Want to Tell You', whilst there are allusions to the skipping chant 'One for Sorrow, Two for Joy', Hot Chocolate's 'It Started With a Kiss', *Clueless* and *Pollyanna*. Watch out for a ROCK THE WORLD! poster at school.

Teen-Speak: Liz: '*Later.*'
   Valenti, to Amy DeLuca: 'So, ya stayin' out of the slammer?'
   Max: 'How's it goin'?' Michael: 'Decent.'
   Metal: '*Whoa! Excellent!*' Octavio: '*Babe-o-rama!*'
   Metal: '*Dude*, relax. This has happened to me, like, ten times, man.'
   Isabel: 'We are *so screwed.*'

Fashion Victims: 'Maria, it's 105 degrees outside, and you're wearing a turtleneck.' A thick red one at that (to hide the enormous love-bite on her neck!) Good stuff: Maria in shorts and a very revealing vest-type blouse (Isabel wears a similar one a little later) and 'Dream' Isabel's tight red dress ('I like the way you look in red,' Alex tells the *real* Isabel later). There's lots of crazy and horrible clothes on display at the party.

Sex and Drugs and Rock'n'Roll: The opening sequence of Maria and Michael is almost pornographic. Maria later describes this to Liz as 'just sucking face'. Liz and Alex find themselves arrested by Valenti after having incriminating bottles of Jack Daniels dumped into their sweaty palms. As Alex complains to Valenti: 'I was at a party! My only wish was that while I was there, I engaged in some sort of depraved activity, like drinking or sex, but I didn't!'

After Liz announces her revelation about Max and the others, Alex notes: 'Part of me feels like you've gone insane, and the other part of me feels like I want some of the massive doses of hallucinogens you've obviously been taking.'

Logic, Let Me Introduce You to This Window: In the opening scene, Michael pushes open the door from the outside, even though the sign says 'push' from the inside. When Liz is walking down the school halls at the beginning she is wearing her hair loose, yet when she bumps into Kyle and Vicky she has a ponytail. When Liz is trying to get the slugs to mate, she has surgical gloves on, then when she caresses Max's hand, she doesn't. In the jail scene when Liz is considering revealing Max's secret to Alex, her hands are on the bars when the camera is facing Alex, then down at her side when the camera is facing her a split second later.

Quote/Unquote: Valenti: 'Being a single parent myself, I know how difficult that can be.' Amy: 'Looks like we finally have something in common!'

Max: 'We agreed to discuss before we acted on any . . . urges.' Michael: 'I hate to tell you this, but when I have *urges*, you're not exactly the first person I think about.'

Alex: 'So what, you're saying the FBI is all over them because they're illegal aliens?' Liz: 'Yeah, sort of.'

Notes: 'A couple of weeks ago, if someone would have asked me who I would trust with my life, other than my parents, I would have said you without skipping a beat. And now, it's like I don't even know who you are.' Nicely sensual in all sorts of unexpected places, 'Heatwave' is probably the closest that *Roswell* gets towards *Buffy the*

Vampire Slayer's mixture of teen-angst, comedy and weird-ness. Diane Farr is a particular delight (it's lovely to see that Maria's mom is as downright peculiar as *she* is). Marvellous direction too.

Isabel has a picture of two young children on her bedroom mirror (probably herself and Max as kids). Alex owns a red Silvertip bicycle and rides it to school (though later in the season he mentions owning a car, see **16**, 'Sexual Healing'). He doesn't believe in aliens. In addition to lots of pupils coupling up, Ms Hardy (see **1**, 'Pilot') and Mr Krewlick have been spotted together. When she was eighteen, Amy DeLuca was involved (along with twenty other people) in a demonstration to prevent the destruction of 'a 200-year-old piece of Native American architecture'. Valenti arrested only her. Because she was cute. ('You were wearing cowboy boots and a little skirt. I had to arrest somebody, so . . .') This event, she says, scarred her for life. Valenti takes Amy out for a meal at a Chinese restaurant (presumably Senor Chow's, see **10**, 'The Balance', **17**, 'Crazy'). Valenti's ex-wife is called Michelle.

Amongst the names of students seen in the yearbook that Isabel looks at are: Sharon Stadler, Robert Thompson and Wendy Wright.

Soundtrack: 'Situation' by Yaz, 'Put Your Lights On' by Santana (featuring Everlast), 'Got You (Where I Want You)' by the Flys, Lunatic Calm's 'Beatbox Burning', Warren G's 'I Want It All' and 'We Haven't Turned Around' by Gomez. Plus, highlight of the episode, 'Let Me In' by Save Ferris (beautifully performed by the band during Alex's dream in which he dances with Isabel. Lead singer Monica Powell has an uncredited speaking-role. The band make a similar cameo in the movie *10 Things I Hate About You*).

Cast and Crew Comments: 'It's absolutely hysterical,' Diane Farr told an online interview. 'I play this offbeat, new-age, hippy mother who's dating the sheriff, a nemesis on the show. I'm supposed to have had [Maria] at fifteen and she's supposed to be fifteen now. In real life,

[Majandra] and I are only about eight years apart. She's the first daughter I've ever had.'

Did You Know?: One of Save Ferris' members had to mime playing the cello, even though that instrument is not part of the band. In the scene where Michael and Maria are making out in the eraser room, Majandra Delfino was embarrassed at having to moan 'Oh, my God', as though she were making a porno movie.

10
The Balance

US Transmission Date: 15 December 1999
UK Transmission Date: 13 March 2000 (Sky One),
16 November 2000 (BBC2)

Writer: Thania St John
Director: John Behring
French title: *Question d'Équilibre*

Liz is having a wonderful day, but Michael and Maria are in difficulties over their break-up. Michael finds the symbols that River Dog showed Max in the cave and is angry that Max didn't share his findings. Curious, Michael takes his own trip to the reservation. After joining in River Dog's sacred ritual, Michael finds himself in a frightening hallucinatory state. Scared for their friend, Max, Liz, Maria, Isabel and Alex work together to save Michael's life. But at the cost of Max and Liz's relationship.

'Dear Diary ...': 'There are days when everything seems wrong,' Liz notes at the beginning. 'When little things just irk you for no good reason. And then there are days like today when the whole world just sings to you from the minute you open your eyes in the morning, till the minute you shut them again at night. Days when you actually enjoy cleaning the milk shake machine.' Once again, the diary itself puts in an appearance in the final scene.

'I've Got the Power': Isabel tells Alex that when she, Max and Michael came out of the pods, 'we looked just like normal kids. We've never been anything else but what you see. No green skin, no antennas. We have emotions, we feel pain, and we probably have more questions about ourselves than you do.' She then demonstrates her ability to 'manipulate the molecular structure of things' by turning ketchup into what looks like mustard.

Roswell Iconography: There's a further reference to The CrashDown dessert-staple, Men in Black-berry pie (see **4**, 'Leaving Normal'). Liz's parents are away for the weekend at a 'stargazing camp-out. Something about Venus being in the morning sky.'

Isabel says that the UFO Center gives her the creeps. Alex shows Isabel drawings similar to those Max copied from the Indian cave that are from Machu Picchu, in Peru. Isabel is scathing: 'Next you're gonna tell me that spacemen came here thousands of years ago to share all their secrets with cavemen, right? Don't you think we've checked all this stuff out? It's just some stupid rumour, like those ridiculous crop circles and the rest of the lies people tell to make a buck.'

Max says that the first time he saw Michael, it was in the desert the night that they came out of the pods. The sky was, he notes, bright with stars and a full moon. Isabel and Max found each other first. They didn't know how to speak, but could communicate anyway (presumably telepathically). Michael saw them from a distance, but was afraid so he watched them for a long time before revealing himself by standing on a rock. 'Just like you'd expect from Michael. "Here I am. Deal with me",' Max says. 'He said it was the hardest thing he's ever had to do. Trust us.' Compare this with what Max told Topolsky about not being able to remember anything before the orphanage in **3**, 'Monsters', and with the flashbacks seen in **19**, 'Four Square'.

Max describes what happened next: 'We all saw the headlights at the same time. Isabel took my hand. We

knew we'd be safe as long as we stayed together. I held my
hand out for Michael. He wouldn't take it. So we just
looked at each other for a long time. Wouldn't see him
again for three years. Isabel would cry every night,
wondering where he was.' This fits in with Max and Isabel
being found by the road by their parents, mentioned in **1**,
'Pilot' (but, see **11**, 'The Toy House').

The Conspiracy Starts at Home Time: River Dog tells Max
more about the alien who lived in the cave on the
reservation when he was a boy (see **7**, 'River Dog'). Some
of the elders of the tribe believed that the alien was an evil
spirit, so they decided to test him. He was invited into 'the
sweat', just as River Dog does with Michael. The alien's
reaction was quick and severe, his eyes turning white and
he developed a fever, but survived. The young River Dog
became friendly with the alien who called himself 'a
visitor'. 'In my language,' notes the old man, 'the word is
"Nasero"' (see **Logic Let Me Introduce You to This
Window**). He gave River Dog the healing stones which
Max, Isabel, Liz, Maria and Alex use to cure Michael.
'They are from his place,' says River Dog. 'They carry an
energy inside them . . . He said that his body carried the
same energy that's in these stones. He called it *The
Balance*.' The stones subsequently prove to be part of a
wall map charting a particular constellation in the sky.

Dudes and Babes: Liz can't stop smiling at the start of the
episode. In fact, it looks like she slept with a coat hanger
in her mouth.
    Maria and Liz discuss kissing aliens: 'It was like every
cell in my body felt the same cell in his and started heating
up,' notes Maria. Liz says she felt dizzy when kissing Max,
and that it was nothing like she felt with Kyle. Maria went
out with a boy called Doug Sohn in the eighth grade. He
was, she says, an 'amateur' compared to Michael.

Behind the Camera: John Behring directed episodes of
Charmed and *My Indian Summer*.

References: Maria refers to Max and Michael as 'Prince Charming and Quasimodo' (from *Cinderella* and *The Hunchback of Norte Dame*, respectively). Also, a quote from Frank and Nancy Sinatra's 'Something Stupid' and an allusion to the Kinks' 'Lola'. Max has a poster for Moby's 'Play' on his bedroom wall (see **5**, 'Missing'). Visual references to *Cocoon*, *E.T.* and *The Doors*.

Teen-Speak: Maria: 'God, this day sucks.' And: 'Me? I'm *Teflon*, babe. Michael starts acting like a total loser, I just walk away.'

Eddie: 'Told you it was intense.'

Fashion Victims: Isabel's black leather trousers put in another appearance. Check out, also, her matching boots.

Sex and Drugs and Rock'n'Roll: Alex's two theories about Liz and Maria's revelations concerning Max, Isabel and Michael (see **9**, 'Heatwave') are that either they have both been 'brainwashed by a drug cult' or, that he is trapped 'inside some extremely long, extremely weird nightmare.' Maria bitterly comments on her relationship with Michael to Alex: 'Granted, the passion was outrageous, but in the end, they're pretty heartless.'

Logic, Let Me Introduce You to This Window: Where does River Dog disappear to during and after the healing of Michael? When Max tells Michael and Isabel that Liz is coming over, Shiri Appleby can be seen outside the open door awaiting her cue. Something clearly audible is dropped on-set during Michael and Maria's scene at the episode's climax. Brendan Fehr is distracted, but continues with the scene. River Dog calls the alien he knew in the fifties 'Nasero'. All subsequent reference to the character are as Nasedo.

Quote/Unquote: Liz, to Max: 'Cherry cola. On the house.' Maria, to Michael: 'Yours is a dollar, twenty-five!'

Alex: 'Why on earth would . . . Excuse the phrase. Why would you be sent here to begin with? I mean, what purpose could you possibly have?' Isabel: 'To wipe out the world, one annoying teenager at a time.'

Notes: 'I'm not going to let Max's mistakes stop me from finding what I need to know.' An excellent, surreal episode from Thania St John. Michael crossing into the dreaming state, and his friends following him to guide him back to reality being a superb example of how hallucinatory sequences can be funny and scary at the same time. An end of the innocence of the early episodes in many ways, with broken relationships to the fore, with the future promising revelation and discovery. A little classic. And with some nice directional touches too (isn't that shot of the red desert sky something special?)

Liz notes that Max likes cherry cola. Maria says that Michael enjoys the same 'with arsenic'. Liz and Max go for a date to Senor Chow's Chinese Restaurant (see **17**, 'Crazy'). Liz appears to be an excellent pool player. She owns a telescope. Maria tells Alex that the first couple of days after finding out about the aliens 'were pretty tough for me too, but trust me, they will not hurt you. I mean, physically.' Maria has had chicken pox and developed a terrible fever which her mother cured by giving her an ice bath. She wears a lapel button on her CrashDown uniform that says WAITRESS FROM HELL.

Soundtrack: 'Troubled Times' by Fountains of Wayne, Third Eye Blind's 'Deep Inside of You', Angie Stone's 'Everyday', 'Incantation' by Cirque du Soleil (the chant that the Indians and Michael perform), 'Everyone Can Fly' by Gigolo Aunts, and Jewel's 'Absence of Fear'.

Cast and Crew Comments: According to Laurin Sydney, CNN's Entertainment News correspondent, in a piece for *CNN Showbiz*, 'viewer alienation is not a problem for *Roswell*'. Interviewed, Jason Behr noted that the series is 'about a bunch of high-school students and their friends and how they relate to each other and how they deal with the whole dynamic of that relationship when it's taken an unexpected turn. It's kind of like a love story, but it's about two different people that shouldn't be together but want to be.' But Jason was also weary of the show's sudden success which, he noted ironically, 'feels alien. It's a weird feeling, like I woke up in somebody else's bed.'

Did You Know?: Shiri Appleby actually *did* wake up in somebody else's bed the day that *Roswell* was commissioned by the network. She was staying at a friend's house so that she wouldn't feel as though she was waiting for the phone to ring. 'I woke up at 11:30, I'm, like, "I'm just going to check the machine". I had three messages. They're [all] "We've been picked up! Call for details".'

11
The Toy House

US Transmission Date: 19 January 2000
UK Transmission Date: 20 March 2000 (Sky One),
23 November 2000 (BBC2)

Writers: Jon Harmon Feldman, Jason Katims
Director: Michael Fields
Cast: Gil Colon (Firefighter One)
French title: *Retour vers l'Enfance*

When a grease-fire breaks out in Max's kitchen, he uses his powers to save his mother from being horribly burned. Her suspicions heightened, Mrs Evans confronts him about his special abilities. Scared that she may find out the truth, Max enlists the help of Isabel and Michael. Things become even more complicated when Sheriff Valenti starts to ask questions about the fire. Still heartbroken from her breakup with Max, Liz feels sympathy for her ex-boyfriend Kyle and all that he has been through. It appears that the two may finally be able to become friends. Meanwhile, Michael chooses a strange way to thank Maria for saving his life.

'I've Got the Power': Max has the ability to extinguish a huge kitchen fire, thereby saving his mother's life. Ten years ago when Max was six, on a family holiday, he healed a pigeon's broken wing, allowing the bird to fly away, an event witnessed by his parents and captured on video tape. From his description of the event to Michael it seems that this may have been the point where Max (and, by implication, Isabel) first realised that they possessed extraordinary powers. Isabel applies lipstick with a wave of her hand.

Roswell Iconography: The school locker next to Max's features a cute, alien-head sticker.

High School Life: Max describes his Biology homework as 'everything you always wanted to know about a dead frog'. He tells his mother that this is not his strongest subject, but that he has a good lab partner (called Liz). After Kyle injures his ankle in the school basketball game Liz takes him a CrashDown pie (which she knows he likes) along with some study notes for Ethics, thinking he might need them for the mid-term.

Dudes and Babes: Maria's description of the events of the previous episode is: 'Michael, we saved your ass. You were *all-flunked-out*, sweating, running a 112-degree temperature and, like, *dying*. I could have walked away and never looked back. But I didn't . . . There I was, dragging your sweaty, gross body through the Indian reservation, getting my clothes all muddy and worrying . . . I went out on a limb for you and you hug Max and Isabel and it's all about the three of you. I mean were you even going to *thank* me?' Michael later explains to Maria, 'I can't get entangled. I've got to be a stone wall. When I'm around you sometimes, I don't feel like a stone wall any more.'

In one of the great moments of the series, Isabel argues with Max and Michael about whether they should tell Diane about their secrets. Michael is dismissive of Isabel's overt sentimentality, concluding that although her mother may love her right now, 'there's no such thing as unconditional love'.

Denial, Thy Name is Diane: We witness *Roswell*'s first case of JOYCE-SUMMERS-SYNDROME as Diane Evans (and, by implication, her husband too) have spent the last ten years in denial over the miracle that they saw their young son perform: 'I've thought about it. I mean, it's just one of those things that happened. I never really understood it, but there was nothing I could do about it at the time. So I tried to forget about it. But some things you never forget about. And when that kitchen fire happened I thought about it all over again.'

Diane says that whenever her husband is away on a business trip, she always eats fried foods and red meat. She doesn't reveal why. Max also comments that in such circumstances she tends to watch old family videos and get sentimental for no obvious reason.

'You Might Remember Me from Such Films and TV Series As . . .': Gil Colon was Tom Prescott in *The Young and the Restless*.

Behind the Camera: Michael Fields' work can be seen on *DC*, *Third Watch*, *Felicity*, *Sex and the City*, *Homicide: Life on the Street* and *Noon Wine* (which he wrote and directed).

References: The episode contains two quotations from Nirvana's 'Smells Like Teen Spirit'. Michael uses Joey Tribbiani's catch-phrase from *Friends* ('How *you* doin'?') on Maria. Isabel has a poster for the band Sebadoh on her bedroom wall. Also, home improvements guru Bob Vila, controversial afternoon talk-show diva Sally Jesse Raphael (the episode that Kyle watched was called 'Ex's on the Rampage') and Doctor Dolittle. Max misquotes from Dido's title song ('I am who I am'). There are visual references to *Heathers* and the *Buffy the Vampire Slayer* movie (the basketball game). The poster beside Michael as he waits for Maria says 'Today I will commit one random act of senseless kindness . . . Will you?' Ironic, as he just has.

Teen-Speak: Isabel: 'You were right to put the brakes on the Liz thing.' Max: 'You mentioned that, *like*, ten times.'
Michael, to Maria: 'Hey.' Maria: 'Yeah, *whatever*.'

Maria, at the basketball game: 'Sorry. I retract that last "whooh".' And, to Michael: 'You should get yourself massive doses of therapy, like, immediately.'

Fashion Victims: Isabel's red top puts in another appearance. Also her orange sweater. Maria is wearing the leather pants this week. Liz's very short, very tight black skirt is notable and the episode is an entire cheerleader-fest.

Quote/Unquote: Michael: 'Dealing with *Frick-and-Frack* is one thing, but we can't bring adults into this and expect them to handle it. Adults are the enemy, Max. Remember that.' Max: 'You say *everyone* is the enemy.' Michael: 'They *are*.'

Kyle: 'I was hoping for something high in both fat and cholesterol and lacking in any inherent nutritional value.' Liz: 'I think you're just in luck.'

Michael: 'You healed a pigeon? Great. Now you're Doctor Dolittle!'

Notes: 'Have you ever noticed anything about your brother? Anything unusual?' Another quality script which (as with **8**, 'Blood Brother') asks an *obvious* question about the aliens' back-story (how come Max and Isabel's parents have never spotted anything odd about their children?) and, with the aid of an astonishingly dramatic climax, closes the issue for all concerned amid deceit (on one side) and denial (on the other). Just like a real-life relationship between a parent and a teenager in other words. A real rabbit-out-of-the-hat trick which turns an otherwise fairly ordinary episode into something utterly valid and aware. And the final scene has Katherine Heigl acting her socks off.

Maria's final woodwork project of the term is a practical. She is making a napkin holder (and not a shoe tree as Michael believes). As a 'thank you' gift for saving his life, Michael creates (without the aid of his powers) a beautifully crafted, spring-activated device. 'It redefined the term "napkin holder",' he boasts. But Maria doesn't use it. She has a poster for her mother's shop (called DeLuca's Alien Collectibles) in her school locker.

Max calls Isabel 'Iz' for the first time in the series (in Melinda Metz's novels, she is regularly called both 'Iz' and 'Izzy' by her friends. See **The Roswell High Novels**). When Diane asks Isabel what she remembers as a child, she replies: 'The orphanage. I most clearly remember seeing you and daddy the day that you came to adopt us. You were wearing this yellow sweater. And I remember thinking that it looked like the sun ... The day that you and daddy came for us, that's when our lives began.' This does not seem to tie in with the suggestion (in **1**, 'Pilot') that Max and Isabel were found *in the desert* by their parents. Larry and Jennifer (see **1**, 'Pilot', **13**, 'The Convention') are mentioned by Valenti when he tells Mrs Evans about the events of Liz's shooting in **1**, 'Pilot' ('they're a couple of tourists with a serious credibility issue'). Max reminds his mother that during his first few nights in his adoptive home he would lie in bed and cry. 'For Isabel it was different. She saw you and dad, and from the very first moment, she knew she was home.' To help the young boy adjust, Diane gave Max a toy house that she said was 'magic' and that if he held onto it, it would take him home. 'But the thing is,' Max tells his mother, 'it would *never* bring me home, because I don't know where home is.' He has a picture of his parents in his bedroom. The meal that Diane Evans is cooking at the start of the episode seems to be a stir-fry of some description containing carrots, red and green peppers, mushrooms, onions and garlic.

Soundtrack: Three Dog Night's 'Shambala', 'Get Up' by Amel Larrieux, Third Eye Blind's 'Never Let You Go' (at the basketball game), 'Amy Hit the Atmosphere' by Counting Crows (Isabel notes that Max always listens to them when he's upset), 'The Woman in Me' by Jessica Simpson (featuring Destiny's Child), Buckcherry's 'For the Movies' and G Love and Special Sauce's 'Rodeo Clowns'.

Cast and Crew Comments: 'This was the episode that helped us *ground* the series,' Jason Katims told a *Roswell* Internet site.

Did You Know?: Colin Hanks' first movie experience was as a set production assistant on Ron Howard's *Apollo 13*.

12
Into The Woods

US Transmission Date: 26 January 2000
UK Transmission Date: 27 March 2000 (Sky One),
30 November 2000 (BBC2)

Writer: Thania St John
Director: Nick Marck
Cast: Tom McCleister (Rocky Calhoun),
Tony Papenfuss (Coach Clay),
John Michael Vaughn (Deputy Stone),
Stan Sellers (Receptionist), Trevor Wright (Cute Guy)
French title: *Le Message*

Rumours of a UFO sighting spread at the same time as the annual West Roswell High 'Fathers' Camping Trip' takes place in the same woods. The weekend ends up more exciting than Liz expected, when she and Maria are involved in the aliens' journey to investigate the sighting. River Dog appears again to help Michael investigate the clues, whilst Valenti must chose between his work and his family.

'Dear Diary . . .': The return of the voice-over: 'I hate the start of a cold. That little tickle that tells you something's about to happen that you know you can't prevent. Something that could be mild if you do all the right things, or could knock you off your feet if you're not careful.'

'I've Got the Power': Max can change playing cards to win at poker. Or, in this case, lose so as not to annoy Jeff Parker. Michael heals River Dog's broken ankle.

Roswell Iconography: Milton is found wandering around the woods with a metal detector. Looking for spaceships, seemingly. There are several references to one traditional 'logical' explanation for UFO sightings, dry lightning. At the camps, Kyle tells one of his grandfather's favourite animal mutilation stories, concerning five cows on Haddie Wexler's farm and the sad story of Haddie herself. 'When she died two months later they did an autopsy, and sure enough, they found perfectly bored holes in her skull just where she claims the aliens made them when they abducted her that night. That skull is now buried deep somewhere within Area 51.'

Isabel Names the Stars: Teaching Alex rudimentary astronomy, Isabel points out the Milky Way, Orion, the north star (Polaris) and the Cygnus constellation.

The Conspiracy Starts at Home Time: Agent Stevens is mentioned. He called Valenti after the sighting. Mayor Higgins (see **1**, 'Pilot') also rings the sheriff for news. Kyle asks his father, 'How many times [did] you sit at home listening to grandma cry while grandpa spent the night chasing spacemen out in the woods? That's my role now, isn't it?'

High School Life: Alex is passing out fliers for the camping weekend. If he issues enough, he may be able to raise his PE grade from C to B-. He admits that he isn't very athletic, except at dodgeball (see **5**, 'Missing', **8**, 'Blood Brother'). Liz bribes Maria to accompany her on the camping trip with $62.50 and by doing Maria's Maths homework for a week.

Dudes and Babes: Maria goes to school wearing an aqua bra that massively emphasises her prize assets. 'All the fun of implants except without the invasive surgery.' She gets three telephone numbers before the end of second period.

'You Might Remember Me from Such Films and TV Series As ...': Garrett M Brown played Bob Russell in *Uncle Buck* and also featured in *Can of Worms*, *Sisters*, *Zelig* and *Grace Under Fire*. John Cullum will be recognised by *ER* fans as David Greene and as Holling Vincoeur on *Northern*

Exposure. His movies include *Ricochet River*, *The Day After* and *1776*, whilst he is also a writer (scripting *The Secret Life of Algernon*) and director (on episodes of *Quantum Leap*). Tom McCleister appears in *Fletch Lives*, *Midnight Run*, *Twins*, *Cheers*, *Star Trek: Deep Space Nine* and *Matlock* and played Ike on *Married . . . with Children*. Tony Papenfuss's CV includes *Firefox*, *Escape from New York* and *Murphy Brown*. He was Bob Newhart's brother Darryl on *Newhart*. Ted Rooney played Doctor Tabash in *ER* and Morey Dell in *Gilmore Girls*, and was also in *The Flintstones in Viva Rock Vegas*. John Michael Vaughn's movies include *In Dreams* and *The Chaos Factor*. Stan Sellers was in *Doctor Dolittle* and *Caroline in the City*.

Behind the Camera: Nick Marck has directed episodes of *Malcolm in the Middle*, *Charmed*, *Buffy the Vampire Slayer*, *Get Smart*, *The X-Files*, *American Gothic*, *Northern Exposure* and *Dream On*. Previously, he was an assistant director on movies such as *10*, *The Postman Always Rings Twice*, *Wavelength* and *City Killer*, and on *Battlestar Galactica*.

References: The title is a Steven Sondheim musical. *Close Encounters of the Third Kind* (both visual and dialogue references), *The X-Files* (ditto), Italian film auteur Federico Fellini (1920–93) the director of *La Dolce Vita*, *8½*, *Satyricon* and *Intervista*. The movies *The Great Outdoors* and *The Abyss*, newspaper *USA Today* and current affairs TV show *Dateline*. Maria and her mom's 'don't-ask, don't-tell-policy' seems similar to that recently adopted by the US military, with regard to the sexual orientation of their personnel.

Teen-Speak: Liz: 'Skewering my navel is not exactly my idea of fun.' And: 'You have *officially* lost it.'

Milton: 'Where's Max Evans?' Maria: 'I thought he worked for you, *dude*.'

Guy, on Maria's sudden revelation of breasts: '*Whoa, check it out, man!*'

Alex, on his date with Isabel: 'It's amazing, you know? It's totally amazing. It's too amazing. It's a joke, isn't it?

It's a practical joke. You two are in on it. You *bastards*.'
Liz: 'Alex, your paranoid schizophrenia. It's kicking in.'

Fashion Victims: Jeff Parker's description of Michael is:
'The guy with the hair!' Maria's Julian Cope-style flying
jacket is merely a prelude of a box of delights on display,
particularly that tight pink top. Her red bra is briefly
visible when she reveals her pierced navel to Liz. Liz's bra
can also be seen when Jeff stumbles in on her changing. On
the downside, Alex and Isabel's perfectly ridiculous
bobble-hats and Maria's hilarious white furry boots.

Sex and Drugs and Rock'n'Roll: Maria gives Liz the
medicinal immune-system herb echinacea mixed with
goldenseal to help with her cold. When Jeff Parker sees the
exchange of a large packet of pills for the money that Liz
has bribed Maria with he, naturally, fears the worst. 'You
thought it was drugs?' Liz asks. 'You're so grown-up all of
a sudden,' replies Jeff, sadly. 'I just feel like I'm not a part
of your life any more.' When Michael tells his foster father
that there's no milk for his cereal, Hank's reply is 'use beer'.

Logic, Let Me Introduce You to This Window: Philip Evans
doesn't seem particularly concerned when he finds out that
his children are missing in the woods, whereas Jeff Parker's
reaction is much more believable. Not only that, but the
deputy seems very reluctant to go and search for them.
When Valenti discovers Max and Isabel, why doesn't he
question why River Dog and Michael are with them? Is
that a guitar case that Maria is taking with her on the
camping trip? If so, why?

Quote/Unquote: Maria: 'Today is the first day of the rest of
our lives.' Liz: 'Spending time with your mother again?'
Maria: 'No, I mean it. Aren't you tired of being a slave to
men?' Liz: '*Definitely* your mom.'

Alex, to Isabel: 'I was wondering, do aliens enjoy
cinema?'

Liz, on her dad: 'I love him but, like, in the normal
father role. Which is five minutes at a time, just a few times
a day. Not for an entire weekend with no TV.'

Notes: 'I figured you guys would be having a little woodsy tryst.' And still the impressive run of episodes continues. 'Into the Woods' is a pocket-epic. An amusing (and yet very complex) house of cards built around the central theme of how fathers and their sons (and daughters) have an, at times, shaky relationship. Valenti's back story is beautifully shaped by his own (and, more importantly, Kyle's) realisation that he is repeating the mistakes of *his* father during Jim's childhood. In that sense this and other *Roswell* episodes (notably several in the second season) follow a theme popular in both *Buffy* and *Friends*, that we all *become* our parents as we grow older.

Witnesses to the alleged UFO sighting that occurred in Frazier Woods (see **34**, 'We Are Family') include 'some guy named Buzz', two motorists, a family camping in the area and Rocky Calhoun, a fly fisherman. Maria again refers to the aliens as 'Czechoslovakians' (see **2**, 'The Morning After'). There's a Fellini retrospective at the art house theatre on Friday night which Alex suggests taking Isabel to. She's not enthusiastic, preferring to watch a 'proper movie' instead. Alex's middle name is Charles. Kyle says that the camping trip is the only two days a year that he and his father get to spend together. One of the local newspapers is called the *Roswell Gazette* (see **1**, 'Pilot'). Amongst the names of the other camp participants are: Bennett, Butler, Coleman, Daskal, Hausman and Kalinowski (Greg Coleman was referred to in **2**, 'The Morning After'. The other three names were all mentioned in **6**, '285 South').

Soundtrack: Matthew Street's 'Faith In You', 'Theories' by Edwin, 'Stranded' by Plumb, Vertical Horizon's 'Everything You Want' and Van Morrison's epic 'Sometimes I Feel Like A Motherless Child' at the end.

Critique: By this stage the series had been sold around the world and was receiving critical analysis from all sorts of locations. Tom Cardy of the *Evening Post* in New Zealand wrote: 'What is it about teenagers and aliens? It's stating the obvious that when you're a teenager you feel alienated.

And *Roswell* is another in a long line of films and TV shows to overdo the metaphor. One of the best, from the 1950s, was *Teenagers From Outer Space*. It had a poster that read: "Teenage hoodlums from another world on a horrendous raygun rampage! They blast the flesh off humans!" *Roswell* takes a more subtle approach . . . Mixed into *The X-Files*-drama is plenty of teenage-angst and soap-opera. Max always had the hots for Liz and now that she knows men really are from Mars and women really are from Venus, he throws in the intergalactic pickup line . . .'

Cast and Crew Comments: 'As an actor it's great stuff to play,' Bill Sadler told *Starlog*. 'If he ever gets his hands on those kids, they're in trouble. But his reasons for wanting them are very human. And the fact that he has a teenage son, who he has trouble with, makes him more human too. They don't communicate very well and that's real too. We've done an episode [**12**, 'Into the Woods'] in which Kyle makes me confront the fact that there's something else in my life that's as important or more important to me than my own son. At the episode's end, I go to see my own father because I've realised what I've been doing all this time.'

Did You Know?: The area used for many of the locations in this episode is Topanga State Park in the Santa Monica Mountains close to the Mulholland Freeway.

13
The Convention

US Transmission Date: 2 February 2000
UK Transmission Date: 3 April 2000 (Sky One),
7 December 2000 (BBC2)

Writer: Emily Whitesell
Director: Tucker Gates
Cast: Tom Bower (Everett Hubble),
Deron Michael McBee (Wrestler),

Paul Tigue (Zinaplox), Andrew Morrow (The Kid)
French title: *Le Festival*

When Milton organises the Tenth Annual UFO Convention in Roswell, Max spends most of his time dealing with the convention's special guest, Jonathan Frakes (of *Star Trek: The Next Generation*). At the same time, he must avoid the suspicious couple who witnessed his powers when he saved Liz. Sheriff Valenti has his own problems when Everett Hubble, the man who ruined his father's life, comes back to Roswell seeking revenge for his wife's death.

'I've Got the Power': Michael's ability to give someone itchy skin (previously seen in **4**, 'Leaving Normal') is again demonstrated. Max moves the gun away from Hubble as they struggle for it in the dirt, but Valenti has to shoot Hubble to prevent him killing Max and Michael.

Roswell Iconography: Hanson says that there have been 14 calls this morning about the UFO sighting last week (see **12**, 'Into the Woods'). Valenti repeats the 'official explanation' of dry lightning. On the menu at The CrashDown: Green Eggs with Moon-Rock Hash, an Alien Encounter milkshake and a Convention Special. Amy's exhibition at the festival is the wonderfully named *Alien Takedown*, an intergalactic wrestling match. (Michael: 'I'm tired of having to wade through the kooks like you and the freak shows like this . . .' Amy: 'Nothing personal, but this freak show keeps my kooky daughter and myself off the streets.') This will feature a match between 'Raging Ray' and 'Ernie, the Alienator'.

The Conspiracy Starts at Home Time: Milton describes Everett Hubble as 'a legend . . . an enigma' and one of the few men rumoured to have made direct contact with aliens. He disappeared almost 30 years ago. Milton comments: 'People in the community believe he went after [an alien]. He found one and he's been tracking him ever since.' Hubble says he has been watching events for the last few months, including Liz's shooting in September.

In 1970 an alien killed his pregnant wife, Sheila. Hubble believes the alien is still active and has caused carnage all over the southwest for the past 40 years. 'Hand prints are the only trail he leaves. It only lasts for a day or so, and then it disappears.' In December 1972, with the aid of Valenti's father, he tracked down a drifter that they believed to be the alien. The newspaper that Valenti finds (dated 8 December 1972) has the headline ROSWELL SHERIFF TAKEN IN FOR QUESTIONING FOR THE SILO MURDER. According to the search engine that Max accesses: 'This unsolved murder of a vagrant is most noteworthy for forcing the resignation of Roswell sheriff James Valenti Snr, due to his alleged involvement in the incident.' Valenti senior was committed to a mental hospital by his son. Valenti finally unravels the real story with the aid of his father: 'Hubble came to you. He told you he found his wife dead and she had a handprint on her, just like the one that you'd seen on that corpse in 1959.' Hubble shot and killed the man, who turned out to be an innocent human, and let Valenti take the blame.

Convention Life: The final event on Sunday evening is a roundtable discussion. There is a *Theories on '47* exhibit. Jonathan Frakes hosts a 'Direct Contact' panel discussion at which an expert speaker talks about a well-documented abduction experience of a man named Grabowski who encountered a 'smooth-skinned ovoid EBE'.

Dudes and Babes: Michael tells Max that he thinks about 'mud' when he is with Maria to stop himself getting emotionally involved. When a heartbroken Alex asks for an orange soda on the rocks, Liz, Maria, Amy and Jennifer give him a really rather cruel five-minute rant about how men are all obsessive, inane and afraid of commitment. Subtext-rapidly-becoming-the-text here, girls. I think I speak for my entire gender when I say my sister is not my enemy. Stop treating all men with such contempt! (Especially considering Michael's selfless act that saves Amy's business).

'You Might Remember Me from Such Films and TV Series As . . .': Tom Bower's numerous TV and movie appearances include *The X-Files*, *China Beach*, *Murder, She Wrote*, *The Waltons* (as Doctor Willard), *The Rockford Files*, Oliver Stone's *Nixon* (as Richard Nixon's father), *Die Hard 2* (as Marvin) and *Raising Cain*. Deron McBee can be seen in *Elvira, Mistress of the Dark*, *Batman Forever* and *Immortal Combat*.

Behind the Camera: Before she became a writer/producer, Emily Whitesell was an actress, appearing as Howdy Doody Mom in *Calendar Girl*. Director Tucker Gates's previous work includes *Angel*, *Strange World*, *Buffy*, *The Commish*, the US version of *Cracker*, *21 Jump Street*, *Wiseguy*, *Dark Skies*, *Profiler*, *Nash Bridges* and *Space: Above and Beyond*.

References: Jonathan Frakes refers to unseen convention guests William Shatner, Leonard Nimoy and his *Next Generation* costar Patrick Stewart (two of whom, it seems, got better hotel suites than him). The date/place captions are an obvious tribute to *The X-Files*. Larry mentions legendary guitar hero Eric Clapton, and his rant about 'the missing bullet' is outrageously *JFK*. Everett Hubble is named after Edwin Hubble (1889–1953) the US astronomer noted for his investigations of nebulae and the recession of the galaxies, and after whom the Hubble telescope is also named. Jennifer is reading John Gray's 1992 bestseller *Men Are From Mars and Women Are From Venus*. Also *Goosebumps* and *Dream On*.

Teen-Speak: Hubble: 'Junior, I expect more from you than dumb-ass small-town threats.'

Isabel, on the convention: 'I'm sure it's a real Mecca for factual information.'

Maria: 'That was some guffaw.'

Michael: 'There's the geek from The CrashDown.'

Frakes: 'That's enough, monkey man!' Larry: 'Listen, cool it, Frakes!'

Fashion Victims: Michael's West Side Warriors sweatshirt and Cuba '71 red T-shirt. Max in PVC, Larry's trampy red track suit top. Love the scantily-clad convention girls in purple hot pants and silver wigs.

Logic, Let Me Introduce You to This Window: Larry says that Liz's shooting took place on 17 September. In **1**, 'Pilot' Liz's diary entry is dated 23 September and notes 'five days ago I died'. That would place the shooting on 18 September. If Hubble tries to shoot Max and Michael, what's the problem? They can surely use their powers to deflect the bullet? Why is there a dartboard in Milton's office? The *Bitter Lake Daily Journal* features the rather unlikely longwinded headline SHEILA HUBBLE FOUND MURDERED AT PEPPER'S GATE IN BITTER LAKE.

Quote/Unquote: Frakes, on Max: 'He may not be the best convention coordinator, but I would hardly call him an alien!'

Milton: 'Can you feel it, Evans? The energy, the synergy . . . It's kismet . . . The sighting has attracted some of the leading experts in the field. This is shaping up to be one of the most important gatherings on the paranormal in history. We're not just a joke any more.'

Larry: 'Listen, I have had an epiphany.' Jennifer: 'Really? I thought you said it was an allergy attack.'

Notes: 'Dead man walking. That's what I felt all those years. Only thing kept me alive was you.' The pinnacle of the first season though, ironically, this was probably the episode that more than any other convinced the network to change the emphasis of the series to more otherworldly matters. 'The Convention' works as a brilliant satire for everybody who's ever attended a convention of any description (the obnoxiousness of some guests and attendees, the sense of dislocation and of the horrid outside world occasionally intruding). In many ways it's a wonderful companion piece to a Neil Gaiman issue of *Sandman* about a convention of serial-killers. But the episode is also a very serious study about male obsession (every male character from Hubble and Valenti's father, through Valenti himself, Max, Michael, Larry and Alex either have, or potentially could, spend their lives chasing an impossible dream) and its mirror image, female denial. Jonathan Frakes's gentle debunking of his own persona is an added bonus whilst the ending, and its revelations for Jim Valenti, is a key moment in the development of the series.

Milton puts Max in charge of 'Celebrity Relations' at the convention. The local hotel where the guests are staying is called the Tumbleweed Inn. It only has two suites. Milton suffers from sciatica. Hubble was born on 14 November 1947. The 1970 New Mexico number plate 89013 was registered to Sheila Hubble of 477 Skyhawk Road, Bitter Lake, New Mexico, 24952.

Soundtrack: A fittingly eclectic bunch for such a strange setting: 'Waiting for the Alien' by the Toyes, the classic 'Planet Claire' by B-52s, Owsley's 'Coming up Roses', Klaatu's cover version of the Carpenters' 'Calling Occupants (of Interplanetary Craft)', Lit's 'Miserable', Sheryl Crow's 'My Favorite Mistake' and 'Alien' by Pennywise (see **8**, 'Blood Brother').

Cast and Crew Comments: Concerning the, at that time uncertain, renewal for another season Jonathan Frakes told *Starburst* magazine: 'I think that *Roswell* is going to make it. It seems to have the teenage girl demographic, which is what the WB has circled as their goal, so I have very high hopes that we will be back next year. I talked to Jason Katims yesterday and he was told that the decision won't be made until May. We have a big four-or-five-episode arc at the end of the season that will hopefully attract attention.'

Did You Know?: Asked by the *New York Post*, about his worst day ever, Colin Hanks replied: 'It was a week. A roommate had accidentally not closed the door when he left for work, and my dog got out. It was about a week later I found out that the pound had put the dog to sleep – on my birthday, in fact. That day sucked.'

14
Blind Date

US Transmission Date: 9 February 2000
UK Transmission Date: 10 April 2000 (Sky One),
14 December 2000 (BBC2)

Writer: Thania St John
Director: Keith Samples
Cast: James O'Shea (Radio DJ),
Michael Yurchak (Doug Shellow),
Jonathan David Bouck (Marcos),
Derrex Brady (Chris), Ben Busch (Nicky),
Patricia Skeriotis (Female Judge),
Joshua Hutchinson (Male Judge),
Matt Walden (Matt Walden), Krysta Burgos (Girl #1)
French title: *Rendezvous Galant*

After Maria enters her into a blind date contest, Liz
becomes the most popular girl in town. While Liz is on her
date with the contest winner, Max and Kyle find themselves getting drunk and bonding. Meanwhile Alex's band,
the Whit's, are chosen to open for a popular beat combo
playing a gig in Roswell. Desperate for a lead singer, they
turn to Maria. Michael talks Isabel into helping him send
a signal to the fourth alien.

'I've Got the Power': When he's drunk, Max uses his power
to superimpose his face on a picture of Liz, Maria and
Alex, and to do strange things to parking meters and street
lighting. After Michael has burned the 'eye' signal for
Nasedo in the grass, Isabel removes it. Max can also set off
a car alarm just by touching the car. But then, most people
can do *that*.

Naming All the Stars: Michael identifies the constellation
he saw in his dream as Aries, the ram, the first sign of the
Zodiac. This contains four stars, including the binary star
Gamma Arietis, and the bright and spectacular Alpha

Arietis (the big one in the middle). Michael notes that if you take a map of Roswell and position it when Aries is directly overhead, in April, all of the symbols from Nasedo's map take on locations in town, one of which is the library.

Dudes and Babes: Liz says she prefers brunettes, out-of-towners and Brainiacs as opposed to class clowns. Who does this remind us of? Her blind date, Doug Shellow, is a freshman at the University of New Mexico who studies ancient languages and wants to be an archeologist. They go for a romantic dinner at Chez Pierre (presumably Roswell's French restaurant).

Kyle asks Max how far he and Liz went. 'We saw into each other's souls,' notes Max. 'How about you?' 'Second base,' replies a gutted Kyle.

The Base System: For those readers unfamiliar with baseball or contact with the opposite sex, or both, it goes like this: first base is kissing; second base is groping; third base is oral sex ('Ah, *third base*,' remembers Chandler fondly in *Friends*; see also the movie *American Pie*); and fourth base is actual intercourse itself.

'You Might Remember Me from Such Films and TV Series As ...': James O'Shea was in *Fear Runs Silent* and *Charmed*. Michael Yurchak appeared in *Puddle Cruiser*. Jonathan David Bouck played Brad in *Small Soldiers* and crops up in *Parenthood*. Patricia Skeriotis's movies include *The Sexperiment* and *Dreammaster: The Erotic Invader*. Joshua Hutchinson was the computer and video effects assistant on *Lost in Space*.

Behind the Camera: Keith Samples also directed episodes of *Felicity*, *Freddy's Nightmares* and *A Smile Like Yours* and was a producer of *Election*, *Turbulence*, *Sydney*, the classic *2 Days in the Valley* and *Three Wishes*.

References: Among the rock bands rumoured to be the surprise mystery guest at the concert are US grunge combos Smash Mouth, barenaked ladies and Foo Fighters ('too big for Roswell' according to Markos). And, bizarre-ly, Manchester's Oasis (the possibility of Liam and Noel turning up in Roswell is, the author has to admit, a huge opportunity missed). Maria is compared to both Celine Dion and Alanis Morrisette. Kyle quotes Daryl Hall and John Oates's 'Man Eater', John Paul Young's disco-classic 'Love Is In the Air' and uses Mr T's catchphrase 'I pity the fool . . .' Also, Brianiac from *Superman*, the Pizza Pan chain, karaoke, *Bill and Ted's Bogus Journey* (Alex gives the 'horned beast' sign), *The Hunger* and *Lost Civilisation*.

Teen-Speak: Alex: 'Man, am I gonna kick some ass.' And: 'We *are* high school geeks.'

  Liz: 'Okay you guys, time-out, all right?'

  Maria: 'Get your butt down there, girl.'

  Kyle, on Max: 'What a wussie!' And: 'Whatever. Get down before you break your neck and everybody blames me for getting you trashed.'

Fashion Victims: The outfits that Maria buys for the guys' concert appearance cost her 50 dollars at a thrift shop ('that's their whole problem, they have no style'). Also, Maria's studded demin-jacket, Liz's shades-and-floppy-hat movie-star look, Alex's grey hooded top and Isabel's leather pants which put in another appearance.

Sex and Drugs and Rock'n'Roll: Whoever it is that the Whit's (note the illogical spelling!) are supposed to be opening for, they never make it. 'The drummer got arrested for disorderly conduct at Albuquerque airport,' says the promoter. 'It's always the drummers, isn't it?' notes Alex. Maybe it *was* Oasis all along! The Whit's original singer, Wendy Lavely, 'got mono' from Peter Gulla. 'She's lucky that's all she got,' notes Maria. The rest of the line-up is Nicky on lead guitar (playing a superb Gibson Les Paul), Chris on drums, Markos on rhythm guitar and Alex on bass. They describe themselves as 'alternative' and their song titles include 'Love Kills' and 'Hurt by Love'.

  Max and Kyle, amusingly, get drunk together in an attempt to bury the hatchet. Max has never had alcohol before and, though only drinking a small amount, the results are spectacular. Later, when they are in Liz's bedroom, Kyle messes about with her lingerie. Liz and Doug drink white wine at dinner. But isn't she too young to be served alcohol?

Logic, Let Me Introduce You to This Window: Michael sets fire to the library lawn as a signal. Why don't the fire department show up? Why isn't Kyle surprised when Max gets violently drunk on one tiny sip from his hip flask? The glitter on Liz's face disappears on a couple of close-up shots when she is in the street with Max. The microphone that Maria is singing into moves backwards and forwards between her hand and the mic-stand. Liz's gloves appear and disappear between shots in the opening scene. Liz slips on one shoulder of her sweater, but next shot, she has bare shoulders again.

Quote/Unquote: Alex: 'What's wrong with "the Whit's"?' Maria: 'Just an "s" away from what you really are.'

Alex, to Liz: 'Your answering machine's fixed. It just needed to be reset after the hundredth call. There are a lot of desperate guys out there.'

A drunken Max: 'I've been hiding for years, Kyle. But it's time the *real* Max comes out.' Kyle: 'He wouldn't be gay, by any chance, would he?'

Kyle: 'This is none of your business, *Shallow*. And you're looking at one hundred and sixty pounds of varsity Greco-Roman wrestler who's gonna keep it that way.'

Notes: 'Both of you sit here with your Cherry cola and your high school fantasies. I'm going to find him.' Sadly, the nadir of the season and the series. A silly story that gets embarrassing as the episode progresses. It might have looked good on paper but, a few good lines of dialogue aside, this is a shocking waste of the talent on display.

There are continuity references to the events of **13**, 'The Convention'. The winner of 'the KROZ blind dream date' gets an evening of 'fantasy and romance that ends in the most exciting concert of the year. An intimate club date with a surprise mystery band that'll put this town on the map for more than just the crash.'

Max eats potato chips with Tabasco sauce. There is a restaurant in Roswell called Night on the Town. Amy's alien-themed cocktail stirrers (see **9**, 'Heatwave') can be seen prominently in The CrashDown.

Soundtrack: At least the music's good: Dramarama's 'Anything, Anything (I'll Give You)', 'Is Anybody Home?' by Our Lady Peace, 'The Truth' by Joe 90, Blink 182's 'Adam's Song', '24/7' by Kevon Edmonds, 'Stand By My Woman' by Lenny Kravitz and Majandra Delfino's note-perfect cover of the Phil Collins MOR standard 'In the Air Tonight'.

Critique: *Cinescape*'s review of the episode concluded: 'The authority-figures-as-villains and issues of who-do-you-trust are soap opera-like. **14**, 'Blind Date' revolves around Liz (not an alien) having issues with dating someone 'not normal'. She wins a radio contest, ending up with a college guy. They get tired of every word and action being aired by an annoying radio personality and run off. Max has his first experience being drunk, which is much more interesting than the blind date. The show's music is great and they impressed me by plugging the bands at the credits. I loved the suspenseful ending with the dark man going back to the extinguished signal fire and, with a touch, igniting it again. I'd like to see more intrigue like that than the sappy lovelorn scenes. The alien slant to Roswell is what it has going for it. I hope they give us more.'

Cast and Crew Comments: By adding a hint of Hispanic authenticity, Majandra Delfino also helps to anchor the series in real-world-Roswell's Southwestern (and, hence, Latino) roots. Both David Nutter and Jason Katims have expressed a desire to make their *Roswell* reflect New Mexico's varied ethnic map, with Nutter talking about a 'responsibility and challenge to examine ethnic diversity'. This also extends to the show's adult characters, with Michael Horse, an actor of mixed Pueblo-descent and the various Native American characters from the episodes **7**, 'River Dog' and **10**, 'The Balance'.

Did You Know?: Colin Hanks is, in fact, a very good bass player.

15
Independence Day

US Transmission Date: 16 February 2000
UK Transmission Date: 17 April 2000 (Sky One),
21 December 2000 (BBC2)

Writer: Toni Graphia
Director: Paul Shapiro
Cast: Eddie Kehler (Driver), Amy Connolly (Teacher)
French title: *Indépendance*

After a violent confrontation between Michael and his foster father, Max and Isabel try to include Michael in their family. However, their efforts go to waste and Michael feels even more isolated. Things start to look up for him, however, when Philip Evans shows Michael how he can take his life in a new direction. Maria is disgusted when Sheriff Valenti's flirtations with her mother become more intense.

'I've Got the Power': Liz tells Max that when they kissed, 'I could *feel* the universe.' Max uses his powers to hide Michael's black eye. When Isabel suggests that Michael use his powers to stop his foster father from beating him, Michael notes: 'I can't control my powers like you and Max. Especially in the state of mind I'm in. If I did anything, I'd probably kill him.' When Michael *does* unleash his powers on Hank, it's in a terrifying maelstrom of violence. Michael can also cook, but that's more of a hidden talent.

Roswell Iconography: The trucker who picks up a fleeing Michael brings a bit of homespun common sense to the whole 'Roswell Incident' field: 'Ain't no aliens in that town . . . If you were an alien, you can go anywhere in the world, would you pick *Roswell*?!'

High School Life: Michael is told that once he is granted a petition for emancipation he will be solely responsible for his own financial, educational, and medical decisions. Which, given that he's got himself an apartment by the beginning of the next episode, means that he'll be needing a job pretty quickly too (see **17**, 'Crazy').

Dudes and Babes: Michael is at his most darkly brooding in this episode (given the subject matter, that's inevitable). The comedic scene of Liz and Maria almost walking in on Amy and the sheriff making out is one of the series' highlights (*love* Bill Sadler's cheesy grin as he emerges from the bedroom tucking his shirt into his pants). 'Once [men] get what they want, they disappear,' notes Maria during an impassioned scene with her mother concerning Valenti and Michael, respectively. 'I hope you're not talking from experience,' Amy pleads. 'Just *yours*,' replies a bitter Maria. Amy is understandably upset when she finds Maria and Michael in bed together ('My baby girl's having *sex*!').

'You Might Remember Me from Such Films and TV Series As . . .': Robert Katims, Jason's father, played Deensfrei in *Seinfeld* and has appeared in *Presumed Innocent*, *Broadcast News* and *The Bride in Black*. Eddie Kehler was Deputy Bobby in *Vampires Anonymous*.

Behind the Camera: Toni Graphia was a former producer on *Orleans* and has written for *Melrose Place*, *Victory Kiss* and *Doctor Quinn, Medicine Woman*. Paul Shapiro has worked on *Millennium*, *The X-Files*, the 90s remake of *The Invaders*, *Heads* and *The Lotus Eaters*. He was writer/director on *Hockey Night* and *Rookies*.

References: An allusion to *My Favourite Martian*. Also, Monopoly, the Who's 'Who Are You?', *Hello Dolly*, *Bonnie and Clyde*, *The Burns and Allen Show* ('Say goodbye, Max') and *Judging Amy*. There's an I'M A PRINCESS, I DON'T DO DISHES poster in Amy's kitchen.

Teen-Speak: Maria: 'Excuse me while I go and throw up.'
Liz: 'I am *so* wiped out.'
Isabel: 'You didn't have to be so rude to my dad.'
Michael: 'He was sticking it to me for no reason.'

Fashion Victims: Another of Isabel's seemingly endless supply of extremely tight sweaters (this one is royal blue). Also, Maria's horrible multi-coloured top.

Sex and Drugs and Rock'n'Roll: Maria slips Liz some 'Grief Relief', a herbal remedy that 'shocks the body back into reality when the mind's gone into overload. Veterinarians use it to calm wild animals.' Michael tells Hank that Isabel doesn't drink after his foster father makes lewd suggestions to her. When Hank apparently returns to Roswell and visits Valenti, he tells the sheriff he has been 'down in Carlsbad. Landed in a bar. Met a lady. What can I say?' But, of course, he is really Nasedo.

Logic, Let Me Introduce You to This Window: Serious logic flaw: how did a violent, alcoholic child-abuser like Hank Whitmore ever get to foster anyone? Don't New Mexico Social Services (in the *Roswell*-universe, anyway) do background checks? Nasedo swallows what look like mints immediately before and after shape-changing (this also occurs in **16**, 'Sexual Healing'). It isn't explained whether this is another dietary quirk or not. When Michael is throwing stones at a passing train, something falls from his jacket. Mrs DeLuca carries a bunch of pies into The CrashDown. Later Maria picks up the boxes which appear to be empty. When Michael is using his powers in front of Hank, the shadow of someone on the production team can be seen behind him.

Quote/Unquote: Isabel: 'Something's up with Michael. He's acting weird.' Max: 'Weirder than usual?'
Amy: 'There are, like, three single guys in all of Roswell. And two of them live in the Desert Inn retirement

community. Jim's a nice guy. He has a good job, he's responsible, and he's fun.' Maria: 'He's a *cop*. And you're a hippy!'

Amy: 'No, not 'whatever'. Maria, as you so subtly pointed out last night, my history with men has pretty much been a train wreck.'

Maria: 'You know the boy that I slept-but-didn't-sleep with?' Amy: 'Unfortunately, the shock has indelibly printed his face on my brain.' Maria: 'He's in jail.' Amy: 'This just gets better and better.'

Notes: 'Be a poster child for domestic abuse? It's not gonna happen.' Wow, *strong* stuff. American television's fascination with stories that touch on child abuse is never far from the surface (*Buffy*'s done the theme a couple of times, for instance. So have most of the other WB teen series). But here, without a glib solution in sight, *Roswell* picks at a raw scab on the American dream. What follows is not wholly successful but is, nevertheless, unflinching and has its heart in the right place. And for that, it deserves much praise.

Valenti likes coconut pie (hell, who doesn't?). Amy mentions that New Mexico has a 'three strikes' law (though she's actually referring to Valenti having let her down on previous dates. See **9**, 'Heatwave'). Amy refers to Michael as 'my favourite wrestler' (see **13**, 'The Convention'). There are continuity references to the events of **10**, 'The Balance' (River Dog's healing stones) and **13**, 'The Convention' (what Hubble told Max about Nasedo).

Philip Evans is a lawyer.

Soundtrack: Euphoria's 'Delerium' again (see **6**, '285 South'). Also 'Detour' by Bis, 'Run' by Collective Soul, '40 Miles from the Sun' by Bush, Jars Of Clay's 'Hand' and Radford's 'Closer to Myself'.

Cast and Crew Comments: Predictably, this fine episode is Brendan Fehr's favourite: 'Just because of what I got to do. With the home situation and the crying,' he told *Popstar!* In the same interview Brendan revealed that he has a Rottweiler named Opa, but no girlfriend, that his first kiss 'was with this girl named Andrea that I had met at camp', when he was 'seven or eight' (*seven*? There's nothing like starting early, is there?) and that he's a fan of actor Sir Anthony Hopkins and thrash metal band Metallica (in a website interview, Brendan also noted an admiration for country legend Johnny Cash and Canadian rockers Tragically Hip). Asked if he would date a fan, Brendan responded: 'That's a tough call. I was walking around the mall before and you might get a look or two but no one really cares. Then you suddenly become big-time and you're *better looking*!'

Did You Know?: The CrashDown café set is located on a sound-stage at Paramount Studios on Melrose Avenue in Hollywood, not too far from the *Star Trek: Voyager* bridge. Both sets are also very close to the Angel Investigations building from *Angel*. Paramount was also the studio where legendary sitcoms like *Happy Days* and *Mork & Mindy* were filmed.

A Switch in Time Saves The Show: Despite promising initial ratings, a vocal fan following and very respectable critical acclaim, by the early months of 2000, *Roswell* was beginning to struggle in the ratings, largely because it was scheduled against NBC's award-winning drama *The West Wing* and, even more critically considering its demographics, *Star Trek: Voyager*. The decision was therefore taken to move *Roswell* to Monday nights from 10 April, airing immediately after the WB's most popular show, *7th Heaven*.

16
Sexual Healing

US Transmission Date: 1 March 2000
UK Transmission Date: 24 April 2000 (Sky One),
4 January 2001 (BBC2)

Writer: Jan Oxenberg
Director: David Semel
Cast: Rosie Taravella (Gym Teacher),
Tara Boger (Girl #1)
French title: *À Fleur de Peau*

After avoiding each other for weeks, Max and Liz finally give in to their attraction. During a kiss, Liz sees visions of stars that she believes may help Max solve the mystery of his origin. Michael and Isabel, realising that Liz may be a link to their past, pressure Max to use Liz and her visions. Liz and Max drive out to the country where they find a mysterious glowing rock buried in the ground. After spending a night together, the two head back to Roswell to face their parents and their peers.

'Dear Diary . . .': 'It's February 20th. I'm Liz Parker and lately I've been having these feelings, like I'm changing inside. And part of me doesn't want to change. Part of me always wants to be my mom's little girl.'

'I've Got the Power': Isabel, brilliantly, can ignite a room full of candles to provide a romantic setting for Max and Liz's liaison.

Roswell Iconography: When Liz and Max connect, Liz sees images of the 1947 crash and of Earth from space. Also through this process, she discovers the whereabouts of a buried device near a radio tower by Highway 42 in Lincoln County.

High School Life: Mr Seligman, the science teacher, notes that hydrogen, oxygen and carbon were created in the millisecond after the Big Bang. These simple molecules are the basis of all life in the universe (present *and* unaccounted for). 'The conceit that alien life forms would be like us in any essential way [is] the wishful thinking of a lonely planet that once believed it was the centre of the universe,' he says pointedly.

Max follows Liz into the girls' locker room to see if it matches what he saw in Liz's fantasy. Seems like the girls

High Times

are preparing to play football, judging from the ball that the gym coach is carrying.

Naming All the Stars: Liz and Mr Seligman discuss the Whirlwind Galaxy (also known as the Whirlpool Galaxy), a spiral cluster with a bright nucleus in *Canes Venatici*. Liz asks, from images that she gets from contact with Max, if there is a red star in that area. Which leads to a discussion on red giants (stars that are in the last stages of their life cycle).

Dudes and Babes: When Maria and Michael make out, Maria says she sees 'a cluster of stars shooting through space. Incredible sunset, near the rings of Saturn.' 'I saw you as a little girl trying to tie shoelaces on her red sneakers,' replies Michael. They both later say that they're faking it, although Michael eventually admits that he *did* experience flashes; one of Maria's sneakers had a Kermit patch on it, and the shoelaces were blue. Maria's Dalmatian dog was also in the vision. The dog died when Maria was seven, soon after her father left home.

Liz and Max are caught kissing in the eraser room (see **2**, 'The Morning After'). Their mothers are called to see the Principal. At one point Liz daydreams of being naked in the shower with Max watching her. We get another look at Jason Behr's less-than-hairy chest (see **8**, 'Blood Brother').

'You Might Remember Me from Such Films and TV Series As . . .': Michael Chieffo's previous work includes *Come On, Get Happy: The Partridge Family Story*, *Mystery Men*, *My Favorite Martian*, *Mercury Rising*, *Apollo 11* and *Ellen*. Rosie Taravella was in *Ballistic* and *Who's the Boss?* and wrote the comedy thriller *Carlo's Wake*. Tara Boger played Leslie in *Perfect Body* and was on the sound crew of *Scream*.

Behind the Camera: Jan Oxenberg was the writer/director of the movies *Thank You and Goodnight* and *A Comedy in Six Unnatural Acts*, and creative consultant on *The Celluloid Closet*, a movie in which she also acted. A long-held fan rumour is that one of the uncredited extras in The CrashDown is legendary Hollywood helicopter pilot and cinematographer Bobby Zajonc (whose work includes *Mulholland Drive*, *3000 Miles to Graceland*, *Double Jeopardy*, *Face/Off*, *American Beauty*, *Romy and Michele's High School Reunion*, *Striptease*, *Jurassic Park*, *Pretty Woman*, *Indiana Jones and the Last Crusade* and many others). This has proved impossible to verify.

References: The title is from Marvin Gaye's smoochy 1983 classic. Michael mentions soul diva Chaka Khan. There are name-checks for *Friends*, Captain Kirk and the Klingons from *Star Trek*, and a possible oblique reference to the *Buffy* episode 'Lie to Me' in which Jason Behr appeared. Posters: Max has one in his bedroom for French pop-duo Air, whilst Michael's apartment includes one for Metallica (the actor's own, apparently) and another for Staind's 'Dysfunctional'.

Teen-Speak: Liz: 'Um, like, *beyond*.'
Max, to Liz: 'You have a hickey . . . And it's glowing.'

Fashion Victims: Maria has an impressive short red and black hooped skirt and black leather boots. Also, Liz's sharp red top and Isabel's sky-blue drawstring blouse.

Sex and Drugs and Rock'n'Roll: Michael gives Max some wise advice: 'Listen Maxwell, you're a sensitive guy and you have available to you one of the top three seduction lines with "It's going to help me find my home planet." And you're refusing it. No guy's *that* sensitive!'
There are continuity references to Max getting drunk in **14**, 'Blind Date', and the fact that he has hardly spoken to Liz since. Liz tells Maria 'when I actually *do it*, it is not gonna be in-between a plate of kielbasa and a deep fryer', indicating that she is still a virgin (see **27**, 'The End of the World').

Logic, Let Me Introduce You to This Window: Jason Behr almost starts laughing during one scene with Shiri Appleby. When Isabel is unloading groceries, a bag is on the kitchen counter. The shot cuts to Michael then back to Isabel and the bag has now vanished and Isabel is drying a glass. When Michael and Maria make out in school the previous scene had been set during the evening after school had finished. Alex's hands change position between shots during the scene in which he comes out of school and sees Isabel.

Quote/Unquote: Liz: 'What are you doin' here?' Max: 'I have orders from my planet to take over the Earth.' Liz: 'Besides that . . .'

   Alex: 'I was just wondering, in the interest of science, kissing being purported to provoke these certain insights. I wanted to, you know, offer myself as a human subject available for experimentation.' Isabel: 'It's not gonna happen, Alex!'

Notes: 'Some girls would give a lot to see themselves fly through outer space. I'm sure it doesn't compare to other things you could be doing, like watching Kyle barf after a beer blast.' Good episode, and one that uses its comedy set-pieces (particularly a gorgeous little scene of Isabel turning up on Alex's doorstep and asking him to kiss her in the interests of research) to counterbalance the sensual nature of Liz and Max's growing infatuation. Good work on display in Liz's relationship with her overly-protective mother.

   Alex now has a car, seemingly (it may belong to his parents but he does say 'my car').

Soundtrack: 'Sex and Candy' by Marcy Playground, Tara MacLean's 'If I Fall' and Sarah McLachlan's 'Fumbling Towards Ecstasy'.

Cast and Crew Comments: '*Roswell* is among the latest wave of teen shows unleashed by the WB network, home to *Felicity*, *Dawson's Creek* and *Buffy the Vampire Slayer*,' noted Manuel Mendoza in the *Dallas Morning News*. 'Closest in tone to the latter, it uses aliens as a metaphor for teen-alienation just as *Buffy* uses vampires as a metaphor for the horrors of adolescence.' Both Majandra Delfino and Katherine Heigl told the reporter that they have been recognised in public since the show started, mostly by little girls in shopping malls. Delfino has also been noticed in her Miami hometown. 'In South Beach, I'm big with the gay men,' she notes. 'I walk down Lincoln Road, and they're like, "Oh my God, we love Maria!" But Miami's weird.' Bill Sadler was also questioned about Valenti's interest in Maria's mother and how the character was becoming more than a standard bad guy. 'That was my big question,' Sadler noted. 'Where's this guy going? At the end of every episode, is he going to be standing in the dust, going, "Curses!" That would've gotten old real fast. What I'm finding fascinating, is how they're sewing together two genres, the *X-Files*-ish suspense and the relationships. I have not seen it done anywhere else.'

Did You Know?: Shiri Appleby's idea of a good night out? As she told Paul Simpson and Ruth Thomas: 'My girl-friends, sushi, and our guy friends come to meet us, and go and hang out at a bar.' A good night *in*, on the other hand, involves: '*Friends*, *When Harry Met Sally*, lit candles, and just hanging-out.' Shiri wasn't a science-fiction fan before working on *Roswell*: 'I was always romance, light comedy. As an actor, it's fun because it's giving you things to play with and it's not just dealing with life.' However she did enjoy the experience of working on episodes of *Xena: Warrior Princess* in New Zealand. 'That was a blast. It was the first time I'd ever left the country. I was nervous – in a new country, and playing this really wild, feisty character. Lucy Lawless was incredible. She kind of took me under her wing.'

Save Roswell: With the very real possibility of cancellation on the horizon, fans were mobilised. A press release from the organisers of the *Save Roswell* campaign stated: 'Fans of the WB teen/sci-fi drama, *Roswell* are joining forces to show their support for this unique Jason Katims Production. "We have incorporated ourselves as ALIEN BLAST," says Kristi Bergman, co-founder of the fan movement.'

A letter-writing campaign began the offensive, with fans asked to write to the WB telling them how much they had enjoyed the show, and why. Letters came pouring in and soon after, Tabasco bottles were also mailed. '*Roswell is HOT*! is another facet of our campaign,' noted Kim Hedland, co-founder for ALIEN BLAST. Support was soon received from all over the world, including France, England, Australia, Puerto Rico and Canada. Word spread over the Internet via *www.crashdown.com* and the *Save Our Show* site, *how.to/save_roswell.com*.

So, was the show actually in danger of being cancelled? 'It has not been picked up by the WB yet,' said Lena Dangcil, co-founder and LA party coordinator. 'We wanted them to know what a huge fan base the show has, especially on the Internet.' The first of the series of ads, paid for by ALIEN BLAST, appeared in the 10 April issue of *Variety*. Thankfully, with the move from Wednesdays to Mondays, audience figures immediately began to pick up and the threat of cancellation receded.

17
Crazy

US Transmission Date: 10 April 2000
UK Transmission Date: 1 May 2000 (Sky One),
11 January 2001 (BBC2)

Writer: Thania St John
Director: James Whitmore Jr.
Cast: Hugh Benjamin (Delivery Guy),
Yelyna De Léon (Waitress)
French title: *Carte Blanche*

Realising that the aliens are in danger, former agent Topolsky returns to Roswell with a warning. However, Max and Liz fear that she may still be an enemy and refuse to trust her. Desperate and afraid, Topolsky is forced to turn to Jim Valenti for help in protecting the kids. Topolsky then approaches Michael and tells him that if he trusts her, she will reveal important information. Michael agrees, but Topolsky is kidnapped before they can meet. Back at school, Isabel finds that she has a lot in common with a new arrival, Tess.

Roswell Iconography: An Eclipse-Burger, a Chilli-Rocket-Dog and Saturn Rings (see **8**, 'Blood Brother') are on the menu at The CrashDown. At the UFO Center, a recording mentions an incident in which two nuns working at St Mary's Hospital in Roswell saw an apparent UFO. Valenti warns Max about 'the crazies. People coming up to you out of the blue, filling your head up with all sorts of conspiracy theories. You know, like Hubble' (see **13**, 'The Convention').

The Conspiracy Starts at Home Time: When Liz asks Topolsky where she has been since **8**, 'Blood Brother', the former agent replies, 'To hell. I've come out to warn you, there's an alien hunter. He's buried deep inside the FBI. Even the President and the Director are on a need-to-know basis. Do you understand what I am saying? He answers to no one. And he will stop at nothing to get what he's looking for.' When Liz asks what he *is* looking for, Topolsky replies: 'Max Evans. And anyone he thinks is involved with him. All six of your names are on the list.' She tells Valenti that she is aware of Hubble's death (see **13**, 'The Convention') noting that all 'UFO nuts' are routinely tracked. When her cover was blown, she was sent back to Washington. That was when, she says, she found out about 'the special unit. Alien hunters. I was the first agent to make direct contact with the subject. I spent four weeks being debriefed by the agent in charge, Pierce. And after what he did to me, I'd hate to see how he'd treat the enemy.' 'Sounds elite,' notes Valenti. 'The problem is they kill people, and there is no one to stop them.' Topolsky continues explaining that the only reason that they haven't swooped in for Max, Michael and Isabel already is that they have no solid proof and are afraid of the aliens and their powers. She also alludes to Pierce having had Agent Stevens killed as an example to the rest of the unit (this must, presumably, have happened shortly after Stevens called Valenti in **12**, 'Into the Woods').

Topolsky tells Michael that the orb that Max and Liz found in **16**, 'Sexual Healing' (and have given to him for safekeeping) is a communication device, and that there is another just like it. 'I took it from the special unit evidence vault in Washington. I know they only work when they're together, so if I bring you the other one . . . I need to know that you will take me with you when your people come to get you.' But she inadvertently leads Pierce directly to the aliens, and seemingly pays the ultimate price for it (see **18**, 'Tess, Lies & Videotape').

High School Life: Isabel and Tess have at least two classes together, English and Phys. Ed. Maria is a member of the French club and went to one of their meetings instead of liaising with Michael in the eraser room, much to Michael's disgust.

Dudes and Babes: Tess breezes into the series like a sultry sexbomb and you can hear all of the boys sigh deeply, despite the rad-fem anger of some of her lines ('. . . [Men] say they understand you and just want to be your friend, but all they really want is fifteen minutes alone in the janitor's closet'). A hint, however, about what she may turn out to be is given when she pours sugar into her yogurt ('nothing can ever be too sweet'). Reading between the lines, it seems that Alex has never seen a girl naked before, which presumably means that he's also a virgin.

'You Might Remember Me from Such Films and TV Series As . . .': Kevin Cooney appears in *Austin Powers: The Spy Who Shagged Me*, *Primary Colors*, *Switchback*, *Dead Poets Society*, *Clockwatchers*, *Independence Day* and *Brimstone*. Australian-born Emilie de Ravin played The Demon Curupira in *Beastmaster*.

Behind the Camera: The son of a famous actor father, James Whitmore Jr's TV credits include *Melrose Place*, *Quantum Leap*, *The X-Files*, *Nowhere Man*, *Young Americans*, *Get Real*, *Buffy*, *Models Inc.*, *Ferris Bueller*, *Charmed*, *21 Jump Street* and *The Pretender*. He is also an actor playing Bernie Terwilliger in *Hunter* and appearing in

Purple Hearts, The Long Riders, The Bastard, Beverly Hills 90210, Scarecrow and Mrs King, TJ Hooker, Highway to Heaven and *Hill Street Blues.* Julie Benz's stunt-double is Gloria O'Brien whose work can also be seen in *Scream 3, Deuce Bigalow: Male Gigolo, Brimstone, The Love Boat: The Next Wave* and *Buffy* (as Amber Benson's stunt-double). She was also the 'boat wrangler' on *Wild Wild West* and a safety diver on *Resurrection.*

References: The title is from Patsy Cline's country standard. Topolsky's warning to Max 'don't trust anyone' is an obvious tribute to *The X-Files.* Tonight's entertainment, for Alex, is 'a box of raisinettes and *Scream 2*', and his 'chick-flick' back-up is *Notting Hill. Love* Tess's assessment of Hugh Grant – 'little English wimp!' Also, oblique references to James's pop classic 'Sit Down', Beck's 'Loser', *Gidget* (a 1960's Sally Fields-sitcom based on a novel by Frederick Kohner), *Judge Dredd* ('I am the law'), *Heathers* ('Hated it!') and Boy Scout merit badges. Valenti's 'you must get a lot of strangers around here', is a clever play on a Hammer movie cliché.

Teen-Speak: Maria: 'You got some flowers from moondoggie.'

Michael: 'Can't you people smell a set-up, or am I the only one thinking straight here?' And: 'You know, this whole dating thing really *bites.*'

Alex, seeing Maria and Liz changing: 'Whoa! Peep shows!'

Tess: 'I am *so* un-hungry right now.'

Fashion Victims: Good stuff: Alex's baggy red-hooded top, Isabel's gorgeous pink and white sweater and her orange sweat shirt which we've seen before. Bad stuff: Michael's bandanna. Michael and Alex both sport ridiculous-looking woolly ski-hats.

Sex and Drugs and Rock'n'Roll: Michael describes Max and Liz as 'a couple of horndogs looking for a place to make out'. Tess introduces herself to Isabel and Alex by saying how hard the first day at a new school always is. 'The guys are usually nice because they want to jump my bones. The girls are nice because they want to find out if I want to jump their boyfriends' bones.' Max's advice to Michael on how to get romantic with Maria is: 'When you're with her, act like she's like the only girl in the room,' and 'try taking her out someplace nice. They love surprises. Little things, like a note in her locker, or a flower in the middle of the day.' Smoothie.

Later, when he and Michael take Liz and Maria on a double-date to a Mexican restaurant, Max buys Liz bubble bath whilst Michael gives Maria a bottle of shampoo-and-conditioner-in-one ('it's a real timesaver!'). In a brown paper bag. When Alex discovers that Isabel and Tess have plans for a girls' night he sadly notes 'guess I've got the wrong hormones for *that*.' Valenti drinks Jack Daniels in his office.

Logic, Let Me Introduce You to This Window: There are all sorts of problems with Nasedo's actions in this episode, given what we find out about him a few episodes further down the line. How, for instance, did he find out about Topolsky, and her involvement with the special unit? And which medical facility she has just escaped from? And the name of her doctor? How does he manage to convince Valenti that he *is* Doctor Margolin? Valenti says he checked it all out. 'The doctor is who he says he is, and Topolsky spent the last month in a mental hospital.' He doesn't seem to have done a very thorough job in checking Margolin's credentials since he manages to speak to the, presumably, *real* doctor in the next episode.

Although Topolsky describes Stevens as Valenti's friend, previous meetings between the two haven't suggested anything more than an, at best, standoffish relationship between the agent and the sheriff. Yet we find that Valenti had this senior FBI agent's home address and telephone number in his desk-file. Pierce's car seems to have no number plates. Also, blackened glass in a car is illegal in several US states because of the possibility of concealed weapons, so it's a bit of surprise to find a law enforcement car, which must have driven through a number of states to get to New Mexico, with such windows.

As Michael and Maria make out, she has her shirt completely unbuttoned but, during a switch in camera angles, several buttons miraculously do themselves up.

Quote/Unquote: Maria: 'Is that so hard?' Michael: 'What?' Maria: 'Acting like a real couple, kissing, arms around each other's shoulders, actually excited to see one another.' Michael: 'Overrated.'

Max, on Topolsky: 'She said we were in danger. And to just act normal until she contacts us again.' Alex: 'Would that be alien-normal or just plain we're-the-subjects-of-an-FBI-manhunt-normal?'

Notes: 'Roswell attracts all kinds. You never know who's gonna turn out to be your friend or your enemy.' Another absolutely cracking episode. Julie Benz returns with a new hairstyle and puts in a truly *great*, twitchy, paranoid performance which sets the tone for the whole episode. In many ways this story, with its introduction of Tess (and, obliquely, Pierce), is the end of the beginning and a pilot episode for the way in which *Roswell* went on to develop. A swift and decisive move away from literal stories of teenage-alienation and into the more murky waters of *noirish* science-fiction. Less *Buffy*, more *X-Files*.

Michael is now working as a cook at The CrashDown. He gets paid on Tuesday and is, thus, unable to pay for Maria's meal when he and Max take the girls out. The secluded place that Max and Liz go to instead of the movies is Buckley Point, a local beauty spot. Topolsky tricks Liz into going to Senor Chow's, the restaurant where Liz and Max had their first date (see **9**, 'Heatwave', **10**, 'The Balance'). Malcolm Margolin is said to be the psychiatrist treating Topolsky for the past six weeks at a facility in Bethesda, Maryland. 'She had a breakdown,' he notes. 'She's paranoid-delusional. That means that she's desperately afraid of things that don't exist.' But the final scenes reveal Margolin to be Nasedo in yet another assumed form (see **18**, 'Tess, Lies & Videotape').

Agent Stevens's FBI address was 106 Hudson Ave NW, #3865, Washington DC, 20001 and his telephone number

(202) 555-0107. All FBI agents seem to have this 555 code. In *The X-Files*, both Mulder and Scully's home telephone numbers include it, whilst the Smoking Man's Conspiracy group's number is 555-1012. Maybe they're part of the same organisation? (In reality, the reason that 555 is used as a telephone prefix in many US TV shows is that it's one of the few three-figure numbers that isn't a real area code somewhere.) Stevens's home address was 6025 Murray Lane, Alexandria, VA 222313, and the phone number was (703) 555-0169. His widow still lives there. (6025 Murray Lane subsequently becomes Max and Isabel's address in **21**, 'The White Room'. Which member of the production team *really* lived at such an address, I wonder?)

Soundtrack: 'Picture Perfect' by Angela Via, Getaway People's 'She Gave Me Love', 'Gypsy Queen' by 7th House, Lori Carson's 'Take Your Time' and Radford's 'Don't Stop'.

Cast and Crew Comments: Jason Katims, in a revealing interview with Kate O'Hare, noted that the change of airdates 'gives us an opportunity to get the *Voyager* audience, which is good. As we've been moving further along into the season, the science-fiction elements of the show have become more prominent and important. We feel that there's a real potential audience there. The other thing is, we're going behind *7th Heaven*, and it's the most-watched show on the WB right now. I'm very hopeful about it.' Katims, O'Hare noted, knew all about working on a show with critical support but a small audience, having lived through 'the *My So-Called Life*-experience'. Whilst Katims' former series made Claire Danes a star and ran *ad infinitum* in reruns on MTV, it had languished during its brief ABC run in 1994. '[*My So-Called Life*] was a lot about trying to find the truth of how people are when they interact with each other. *Roswell* is similar in that it's about outsiders who are teenagers, trying to find a place in the world. This is a show that has a metaphor at the centre of it. It's about how, as teens, we are *all* aliens. Because it's based on a metaphor, like *Buffy*, you get to play with much bigger stories, more life-and-death stories, more fanciful storylines.' So, was Katims, a native of Brooklyn, drawing on his own high school memories? 'My high school experience? Yeah, there were a lot of aliens there, and I think I was one of them. Everybody's an outsider on the show and that, to me, is unfortunately my experience of high school, feeling different and isolated, trying to find those moments of connection. Believe it or not, almost everyone – and this includes football heroes and beautiful cheerleaders – feels alienated at some point in their adolescence.'

'One of the seductive aspects of working in science-fiction, fantasy and horror,' Katims also noted, 'is that the issues are larger, often literally life, death and the future of humanity. For a writer used to dealing with the smaller dramas of real life, this can be liberating.'

Did You Know?: Julie Benz wouldn't mind reviving Topolsky at some stage. Talking to *TV Guide Online* Benz revealed, 'A WB executive recently told me they're working on a way to bring me back.' Although Topolsky's body was never found, Benz says, 'they're so far removed from that storyline to get back to it now would be hard.' However, the actress was somewhat traumatised when she checked out some websites and discovered that Topolsky was despised by many fans. 'I was very sensitive to it,' she admits. 'It was wonderful that my character was having that effect . . . But I honestly believed Topolsky was good from the beginning, so I was shocked that people were seeing her as evil. One girl said that her mother used to throw things at the TV when I came on. I felt misunderstood!'

18
'Tess, Lies & Videotape'

US Transmission Date: 17 April 2000
UK Transmission Date: 8 May 2000 (Sky One),
18 January 2001 (BBC2)

Writer: Toni Graphia and Richard Whitley
Director: Paul Shapiro
French title: *Attirance Fatale*

Suspicion about Tess continues as she features in Max's vivid daydreams. He feels an unexplained attraction to her and, though he tries desperately to fight it, kisses her in front of Liz. Hoping to win Max, Michael and Isabel's trust, the sheriff returns the missing orb and reveals that he has learned Topolsky was killed in a fire. Meanwhile, Michael discovers a hidden camera in his apartment and asks Liz to plant it in Tess's home. Liz puts herself in danger when Mr Harding finds her investigating his interest in Max. And everyone is shocked when the camera reveals another alien amongst them.

'I've Got the Power': There's the revelation, at the episode's climax, that Tess is an alien as she repairs the broken Buddha statue. If Liz had been more eagle-eyed whilst having dinner with the Hardings, however, she might have noticed the sauce bottles on their table.

The Conspiracy Starts at Home Time: Ed Harding is, he says, a consultant for the military – helping them convert their abandoned base facilities into storage units. He has a passion for collecting antiques. ' "Consultant" is a fancy word for "spy",' notes Michael, which appears to be justified when Liz finds a box full of surveillance photographs of Max in the Harding house.

High School Life: In Bio-lab they're doing combustibility-as-a-metaphor-for-sex ('two or more chemical elements become aroused culminating in oxidation and eventually burning').

'You Might Remember Me from Such Films and TV Series As . . .': Jim Ortlieb's appearances include a memorable role in *Magnolia*, *Chain Reaction*, *Home Alone*, *Flatliners*, *Running Scared*, *Spin City* and *Early Edition*.

Behind the Camera: Richard Whitley wrote the movies *Pandemonium* and the classic *Rock'n'Roll High School*. Stuntman Harry Wowchuk's career includes *The Adventures of Rocky and Bullwinkle*, *Magnolia*, *The Secret Life of Girls*, *Conspiracy Theory*, *Carpool*, *The Usual Suspects*, *See No Evil, Hear No Evil*, *Alien Nation*, *RoboCop*, *Repo Man*, *Parasite*, *The Entity*, *The Pom Pom Girls*, *Hollywood Boulevard*, *Death Race 2000* and *The Incredible Two-Headed Transplant*. He was also production manager on *Grand Theft Auto*.

References: The title is a play on Steven Soderbergh's movie *sex, lies, & videotape*. Also, the Turtles' 'Happy Together', Sherlock Holmes, Elvis Costello's 'Accidents Will Happen' and *Die Hard* ('If I told you, I'd have to kill you'). The TV reporter covering the hospital fire is called Thania St John (one of *Roswell*'s producers). Kyle is watching a basketball game featuring the LA Lakers on TV.

Teen-Speak: Tess: 'I have to admit, I'm a little bummed your brother is unavailable. I'm sort of into those serious-mooded guys.'
Maria: 'What a jerk.' And: 'That is *so* not like Max.'

Fashion Victims: Tess, as befits the daughter of a rich military consultant, has a top-line in designer gear, including a Gucci watch, a really cool leather jacket, short black skirt and cleavage-displaying red top. Also, Isabel's scarlet blouse and yellow top and Maria's pink T-shirt.

Sex and Drugs and Rock'n'Roll: Maria tells Michael: 'So give it to me straight or you won't be giving it to me at all.' *Love* Alex's grin in the middle of Max's erotic daydream. Wannabe! Equally impressive is Isabel's whiny *Max-loves-Liz* voice.

Logic, Let Me Introduce You to This Window: The TV report states that six people were killed in the hospital fire. Valenti later says 'What if [Pierce] killed Topolsky and six completely innocent people.' That makes *seven* victims. Max sets fire to himself but appears unharmed. He should suffer at least third-degree burns. Ed Harding says 'it's the twenty-first century'. This episode takes place in 2000, so as all true pedants know, it isn't.

Quote/Unquote: Michael, to Max: 'Valenti has the communicator and we need to do something about it. This isn't the time for your sex fantasies.'

Maria finds Michael and Alex playing with the mini-camera: 'What is that, like porn, or something? Ooo, I'm not as flat as I thought I was!'

Notes: 'Before you can expect somebody to trust you, you've got to trust them first.' A mini-Bond movie that twists and turns through a number of red-herrings and cul-de-sacs until the excellent last ten minutes when Liz's visit to the Harding household brings revelation and suspense in equal doses. Fine, dryly-sinister performance by Jim Ortlieb and some lovely direction.

Alex is a whizz at electronics (previously hinted at), taking the mini-camera that was planted in Michael's apartment and producing a wireless integrated device with a microwave transmitter. 'It has a polarised high grain antenna with an automatic iris, and a built-in wide-angle lens.' Apparently. Tess's birthday is listed as 7 May 1983, and her address is 423 Greatview, Roswell. Her school records also state that her mother's name is Sheila. She drinks Cherry Coke with lime and has recently arrived in Roswell from a school in Chicago.

There's another reference to the local cheese factory (see **3**, 'Monsters') and to the Tumbleweed Inn (see **13**, 'The Convention'). So, it *does* rain in Roswell after all!

Soundtrack: 'Everlong' by Foo Fighters, Godsmack's 'Voodoo', 'Zip-Lock' by Lit and a favourite of the author, the ambient masterpiece '6 Underground' by Sneaker Pimps (accompanying the erotic Max/Tess classroom sequence).

Cast and Crew Comments: 'What we're going to do is lead to a climax at the end of the first season,' Jason Katims told Kate O'Hare, 'that shows us that the world out there is much larger and more dangerous than they thought it was. There are still questions and things you want to know, but there will also be a lot of answers. The second season will be about them dealing with that.'

Did You Know?: This plot was originally intended to be the season finale. The fourth alien was to be revealed as the cliff-hanger, but with a compression of the season's story-lines this allowed the writers to bring forward this revelation.

19
Four Square

US Transmission Date: 24 April 2000
UK Transmission Date: 15 May 2000 (Sky One),
25 January 2001 (BBC2)

Writer: Thania St John
Director: Jonathan Frakes
Cast: Henriette Mantel (Secretary)
French title: *Mise au Point*

The gang are convinced that Tess is the shape-shifter, Nasedo, and worry that she may be a threat to their safety. Deciding that they should not be alone, Max, Isabel and Michael stick close together. At the same time, Isabel and Michael are embarrassed about the dreams they are having about one another, and go to extreme lengths to avoid the development of any romantic ties. Isabel finally gives in to Alex's feelings for her and Michael asks Maria for a stronger commitment. Despite all of their efforts, however, the naughty dreams continue.

'I've Got the Power': Isabel tells Max that when she was talking to Tess, 'it was like I lost a few seconds of time and when it was over, I wasn't even sure if what I remembered had happened or not'. (Compare this with Brody Davis's descriptions of 'missing time' during his abduction periods in **24**, 'Ask Not'). Isabel and Michael share the same dreams, of the pair kissing in the desert with the familiar alien symbols on the ground beside them. They also have a child. Their child. Tess can change the molecular structure of walls (which she does to retrieve the hidden alien book).

Roswell Iconography: On the menu at The CrashDown: A Galaxy Melt.

The Conspiracy Starts at Home Time: Ed Harding tells Valenti that his line of work is 'Government consultant, the boring stuff, facilities management. No special clearances, no matters of national security.' Valenti confronts Max with the camera that was used to spy on Tess. It is, he says, 'special issue FBI equipment. You know what it tells me? That Pierce and the alien hunting unit of the FBI are here in Roswell in full force, and they're paying special attention to you.'

Michael and Isabel tell Max about the events of **14**, 'Blind Date', and of their attempts to send a signal to Nasedo. Max is horrified and assumes that this must have worked and that this is why Tess is in town now. Michael discovers that the Pohlman Ranch was the site of the 1947 crash, but that the government have erased all traces of it from maps.

Max accuses Tess of having killed William Atherton in 1959 (see **6**, '285 South'). 'Then who was next? Everett Hubble's wife? An innocent woman died just because she got in your way?' (see **13**, 'The Convention'). 'You've seen my face before,' Tess tells him. 'You know who I am', as Max has a vision of himself coming out of the pod. Isabel and Michael are already out and there is a fourth pod with a girl with blonde hair whom they leave behind.

High School Life: Isabel claims to the School Administrator that she is on the 'Sunshine Committee ... Like the Welcome Wagon for new students. Helps them get along and fit into a new place.'

Naming All the Stars: Aries, Liz notes is the key astronomical point in many ancient traditions involving spring, the equinox, pagan ceremonies and Indian fertility rituals. Max asks her to change the constellation pattern on the computer to specific dates and they discover that the planet Venus, at certain times of the year, completes the familiar V shape. 'It started moving into this formation after the last full moon,' Liz says. 'About the time that Tess showed up,' notes Max (see **31**, 'Max in the City').

'You Might Remember Me from Such Films and TV Series As . . .': Henriette Mantel was Alice Nelson in *The Brady Bunch Movie*.

References: Allusions to the Troggs' 'I Can't Control Myself', Don Gibson's 'Sweet Dreams' and *Something Weird*. There's an *X-Files* influence marbling the dream sequences. Packets of M&Ms and Skittles can be seen in the school snack machine. Briefly glimpsed in the library scene, Arthur C Clarke's SF novel *Childhood's End*.

Teen-Speak: Maria: 'We're on it.' And: 'Official? Like going steady, or something?'

Fashion Victims: Isabel seems to be wearing a pair of carpet slippers with her black ballroom gown in her dream. Weird. Also, Liz's stripy jumper and cream silk blouse, Tess's various slutty tops.

Sex and Drugs and Rock'n'Roll: Isabel and Michael's erotic dreams. Hot stuff! The episode also includes a brief look at the problem of teenage pregnancy (taken further in the next episode). Alex and Isabel in the janitor's closet is both funny and touching.

Logic, Let Me Introduce You to This Window: If the government erased all traces of the Pohlman Ranch in 1947, then why is there still a large sign announcing the place's name on the site when Michael emerges from his pod in 1989? What we see of Max, Michael and Isabel emerging (and Tess *not* emerging) from the pods doesn't tie in with Max's description of these events in **10**, 'The Balance'. Tess has only just started school. Surely even a transfer student wouldn't start that late in the school year?

This episode appears to takes place on 27 May 2000
judging from the date that Liz types into the computer.
However, according to **24**, 'Ask Not', the subsequent
events of **22**, 'Destiny' occurred on 14 May 2000, making
the dating in this episode impossible. Who placed the alien
book in its hidden location in Roswell Public Library?
Nasedo? If so, why, when and how? Young Isabel's hair is
a lot longer and darker in this episode than it was in **1**,
'Pilot' or **10**, 'The Balance'.

Quote/Unquote: Max: 'What plan?' Maria: 'Operation
Never-Leave-Max-Alone-For-An-Instant. That way one of
us is always around in case she works the voodoo on you
again.'

Michael: 'I've been thinking.' Maria: 'Great. This
usually involves me having to get my car towed.'

Maria: 'Enough with the grade crap. Any unusual
evaluations? Like psyche stuff?' Liz (sarcastically): 'Yeah
. . . She's really a shape-shifting alien also known as
Nasedo!'

Notes: 'There are signs all around you.' Mired in an
intricate (possibly over-stretched) plot, 'Four Square' is the
weak spot in the lengthy and impressive story-arc that ties
up the season. The hole where the rain got in, basically.
Top-heavy with information, its comedy moments are a
little arch and the episode doesn't have the depth of other,
better, examples of the series mythology. Some good lines
of dialogue aside, it feels like an exercise in treading water.

When Tess visits the Evans's home, Diane tells her
various stories about Max and Isabel's childhood, including: 'The road trip to Florida. The time Max brought
home that snake. And that silly clown show that the two
of you used to put on for us.' From Tess's school records,
Liz discovers that she had averages of 3.0, 3.2 and 3.4 from
three previous schools (Liz is incredibly jealous of the
latter). Tess's phone number is (505) 555-0143. Her previous school was Glenbrook in Chicago. Her school classes
include English, PE, Science Lab, Home Economics,
Algebra and Creative Writing.

Soundtrack: Folk Implosion's 'No Need to Worry' and 'Automatic' by Collapsis.

Network Critique: Fans were certainly able to take solace in *Roswell*'s ratings after its move to Monday nights. By the end of April, the show was generating season-best ratings in several key demographic categories for a WB series in the 9 p.m. slot. That still wasn't enough to guarantee it would be back next season, but a WB spokesman was keen to stress that 'we are very happy with the ratings. The network has always been behind the show, always loved the show, but they won't decide until after we see how it does in sweeps.'

Cast and Crew Comments: The revamp of the show, around episode fifteen, was intended to move *Roswell* towards a heavier science-fiction emphasis and, hopefully, attract a larger and more adult audience. 'We're relaunching the series,' Jonathan Frakes told the *Los Angeles Times*. 'We want to deal with the mythology of the aliens. When the secret that these kids were aliens got out, there was little for them to do other than stand around their lockers and talk about it. There are enough teen-angst shows already.' Frakes seemingly agreed with WB executives who felt that putting more of an SF-spin on *Roswell* would make the show more compatible with other WB youth-oriented series like *Buffy the Vampire Slayer* and *Angel*. The article also stated that Fox TV presidents Dana Walden and Gary Newman had expressed confidence in the new direction. 'Jonathan brings a real science-fiction credibility to the show,' noted Newman. 'Jason has a strong background with relationship-driven TV, and Jonathan has the edge on science-fiction. Together, they lift this show out of either of its individual genres,' added Walden.

Did You Know?: Given her position as the interloper in the group, Emilie de Ravin found her role opening up some bad memories. 'In Australia I was in ballet school and the atmosphere was really bad,' she told Finnish teen-magazine *Suosikki*. 'Everyone tried to hurt each other. I wanted to be different from all the other girls.'

20
Max to the Max

US Transmission Date: 1 May 2000
UK Transmission Date: 22 May 2000 (Sky One),
1 February 2001 (BBC2)

Writer: Toni Graphia
Director: Patrick Norris
Cast: Drinda La Lumia (Blue Haired Lady),
Gordon Haight (Announcer)
French title: *À la Poursuite de Max*

Isabel, Michael and Max are told that they were engineered and not born as they had believed. Hoping for more
answers, Max goes to Tess for an explanation. Tess tries to
convince Max that she, he, Michael and Isabel are destined
to be together. Meanwhile, Nasedo shape-shifts into Max
and kidnaps Liz in an attempt to trick Agent Pierce into
revealing himself. Scared for Liz's life, Maria and Alex
enlist the help of Valenti to find her. After following
Nasedo to a nearby carnival, Max is captured by the FBI.

'I've Got the Power': Nasedo can make a petrol pump
explode by touching it.

Roswell Iconography: Nasedo has spent a lot of time with
Tess, but she still doesn't consider him as her father. Max,
Isabel and Michael are her real family, she notes. Seeing
images of themselves in the alien book, Max, Michael and
Isabel discover they were genetically-engineered. Nasedo
found Tess soon after she came out of the pod and has
taken care of her ever since. Tess says that he doesn't have
a human body like Max, Isabel and Michael and that is
why he shape-shifts. Nasedo has never let Tess see what he
really looks like (see **26**, 'Summer of '47').

The Conspiracy Starts at Home Time: The terrifying Pierce
arrives in town under the alias of Deputy Dave Fisher
from Santa Fe. He plays on Valenti's insecurities by

claiming that his own father was also a sheriff in Las Vegas, New Mexico, who died in the line of duty and that he is an overachiever because he is trying to escape his father's shadow. According to his file, Edward M Harding is a civilian consultant, transferred to Roswell from Fort McClellan near Birmingham, Alabama. Before that he was with the Army Material Command in Alexandria. He is divorced with one child. With the government's resources behind him, it's easy to see how Pierce could have covered his tracks so thoroughly, but it's never revealed how Nasedo managed to set up such a convincing back-story for himself and Tess. Nasedo dumps an agent's body as a 'clue' for Pierce on Highway 380 to Hondo, near mile marker 67.

'You Might Remember Me from Such Films and TV Series As . . .': Gordon Haight appeared in *American Gigolo*, *Honky Tonk Freeway* and *Near Dark*. David Conrad's movies include *Men of Honor*, *The Weekend* and *Relativity*. Stephen O'Mahoney played Coletta in *Murdercycle*.

References: The title alludes to Willy Bogner's documentary *Ski to the Max*. The Rolling Stones' 'It's All Over Now' is mentioned and there's a misquote from the Verve's 'Bittersweet Symphony' ('I'm a lot of different people'). The 'hall of mirrors' sequence is reminiscent of Scaramanga's toy-house in *The Man With the Golden Gun*. The capture of Max echoes the sinister abduction of Thomas Newton in *The Man Who Fell to Earth*. There are possible oblique visual references to two cult 1960s Amicus horror movies *The Torture Garden* and *Dr Terror's House of Horrors* in the carnival sequences. The location of the alien cave is Vasquez Rocks off Agua Dulce Canyon Road in Santa Clarita, northeast of Los Angeles. A perennial favourite of western TV series like *Bonanza*, readers may recognise the site from its legendary use in the *Star Trek* episode 'Arena', and in *Bill and Ted's Bogus Journey* (in the scene where the Grim Reaper – you know who played *him*, right? – first appears). A Sizzler restaurant can be briefly glimpsed on Roswell High Street (the author is a particular

fan of the chain's excellent 'surf 'n' turf'). The FBI agent
Del Bianco, mentioned by Pierce, is named after Karen
Wyscarver Del Bianco, Jason Katims' assistant on *Roswell*.

Teen-Speak: Maria: 'I heard something, and I gotta ask
you about it. And I hope that the answer is some alien
thing, 'cos I can't imagine any other explanation that you
could give . . .'

Fashion Victims: Michael's K-Mart trousers and denim
jacket are functional rather than sexy. Like The Crash-
Down T-shirt, however. Liz wears her roll-neck sweater
again, and there's a further examination of Tess's slutty-
top wardrobe.

Sex and Drugs and Rock'n'Roll: Although Isabel and
Michael are uncertain as to how aliens (ahem) *perform the
act*, Tess tells Max: 'We have to do it the human way. I
hope that doesn't disappoint you.' 'Tess says the dreams
are just to guide us in our destinies,' Max tells a relieved
Isabel. 'She says the constellations have aligned and
awakened our biological drives but the usual methods still
apply. You can't get pregnant from a dream.'

Logic, Let Me Introduce You to This Window: Is Nasedo
trying to get Max captured or not? There has been
considerable fan-debate on this issue. Because this is such
a fast-moving and confusing episode, it is easy to miss one
of the few bits of dialogue which help to clarify Nasedo's
intentions (a seeming attempt to unmask Pierce in order to
protect Max and the others from capture, when Nasedo
tells Liz: 'I am the bait. Pierce is looking for Max, and I'm
going to draw him to me . . . You're my collateral, my
hostage. He knows what Max did to you at The Crash-
Down. He wants you alive. You could come in extremely
handy in terms of my survival.') The surveillance tape from
Michael's apartment indicates that the special unit now has
evidence of alien activity. So, why haven't they swooped on
Michael at the very least? The alien book contains pictures
of what the aliens look like at their present ages, so why
was Nasedo unsure of who Max was? (That was the reason

given in **19**, 'Four Square', why an approach wasn't made sooner.) The entrance to the cave moves position between this episode and **22**, 'Destiny'. Presumably Nasedo left the pods that he and the other alien survivor liberated from the Air Force (see **26**, 'Summer of '47') hidden at the Pohlman Ranch in 1947 and then periodically returned to the site to check on whether they had hatched (which would explain his presence in the area in 1959, when he met River Dog and killed the suspicious Atherton, and in 1970 when he encountered Mr and Mrs Hubble). Unfortunately, it would seem that he missed Max, Michael and Isabel emerging from their pods, but arrived in time to find Tess. Then they left and spent over a decade wandering America looking for the other three? Why? Didn't it occur to him that they might still be in the Roswell area? Six-year-old children can't wander *that* far, surely?

Quote/Unquote: Max: 'We've got to go to Valenti.' Michael: 'And tell him what? There's two Maxes. The good one's right here, but please help us catch his evil twin?'

Notes: 'I don't even know who you are any more.' A breathless episode with so much going on that, at times, the viewer is in danger of losing some of the more subtle subplots that marble the story. Basically good stuff, though, with Jason Behr putting in a truly memorable double performance. Love the ALIEN BEAM UP sign at the carnival, and the great scene of Michael and Isabel discussing her 'pregnancy' whilst he washes the dishes.

Max mentions Michael's solo pursuit of Topolsky in **17**, 'Crazy'. Max carries a West Roswell school yearbook with him. Michael is seen playing table tennis with an unseen opponent. Nasedo likes candyfloss.

Soundtrack: 'With Arms Wide Open' by Creed, Filter's 'Welcome To The Fold' (as Max enters the mirror-maze), 8STOPS7's 'Question Everything', Beth Hart's 'Just a Little Hole' and 'Open Your Eyes' by the delightfully named Guano Apes.

Cast and Crew Comments: Quoted in the *New York Post*, producer Kevin Brown noted, concerning the final six episodes: 'Fans are going to go bonkers. One of the main characters will get shot and we'll have a grittier, edgier sci-fi emphasis.' Which, the article stated, was the intention all along, Brown noting that the producers didn't want *Roswell* to be 'stories about teens going to dances. This show has always been a combination of *Romeo and Juliet* meets *The X-Files*, but we're certainly not going to lose the emotional relationships between the characters. It's just a coincidence that these six episodes will be more SF-oriented. We started introducing [such] elements with our thirteenth and fourteenth episodes. I honestly think the fans have responded so passionately because the show is the first sci-fi show that they can relate to on a personal level.'

Did You Know?: In the 'Star Woes' section of the November 1999 edition of *Teen People*, in which actors tell of their most embarrassing moments, Majandra Delfino revealed: 'I was at a WB press event with Brendan Fehr. I have this very big crush on an actor I'm friends with who will remain nameless. As he walked in the room, Brendan goes, '*Oooh, he's hot!*' Then the actor came and gave me a kiss and Brendan started making kissing noises . . .' Teenagers!

21
The White Room

US Transmission Date: 8 May 2000
UK Transmission Date: 29 May 2000 (Sky One),
8 February 2001 (BBC2)

Writers: Jason Katims and Thania St John
Director: Jonathan Frakes
Cast: Jason Winston George (Agent Matthison)[15]
French title: *Le Prisonnier*

---

[15] Jason Winston George also appears, uncredited, as Matthison's corpse in **22**, 'Destiny'.

After being captured by Agent Pierce, Max is held prisoner. Interrogation and torture follow as Pierce tries to make him reveal his true identity. In order to save Max, Isabel uses her dreamwalking powers to find where he is being held. She, Michael and Tess set out to rescue him. Scared for Max's life Liz, Maria and Alex decide that it's time to reveal the full truth to Valenti. To Be Continued . . .

'I've Got the Power': Tess asks what powers Michael and Isabel have. They admit that they aren't very advanced. 'We can do easy things, like change simple molecular structure,' Isabel notes. 'But we don't use them very often.' Tess says that being around Nasedo has taught her a great deal, as she demonstrates to Isabel when she seems to be carried off by an agent. 'I made you think something was happening when it really wasn't.' However she cannot do the 'dream-thing' a power seemingly unique to Isabel.

Nasedo proves his strength by sending Michael crashing to the morgue floor. He is further surprised that Michael isn't able to scan images directly into his brain, contemptuously telling him that, instead, he has two minutes to memorise the escape route. However, even Nasedo cannot manipulate the security door which is made of depleted uranium, a metal composed of heavy atoms. 'You have many limitations,' he tells Isabel, and he impressively teaches Michael how to shape-shift his fingerprints. Nasedo tells Michael that humans are wasteful and weak, and that human brains are incredible machines which humanity hasn't even begun to use. 'When you were engineered, you were given the capacity to do everything the human brain is capable of,' he continues. Michael queries whether that is apart from their powers and Nasedo replies 'Those *are* your powers. You were just programmed to be several thousand years ahead of mankind. But from what I saw earlier, you've barely tapped into what you're capable of.'

Roswell Iconography: 'I might not have been around in 1947,' Pierce notes. 'But I know all about the crash. About

the four aliens they captured: two dead, two alive. I've
spent my entire career studying the documentation. Especially the three years of observation they made on the
one held in captivity, right here in this room.' One of the
two living aliens, Nasedo, escaped. The other one must
have too, if what we learn in **31**, 'Max in the City' is
accurate. Tess says that Nasedo has never left her alone
before. Nasedo confirms what Tess told the others in **20**,
'Max to the Max', that he is different from them. 'I can
shape-shift into any of these agents: take their form, even
their fingerprints. That's why they added the X-ray scanner. My bone structure is far from human. I can change
my appearance, but not what's on the inside. Your bone
structure, on the other hand, is one hundred per cent
human.'

Pierce has one of the alien communication orbs which
was found in the crash. 'We have spent fifty years looking
for the other one, and we know you have it. It took a little
persuading, but Topolsky told us.' Inside the UFO Center
photos of the Eagle Rock air base can be seen.

The Conspiracy Starts at Home Time: Max's X-rays reveal
him to have human bone structure, organs, circulatory and
pulmonary systems. His blood cells are 'completely *not*
human', however. Pierce reveals that in 1962 in Delta,
Colorado, Agent Lewis, the first head of this special unit,
was found dead. His internal organs had reached a
temperature of 180 degrees Fahrenheit and a silver handprint was found on his chest. In 1967 in Union City,
Tennessee Agent Del Bianco, his replacement, also died.
On 2 May 1999, Agent Daniel Summers, the man who
brought Pierce into the special unit and whose job Pierce
now has, also died, seemingly by Nasedo's hand. Eagle
Rock Military Base, where Max is held, is where 'they'
were said to have secretly taken the surviving aliens after
the crash (compare with **26**, 'Summer of '47'). It has been
abandoned for years. Nasedo says that the only female
agent on the special unit is now dead, presumably a
reference to Topolsky (see **17**, 'Crazy').

'You Might Remember Me from Such Films and TV Series As . . .': Jason Winston George played Michael Bourne in *Sunset Beach* and Scott in *Titans*. Bo Clancey was Jack in *Easier Said*.

References: The title is the name of a best-selling and hugely influential LP by maverick trance-house collective the KLF. The opening sequences of the hidden interrogator and his victim has so many possible influences it's difficult to know where to start. *The Prisoner* is the most obvious one (much of the opening dialogue, plus Pierce refers to Max as exactly that) and, inevitably, by the works of Franz Kafka (Max as Josef K). Also, *The Avengers* episode 'The Wringer', *Mission: Impossible* ('Good morning, Max'), *Buffy the Vampire Slayer* ('we can do this the easy way or the hard way') and the Show Time channel. *The X-Files* influence on the episode extends from the specific (a sign in the UFO Center saying 'Trust No One') to the oblique (the hallucinatory sequences may have been inspired by scenes in the 1999 movie). The design of the White Room owes much to Ken Adams' revolutionary sets for *Dr No* and other early Bond movies.

Teen-Speak: Michael: 'Will you quit saying that?' And: 'Give me a pointer, huh?'

Fashion Victims: Tess's gypsy dress, Maria's cleavage-revealing top, Alex's hooded New York sweatshirt.

Sex and Drugs and Rock'n'Roll: Pierce tells Max that the serum he has injected Max with is very effective in suppressing the neurotransmitters in Max's cerebral cortex. Experiments on the alien in the 40s taught the special unit that this is where most of the aliens' power comes from.

Logic, Let Me Introduce You to This Window: Max gives his address as 6025 Murray Lane, however in **1**, 'Pilot', his driver's licence clearly says his lives in Newton Avenue. Maybe he's lying to Pierce to protect his family (see **25**, 'Surprise'). Isabel says that she has only done the 'dream-thing' a few times. We've certainly seen her do it at least five times in the previous episodes, and the implication of Max scolding her in **3**, 'Monsters', is that it's her regular party trick. The episode's time frame seems wrong. Liz, Maria and Alex agree at 11.20 to wait until 4 o'clock before telling Valenti that Max has been captured. This means that, presumably, Michael, Isabel and Tess (who are already in the base when this scene takes place) sneak around a heavily guarded installation for over four hours without discovery. Yet mere moments after Liz, Maria and Alex have alerted the sheriff, back in the base Nasedo gets Isabel, Tess and Michael to synchronise their watches and it's 5:47. Why do Michael, Isabel and Tess take time to change clothes after they set off to rescue Max? It's hardly the most appropriate moment. One of the dead bodies in the morgue can be seen breathing.

Quote/Unquote: Pierce: 'We can do this the easy way, or the hard way. What is the name of your home planet?' Max: 'Earth.' Pierce: 'All right. Hard way.'

Michael: 'I've been looking for you for a long time.' Nasedo: 'Not as long as I've been looking for *you*.'

Pierce: '*I'm* evil? I'm risking my life to save my country, my planet from being colonised by alien life. By you.'

Notes: 'I can take you apart piece by piece, and make sure that you stay conscious enough to feel every second of it.' A *very* disturbing episode. The montage of Max being tortured with drugs, ice-baths, isolation, electroshock therapy *et al* is not for the weak of stomach. But it's a really revelatory episode in many ways, and Nasedo, Michael, Tess and Isabel's infiltration of the base is one of the season's highlights. Great direction too.

According to several accounts Jason Katims and Thania St John's script massively overran the required time-slot. In tightening the script, Thania managed to condense a lengthy dialogue sequence into one memorable line: 'Who's inhuman now . . .?' a beautiful summation of the series in microcosm.

Soundtrack: Remy Zero's 'Yellow Light' (which covers The CrashDown scene and Max being tortured).

Critique: 'I hope this constantly well-written series is picked up for a second season,' noted David Mason, TV editor of *Ventura County Star*. 'It's brilliantly unpredictable and well-acted. The cinematography is impressive and the episodes have been consistently more compelling than *Voyager*. Each *Roswell* story is like a small movie, and that's refreshing for television.' A spokeswoman for the WB was quoted by Mason as saying that she didn't know what impact the fan response (and all that Tabasco sauce) was having on the programming department at the WB.

Cast and Crew Comments: Jason Behr told *Teen* magazine. 'The room itself was very small: no windows, one door. It was a very long day and very claustrophobic. Once they shut the door there was no air. They had to pick me up and throw me into the room. Every time we did it, I'm telling the guy "I don't gently shut the clasp, I want you to slam it shut – shove my hand in the thing!" Every time he pinched my skin. I was bleeding from my wrists, but it worked for the scene.' Jason also revealed that 'I'm into fast cars. I drove a stock car once up at California Speedway. There's something about the fact that you're close to death that I like.'

Did You Know?: The green surgical scrubs worn by Jason Behr in the White Room fetched the highest price at an auction held by the *Roswell* fans in the US. It even beat the legendary pink pyjamas worn by Katherine Heigl in **9**, 'Heatwave', and Sheriff Valenti's hat. All proceeds went to charity.

22
Destiny

US Transmission Date: 15 May 2000
UK Transmission Date: 5 June 2000 (Sky One)

Teleplay: Toni Graphia and Jason Katims
From a Story By: Thania St John
Director: Patrick Norris
Cast: Howie Dorough (Alien), Genie Francis (Mother),
Richard Dorton (Agent Levin)
French title: *Un Nouveau Départ*

Valenti is stunned when he witnesses Michael use his powers to save Max from Agent Pierce. After killing Pierce, the aliens locate Nasedo and bring him back to life. Nasedo vows to take Pierce's place in an effort to protect the Royal Four, who finally use the communicators and come into contact with Max and Isabel's real mother. Max's destiny is revealed. And it doesn't include Liz.

'I've Got the Power': Michael demonstrates increasing confidence in his power, disabling the FBI car. 'It's your own energy, Michael,' Tess tells him. 'That's what Nasedo was trying to teach you.' Michael later atomises Pierce to save Valenti's life. Tess again displays her ability to show people things that aren't there, sending the FBI on a wild goose-chase. Nasedo once told Tess that if he were to die, the others had the power to bring him back to life using River Dog's healing stones (see **10**, 'The Balance'). And, memorably, Max heals Kyle from Valenti's inadvertent bullet.

Roswell Iconography: Nasedo tells the aliens that he was not sent to lead them, that's Max's job, but rather to protect them. He warns them that through the communication orbs they will be able to contact their own planet, but that they also risk leading other forces to them (see **24**, 'Ask Not', **28**, 'The Harvest', **31**, 'Max in the City').

The alien mother tells Max, Michael, Isabel and Tess that they have lived before and perished in the conflict that enslaved their planet, but that their essences were duplicated, cloned, and mixed with human genetic materials so that they might be recreated into human beings. Max was the leader of their people and Tess was his bride (see **18**, 'Tess, Lies & Videotape'). Isabel was his sister and

Michael was her betrothed, and Max's second-in-command (see **30**, 'Meet the Dupes').

'It has begun,' notes Howie Dorough as, in different locations around the globe, communication devices are activated (see **31**, 'Max in the City').

The Conspiracy Starts at Home Time: Pierce promises that he can get Valenti, his father and Kyle new identities, protection and government pensions if he delivers the aliens to the unit. After Pierce's death, Nasedo assumes his form to lead the special unit away from the aliens (see **23**, 'Skin and Bones').

Dudes and Babes: Isabel wields a mean piece of wood and thoroughly brains an FBI guy. What a babe.

'You Might Remember Me from Such Films and TV Series As . . .': Howie Dorough is better known as Howie D of teen-pop sensations the Backstreet Boys (so *he*'s an alien? That explains a lot). Soap veteran, and wife of Jonathan Frakes, Genie Francis was Ceara Connor Hunter in *All My Children* (and its spin-off *Loving*) and Laura Vining in *General Hospital*. She also appeared in *3rd Rock from the Sun* and *Roseanne*. Richard Dorton was special effects and make-up artist on *Eat Me!*

References: Liz and Max's escape from the FBI is borrowed from *Butch Cassidy and the Sundance Kid*. Maria quotes from the Smiths' 'What Difference Does it Make?' The scene with Max and Isabel's mother seems influenced by *Superman II*, whilst there are allusions to the movies *Shoot to Kill* and *The Price of Freedom*. Agent Levin is named after Neil H Levin, Thania St John's assistant. We are shown a brief glimpse of Nasedo's true form; not unexpectedly it bears a resemblance to the 'greys' in *The X-Files*. And the Asgard in *Stargate SG-1* (whom Jack O'Neill often refers to as 'Roswell grey'). And the aliens in *Close Encounters of the Third Kind*. (See **26**, 'Summer of '47').

Teen-Speak: Michael: 'You think the government's going to do something about Pierce? He's *part of it*.' And:

'Bottom line, Maxwell, I kill people. You heal them.
You're good, I'm bad.'

Logic, Let Me Introduce You to This Window: Valenti
claims to have a contact in the attorney general's office.
Odd that he hasn't thought of contacting him sooner? As
Michael suggests, this is a lie, isn't it? Liz and Max don't
look very wet after they emerge from the river. Where did
Michael's T-shirt come from? Did Nasedo create his
underwear along with the suit in the previous episode?
Liz's knickers can be seen when she runs from the cave.

Quote/Unquote: Michael: 'Why are you helping us?' Valenti: 'There's a right side here and a wrong side. I don't think
Pierce is on the right side.'

Pierce: 'If you're here to kill me, Sheriff, it won't do any
good. There'll be a new man in charge of the unit in 24
hours.' Valenti: 'If I wanted to kill you, you'd be dead
already.'

Notes: 'Whether I die tomorrow or fifty years from now
my destiny is the same. It's you.' Given that the final six
minutes has to clear up a hell of a lot of information about
who the aliens are, where they come from and what is
likely to happen next, 'Destiny' works remarkably well,
dragging together a lot of different plot-strands. Some of
this is successful – drawing Valenti and Kyle into the
conspiracy, for instance. Some is glib and unsatisfactory –
Nasedo assuming Pierce's role seems like a pat cure-all.
Considering how much goes on in the episode, it's likely to
leave the viewer somewhat drained. But it's got some great
set-pieces and the ending is a brilliant cliff-hanger. Not the
most subtle of stories, but if you can survive the pace, it
has many rewards.

Valenti suggests that the fugitives hide at an old silver
mine in Galitas off Horseshoe Road. Nasedo's body is held
at Jeffords Airstrip near Hobson.

Soundtrack: Dido's 'Here With Me', played at the end of
the episode as Liz walks away from Max.

Cast and Crew Comments: 'When the season started I was just the sheriff in dark sunglasses chasing these sweet young aliens,' Bill Sadler told the *Calgary Sun*. '[The] people in my life have, little by little, been pushing me into the good-guy category. It was something I always hoped would happen, a nice arc.' Concerning his young colleagues, Sadler joked: 'I smack them around. They come around to me and say, "Mr Sadler, I need career guidance ..." I was actually very lucky. We have a talented group of kids. What they lack in experience, most of them have more than made up for in raw talent. They surprise me all the time.'

Did You Know?: 'Basically, what an actor tries to do, whether he wants to admit it or not, is become the most famous person in the world,' Brendan Fehr told the *Winnipeg Sun*. 'Because in becoming [that] you hold a lot of power, and you get to choose what you do and get first crack at all the scripts.'

Roswell – Season Two
(2000–2001)[16]

Jason Katims Productions/Regency Television/
20th Century Fox

Developed by Jason Katims
Co-Producers: Christopher Seitz, Tracey D'Arcy,
Gretchen J Berg, Aaron Harberts, Fred Golan (23–37)
Lisa Klink (38–43)
Producer: John Heath (23–37)
Consulting Producer: Toni Graphia
Supervising Producer: Carol Dunn Trussell
Co-Executive Producer: Ronald D Moore
Executive Producers: Jonathan Frakes, Lisa J Olin,
Kevin Kelly Brown, Jason Katims

Regular Cast:
Shiri Appleby (Liz Parker)
Jason Behr (Max Evans)
Brendan Fehr (Michael Guerin)
Katherine Heigl (Isabel Evans, 23–26, 28–43)
Majandra Delfino (Maria DeLuca)
Colin Hanks (Alex Whitman, 23–27, 29–30, 34–39, 43)
William Sadler (Sheriff Jim Valenti, 23–26, 29–30, 32–43)
Nick Wechsler (Kyle Valenti, 24–27, 29–30, 32–39, 41–43)
John Doe (Jeffrey Parker, 27, 39)
Jason Peck (Deputy Hanson, 23, 33–35, 39–40, 42)
Mary Ellen Trainor (Diane Evans, 25, 29, 32, 39, 43)
Jo Anderson (Nancy Parker, 39)
Diane Farr (Amy DeLuca, 32, 34–35, 38–40, 42–43)
Nicholas Stratton (Young Michael, 43)
Garrett M Brown (Philip Evans, 30, 32, 39, 43)

---

[16] For season two, the series title dropped the word 'High' and was renamed *Roswell* in all markets.

Ted Rooney (Mr Whitman, 39–40)
Michael Chieffo (Mr Seligman, 30, 41)
Robert Katims (Judge Lewis, 33–34)
Emilie de Ravin (Tess Harding)
Jim Ortlieb (Nasedo, 23–24)
David Conrad (Agent Pierce, 23)
Gretchen Egolf (Vanessa Whitaker, 23–25, 28)
Sara Downing (Courtney Banks, 23–25, 27–29)
Jeremy Davidson (Grant Sorenson, 23, 25, 33, 35–36)
Desmond Askew (Brody Davis, 24, 30–32, 35–36, 42)
Miko Hughes (Nicholas Crawford, 28–29, 31, 42[17])
Jenny O'Hara (Ida Crawford, 28–29)
Allison Lange (Laurie Dupree, 33–36)
Keith Szarabajka (Dan Lubetkin, 33–34)
Devon Gummersall (Sean DeLuca, 33–35, 38–43)
Erica Gimpel (Agent Suzanne Duff, 34–36)
Heidi Swedberg (Meredith Dupree, 35–36)
Dennis Christopher (Bobby Dupree, 35–36)
Rosana Potter (Carmen, 35–36)
Jeremy Guskin (Derek, 40–41)
Nicole Brunner (Leanna/Jennifer, 41, 43)

23
Skin and Bones

US Transmission Date: 2 October 2000
UK Transmission Date: 21 February 2001 (Sky One)

Writer: Jason Katims
Director: James A Contner
Cast: Frank Birney (Congressman),
Dennis Lipscomb (Psychologist),
Austin Tichenor (Doctor Bender),
Phil Abrams (John Shanahan),
Kenneth Choi (Engineer #2), Bill Glass (Mitch),
Daniel Fester (Guard), Colin McClean (FBI Agent)

---

[17] Uncredited in **42**, 'Off the Menu'.

Ordering everyone to maintain a low profile, Max disregards Michael's suggestion to actively seek out other aliens. A geologist finds Pierce's skeleton in the desert. The bones are connected to Michael and he is arrested for murder. Despite Valenti's efforts to help him, it is up to Max and the others to save their friend from the FBI and a congresswoman for whom Liz is currently working.

'Dear Psychologist': 'Your parents are concerned about you,' a hired psychologist tells Max. 'I want you to know that however unique you think your problems may be, there are millions of teenagers out there going through exactly what you are . . . Tell me what's been going on?' Max, thus, sets the record straight: 'I'm an alien. A hybrid, actually. Human DNA mixed with alien DNA. My sister Isabel and our friend Michael are also a little green around the gills. For the past ten years, we've been ageing much like humans, but clearly there are differences. From the beginning we had the instinct to keep this to ourselves, to hide in plain sight. Then one day last fall, everything changed. The six of us were connected by the secret we shared. There's also Tess, a hybrid like us. And then there's Nasedo. He's a shapeshifter . . . We used Nasedo's abilities to infiltrate the special unit of the FBI.' Except, of course, that he doesn't say any of this *out loud*. 'It's like you said, just normal teenage stuff.'

'I've Got the Power': Tess helps Michael to hone his 'blowing-up-rocks' power, much to Max's amusement. Tess performs her 'mind-warp-thing' on a room full of scientists to allow Max to change the chemistry of the skeleton, and amend the carbon dating procedure to indicate that the bones had been in the desert for 42 years, instead of merely months.

Roswell Iconography: Nasedo refers to Max, Isabel, Michael and Tess as 'the Royal Four' for the first time. Note the plastic alien head in the background during the scenes in The CrashDown back room and the blow-up green alien lying on the witness stand beside Nasedo at the Congressional Inquiry. Nice use of irony.

The Conspiracy Starts at Home Time: Nasedo appears, as Agent Pierce, at a congressional hearing, stating that none of the seventeen million dollars spent by the special unit was ever authorised by FBI superiors. This helps to get the unit disbanded by Congress, despite the protests of Roswell Congresswoman Whitaker. She argues that, in 1972, the unit investigated a curious murder with silver markings on the skin, which subsequently vanished. The internal organs and tissues of the victim were decimated (see **13**, 'The Convention'). Nuclear analysis of the victim's bones showed traces of a substance dubbed cadmium-X, an element said not to exist on earth. Nasedo tells the hearing that cadmium-X is a hoax invented by the special unit. In fact, Max speculates, it may be an isotope of cadmium created when an alien unleashes its power.

High School Life: Liz mentions the particle physics lab at Las Cruces University which Mr Seligman has spent weeks obsessing about, to Liz's approval. The new cyclotron can measure isotope ratios. 'I'm not a dork,' she tells Max, defensively. 'I just enjoy science.'

Dudes and Babes: Two major new female characters, the slutty, bad girl-temptress Courtney and the bitchy, knows-more-than-she's-letting-on Vanessa Whitaker. Plus hunky male icon Grant Sorenson for all the ladies. Love Maria's whiny Max-voice (reminiscent of Isabel's similar mocking in **18**, 'Tess, Lies & Videotape').

'You Might Remember Me from Such Films and TV Series As . . .': Gretchen Egolf was Fran in *The Talented Mr Ripley* and Amy Dylan in *Martial Law*. Frank Birney played Judge West in *The Practice* and can also be seen in *The Dukes of Hazzard, Jane Austen's Mafia!* and *Don't Touch My Daughter*. Dennis Lipscomb's work includes *Apollo 11, Under Siege, The First Power, Crossroads, Union City, Moonlighting, Little House on the Prairie, CHiPS* and *WKRP in Cincinnati*. Colin McClean appears in *Soul Survivor, The Boy Who Saved Christmas* and *Due South*. Sara Downing was in *Never Been Kissed, Tumbleweeds* and

Titus. Austin Tichenor appears in *Y2K* and *The West Wing*. Kenneth Choi's movies include *Deep Core* and *Halloweentown*. Bill Glass was a make-up artist on *Space Virgins*.

Behind the Camera: New to the production staff, Ronald D Moore was a veteran writer/producer of *Good Vs Evil* and both *Star Trek: The Next Generation* and *Deep Space Nine*. He also wrote the story for *Mission: Impossible II*. Christopher Seitz began his career as assistant director on classics like *Kolchak: The Night Stalker*, *Hawaii Five-0* and *The Paper Chase*. He was producer on *Revolver* and *Flash*.

Director James A Contner's previous work includes *Midnight Caller*, *21 Jump Street*, *Wiseguy*, *The Equalizer*, *Miami Vice*, *The Flash*, *Lois & Clark: The New Adventures of Superman*, *Hercules: The Legendary Journeys*, *American Gothic*, *Dark Skies*, *The X-Files*, *Charmed*, *Buffy the Vampire Slayer* and *Angel* (which he also co-produced). Before that he was cinematographer on movies such as *Heat*, *Monkey Shines*, *Jaws 3-D,* and *Times Square* and a camera operator on *The Wiz* and *Superman* . It's also his camera-work on the groundbreaking 1976 concert footage in *Rock Show: Wings Over the World*.

References: Alex wants to take Isabel to see *One Flew Over The Cuckoo's Nest* at the Revival Theatre. Also, *thirtysomething*, *Goosebumps*, Ward Cleaver, the character played by Hugh Beaumont in *Leave It To Beaver*, the Child Labour laws and atomic tests of the 1950s. Bender is named after the robot in *Futurama*. Nasedo describes Whitaker as a 'foul temptress' (from *Macbeth*). Whitaker alludes to the start of the Indianapolis 500 ('Gentlemen, start your engines'). Maria says that half the movies ever made are about soldiers with chicks waiting at home for them.

Teen-Speak: Maria: 'I am definitely not in the market for a thirtysomething shape-shifter, but I have to admit, the man *rocks*!' And, to Max: 'Girlfriend, like, I know that we bonded over the summer, but I'm *not* quite ready to show you the bod just yet!'

Michael, on Nasedo: 'Great people skills.'

Fashion Victims: Check out Maria's hair! And her *two* criminally short skirts (the gold one and the tasseled red one). Isabel's leather pants show up again, along with a stunning red mini skirt and yet another of Tess's seemingly endless wardrobe of revealing tops.

Skins and Drugs and Rock'n'Roll: Michael's discovery of the disintegrating skin near the place where Pierce was buried is the first oblique reference to a new enemy who kill Nasedo at the episode's climax, the Skins.

Valenti covers for the presence of Michael's dropped penknife at the site of Pierce's burial by claiming that he found Michael and two friends drinking beer, joyriding and taking potshots out into the desert some months previously. Nasedo (as Pierce) and Whitaker have been lovers during the summer in Washington, and resume their relationship on their return to Roswell. Maria says that she has heard that ex-cons are great in bed.

Logic, Let Me Introduce You to This Window: Max's entering into the cyclotron is physically impossible. Common sense dictates that anything placed in a containment chamber is so placed for a reason. Even though Max leaves before the second stage of the cyclotron is activated, his presence in there at all seems ridiculous. Exact carbon dating of bones is scientifically impossible.

The bones Grant digs up don't seem to be buried very deeply, yet when we see a flashback to Valenti, Max and Michael setting fire to and then, presumably, burying Pierce's body, it's in an enormous pit. Maria calls Nasedo a 'thirtysomething shape-shifter'. He's been on Earth since 1947, making him *considerably* older than that. Surely even a congresswoman can't simply invite herself along to the arrest of a murder suspect? What about the arrested person's constitutional rights? There's no channel logo on the TV screen covering the Congressional Subcommittee

Inquiry. Nasedo's blood is red and looks just like human blood. Not very likely, is it?

Quote/Unquote: Liz: 'You are a real hero to me.' Whitaker: 'You don't need to suck up. My paid staff takes care of my enormous ego.'

Nasedo: 'Sheriff Valenti, welcome to the ever-burgeoning "I know an alien" club!'

Nasedo, on Whitaker: 'I know her intimately ... To borrow a rather crude human colloquialism, I've been diddling her all summer.'

Nasedo: 'Tell me how far this information has been leaked. I need to extinguish every human who has this information.' Alex: 'I'm going to assume present company is excluded?'

Max: 'Killing people isn't going to solve anything.' Nasedo: 'A pacifist for a king? Shall we all commit joint suicide right now, or wait for our enemies to show up and have a nice boxed-lunch of us?'

Notes: 'I smell a rat.' A bit *ordinary*, frankly, at least until Nasedo turns up, at which point the episode becomes a riotous series of pithy one-liners and sexual innuendo. There *are* some terrific moments (Valenti helping Michael to come to terms with his murder of Pierce) and a shocking climax. But it does feel as though in the quest for increased ratings, *Roswell*'s concentration on plot and suspense-over-character takes its toll in this episode. Isabel, in particular, is sexed-up and dumbed-down. The writers seem to have latched onto the character's use as a sexy decoy, displayed in episodes like **19**, 'Four Square'. It happens twice here (first with Sorenson, then with the security guard). A rather worrying development.

Liz has been staying with an aunt in Florida for most of the summer. Valenti checked out Sorenson's credentials, discovering that he has a degree from the University of Wyoming and was hired to do field work in the area near the old Clovis highway for radioactivity ('Nasedo had a pretty good cover, too,' notes Isabel perceptively. See **36**, 'How the Other Half Lives'). There's another reference to the cheese factory (see **3**, 'Monsters'). Nasedo refers to the torture of Max in **21**, 'The White Room'. Valenti mentions the deaths of Topolsky and Stevens (see **17**, 'Crazy').

Soundtrack: 'Sour Girl' by Stone Temple Pilots, 'Kryptonite' by Three Doors Down, Bif Naked's beautiful 'Lucky' (also used to great effect in episodes of *Buffy* and *Charmed*) and Richard Ashcroft's 'Brave New World'.

Critique: *Entertainment Weekly*'s Ken Tucker noted on *Roswell*'s return: 'I was willing to give this teens-from-outer-space show the benefit of a first season doubt; the acting was good, the concept intriguing. But after being inundated with 'save *Roswell*' mail this summer, even though the damn thing had been renewed, I've watched the new season closely, and have come up unimpressed. In their zeal to bolster the sci-fi elements of the show, they've sacrificed the one thing that made *Roswell* compelling – the interaction between the aliens and human teens, as friends, lovers, and enemies.'

Cinescape's Kim Bundy, on the other hand, was happy to report that '*Roswell* fans are cheering. The show seems to have found a nice balance between the special effects and relationship aspects of the story', whilst Mike Antonucci in the *San Jose Mercury News* hoped that: '*Roswell* finds success as a niche hit, or as the network's most-improved-and-almost-respectable ratings climber. Something. Anything. It's a largely undiscovered, misunderstood *gem* that's much more than a sci-fi show. It's the most worthy returning program that's in danger of not surviving the season.' The WB, meanwhile, used a simple two-word quote from *TV Guide* in all of their season two trailers. 'Irresistibly gripping'.

Cast and Crew Comments: 'She's growing up,' Shiri Appleby told Paul Simpson and Ruth Thomas when asked how she felt about the way Liz's character was changing. 'I'm trying to make her not quite as vulnerable towards the situations she's put into. I want her to be able to deal with them and stand up for what she thinks. I don't think that the circumstances are necessarily so frightening to her because she's been in the situations before.'

Did You Know?: 'I went for the part of a Mexican girl in a big film,' Majandra Delfino told *TV Guide* in New Zealand. 'I had to pray in Spanish and I did it perfectly with a Latin accent. They said "she's good, but we're going to go with a more authentic Latin"', who turned out to be Rachael Leigh Cook. 'She's, like, Irish or something. It's insane.' Majandra also talked about her role in *Traffic*. 'These kids go to this really nice private school and make straight As and then get wasted on coke and pot.' On the subject of romance, Majandra emphatically denied that she and costar Brendan Fehr are an item. 'We go to things together,' notes Delfino. 'It's bad because we hold hands when we go to an event, but then I'll show up at another one with my friend Wilmer Valderrama from *That '70s Show*. People must think, "What a tramp!"'

24
Ask Not

US Transmission Date: 9 October 2000
UK Transmission Date: 28 February 2001 (Sky One)

Writer: Ronald D Moore
Director: Bruce Seth Green
Cast: JG Hertzler (Mr Lafebar), Bill Jacobson (Welder)

Max realises that he cannot remain a passive leader after Nasedo is murdered, and the arrival of Brody, the suspicious new owner of the UFO Center, is another worrying development. Michael aggravates the situation by questioning Max's authority and breaks into the museum to uncover the truth, barely escaping with his life. This forces Max to make a crucial decision, after Michael and Isabel decide that Brody is a threat and must be eliminated. Meanwhile, Tess finds a new home with the sheriff and Kyle.

'I've Got the Power': Max can now erect a force-field, which he uses to prevent Isabel and Michael from following him into the UFO Center. He says he's had this ability for a while, he just didn't feel like sharing it with the others. Tess uses her power to remove a bruise from Max's face. When Max asks Tess if she remembers their world, she replies: 'Images, mostly. Impressions, feelings. Nasedo taught me a few memory-retrieval techniques.'

Roswell Iconography: Kyle notes: 'I'm just not looking forward to dealing with all the little green men again.' Brody arrives in town, having bought out Milton. An English whizz-kid who helped take an Internet company public, he was driving on the Massachusetts Turnpike seven years ago when he was, he claims, abducted by aliens. 'Then I'm back in my car and two days have gone by and I'm in West Virginia. I would have written the entire thing off as an acid flashback. Then my doctor told me the cancer was gone. It was bone marrow. Terminal.' When Brody talked publicly about his experiences he became a liability to his company, who bought him out for $300 million. 'Two years of recovered-memory therapy and the only thing I can remember about my abduction is the colour of the walls [and] the smell of burned hair,' he tells Max (see **31**, 'Max in the City').

Domestic Arrangements: Following the death of Nasedo, Tess comes to live with Valenti and a rather put-out Kyle, though he eventually suggests that she take his bed and he will be happy to sleep on the couch.

The Conspiracy Starts at Home Time: Max tells the others what Nasedo said as he died: 'The Skins are among us.' And, indeed, as the episode climax proves, they are. They're a race who, as the name suggests, seem to periodically grow a new skin to replace the shedded old one (like a snake).

High School Life: In history class, Mr Lafeber gives a series of precise little essays on the lead up to, and the duration of, the Cuban Missile Crisis: 'In the fall of 1962, John

Kennedy was still a young man. The Soviets thought he was a pushover and at that point most Americans would have agreed. And yet Kennedy would rise to the occasion, face down the Soviets and bring the world back from the brink of nuclear war.'

Dudes and Babes: The opening sequence has Tess, Isabel, Liz and Maria dancing provocatively before a gobsmacked male audience (plus Alex and Michael). Oh momma! Maria has an off-centre view on the Max/Kennedy link, continuing the not-so-delicate prodding of Max and Liz back together seen to great effect in **23**, 'Skin and Bones': 'JFK, he's not so great. Cheated on his wife with tramps. Oh, *there's* something you and Jack have in common!'

'You Might Remember Me from Such Films and TV Series As . . .': British actor Desmond Askew made his TV debut aged eight in a Cadbury's commercial. He's a veteran of *Grange Hill*, played Simon Baines in *Go* and appeared in *Give My Regards to Broad Street* and *Repli-Kate*. JG Hertzler was Klingon General Martok in *Star Trek: Deep Space Nine* and has also been in *Highlander* and *Quantum Leap*.

Behind the Camera: Director Bruce Seth Green's TV work includes episodes of *Knight Rider*, *Buffy*, *Angel*, *Airwolf*, *MacGyver*, *She-Wolf of London*, *V*, *SeaQuest DSV*, *Jack & Jill*, *Xena: Warrior Princess*, *TJ Hooker*, *Hercules: The Legendary Journeys* and *American Gothic*.

References: The title refers to Jack Kennedy's famous 1960 speech in which he urged young Americans to 'ask not what your country can do for you, but what you can do for your country'. There's an oblique reference to the Beach Boys' 'In My Room'. Kyle calls Nasedo 'Noriega', referring to the notorious Panamanian dictator Manuel Noriega, deposed by a US invasion in 1989. Also, *Star Trek* (the planet Vulcan) and *X: The Man With X-Ray Eyes*. There's a *Reservoir Dogs* sight-gag (Max, Michael and Isabel walking towards the camera in slow motion). Notable shop-window signs include the LA Lakers, glam-metal dinosaurs Kiss, teenage popstar Britney Spears and tropical folk singer Jimmy Buffett.

Teen-Speak: Isabel: 'I am *so* not having this conversation.'
    Liz: 'Maria, will you do me a favour? Keep your big fat nose out of this?'
    Whitaker: 'You *go*, girl. Don't you let any man pull that crap on you.'

Fashion Victims: Kyle wears Calvin Klein boxers, much to Tess's approval. Isabel's orange top is seen again. Since we're back in school, there are lots of short skirts on display (Maria's particularly). And, of course, another school year, another set of slutty tops for Tess. Not forgetting, a particular highlight, Valenti's tasteful red dressing gown. Isabel's choice of clothes is occasionally a bit strange. We know that she must really love those leather pants (they show up often enough) but does she *have* to wear them when going to, in theory, *murder* Brody?

Sex and Drugs and Rock'n'Roll: Kyle finally proves he's a normal seventeen-year-old boy with a healthy interest in pornography. And Buddhism. Okay, the last bit's a surprise. He has a copy of *Buddhism for Beginners* under his bed. 'How do you think Buddha would feel about being sandwiched between *Hustler* and *Busty Biker Babes*?' asks Tess.
    Courtney asks Michael his opinion on body piercing. Michael says he isn't into pain. 'It only hurts once,' notes Courtney. 'Then it's about the stimulation.' Ooo ... Saucy.

Logic, Let Me Introduce You to This Window: So Max bruises but he doesn't burn (see **18**, 'Tess, Lies & Videotape').

Quote/Unquote: Whitaker: 'Don't be shy. It's not every day you walk in on your boss drinking and shredding. Then again, you've never worked in Washington.'
    Kyle: 'This is my room and that's my jersey. [Tess, starts to remove it] All right. You wear it.' Tess: 'Kind of uptight

about nudity for a guy who reads *Jugs*?' Kyle: 'Give me that!' Tess: 'The Post-Its? Nice touch!'

Alex discovers that Brody is a dotcom millionaire: 'Note to self, take more computer classes.'

Notes: 'You can tell people you've seen the Virgin Mary and they'll light candles outside your bathroom. But tell 'em you've been abducted by aliens and they'll write you off as a lunatic.' The final revelation that Courtney is a Skin is shocking and helps to hide the fact that, despite some good work on Kyle and Tess (including one of the series' great moments as Tess twangs the waistband of his boxer shorts) and the introduction of Brody, 'Ask Not' is actually a hollow mess that rambles in circles for long periods and muffs its metaphor completely. No cigar.

Liz uses an Apple Mac at Whitaker's office. Kyle has spent the summer at football camp. Alien bodies seem to disintegrate after death.

Soundtrack: Tarsha Vega's 'Be Ya Self' (the song that the girls, ahem, *dance* to), Amanda Ghost's 'Idol', 'Bohemian Like You' by the Dandy Warhols and two songs by Trinket, 'Boom' and 'Superhuman'.

Cast and Crew Comments: According to Ronald Moore, writing 'Ask Not' was his biggest challenge on the show. 'Max is studying the Cuban Missile Crisis in history class,' he told Jim Swallow. 'Thematically, the show is about Max's journey as a leader, trying to draw lessons from President Kennedy and apply them to what's going on.'

Did You Know?: 'In London, I couldn't get arrested,' Desmond Askew told *FHM*. 'I've done my share of crap in the past. When you're young you don't really know good from bad. I was also a butcher at a grocery store for a while. When I arrived in LA, I stepped off the plane and went straight into a meeting on Sunset Strip with the director of *Go*. I sat there facing a dozen people auditioning me, trying to concentrate, and all I'm thinking is, "I'm in Hollywood!"'

25
Surprise

US Transmission Date: 16 October 2000
UK Transmission Date: 7 March 2001 (Sky One)

Writer: Toni Graphia
Director: Fred K Keller

Isabel's friends throw her a surprise birthday party at The CrashDown, but a mysterious headache and a series of disturbing visions of Tess in jeopardy put a damper on her mood. Meanwhile, Liz discovers that Vanessa Whitaker has been recording her personal phone calls at work. Is there a connection?

'I've Got the Power': The Skins seem to have similar powers to Max and Co, judging by Courtney's unorthodox ability to pour drinks. Tess uses her power to contact Isabel and tell her of the danger she is in. Isabel can melt metal. In a terrifying maelstrom of psychic energy, Isabel and Whitaker battle it out until Isabel erects a force-field that reflects a bolt of electricity back at Whitaker and she explodes in a snowstorm of shedded skin. *Excellent.*

Domestic Arrangements: Kyle complains that Tess has 'taken over television, the computer, my phone. If some chick's gonna be yelling at me about keeping the toilet seat down, she better at least be *doin'* me.'

The Conspiracy Starts at Home Time: Liz uses a letter opener to unlock the cabinet that Whitaker locked. There she finds a CD-R labelled *Parker Liz, Date: Sep 6–19* which contains her recorded telephone conversations. When Whitaker confronts Isabel, we learn much about the Skins. Unexpectedly they are from the Royal Four's home planet, representing a rival faction in the revolution that destroyed Max and Co. Whitaker is seeking 'the granilith' an artefact that, she believes, the Royal Four are hiding. The Skins can't exist on Earth, at least not in their natural state, their DNA being incompatible. Their limit is 50 years in one body and Whitaker's time is almost up. She tells Isabel that Isabel's real name was Vilandra. 'You were beautiful, even more than you are now. You had a great love and for him you betrayed your brother, your race.' Whitaker confirms that she killed Nasedo. Isabel discovers the granilith, a cone-shaped device, is in the pod chamber.

Dudes and Babes: A question to all of the ladies. Do any of you actually get turned-on at all by Colin Hanks slapping his own buttocks? *Really*? Courtney describes Tess as 'like Dolly Parton without the jugs!'

Behind the Camera: Director Fred Keller's CV includes writing, directing and producing, amongst others *The Pretender*, *Nash Bridges*, *Veronica Clare*, *Vamping*, *My Dark Lady* and *Eyes of the Amaryllis*.

References: Whitaker says she loves the movie *Run Lola Run* ('story of my life'). Also, *The Full Monty* (Alex's striptease), The Faces' 'Stay With Me', the *Buffy* episode 'Surprise' (a birthday party interrupted by earth-shattering events), *Batman* ('think about the future'), cookery guru Betty Crocker, *NYPD Blue*, country singer Dolly Parton, *Tonight* host Jay Leno, Propellerheads' 'History Repeating', legendary cartoon series *Deputy Dawg* and women's lingerie store, Victoria's Secret.

Teen-Speak: Maria: 'Say that you're surprised, 'cos he was *totally* stressing that you'd figure it out.' And: 'Him, him, him. Ever since you broke up, he's become this pronoun instead of a person.' And: '*No way*. Last time I lent out the Jetta, an Uzi took out the back window.'
   Courtney, to Michael: 'Are you, *like*, high or something?' And: 'Jerk!'

Fashion Victims: Alex spent $150 to rent his police officer costume. 'Do you have any idea how it feels to walk around all day with a thong up your ass?' he asks. Maria and Courtney both confirm that they actually do. Diane notes that sometimes, if one hair is out of place, Isabel won't leave the house. Isabel's red party dress shows up again.

Sex and Drugs and Cake: Michael bakes Isabel a Tabasco-based birthday cake. Courtney: 'So, what's a chick got to do to get a cake out of a guy like you?' Michael: 'Nothing you could handle.' Courtney claims that the reason Whitaker has photographs of her in her office is that she was sleeping with Whitaker's stepson. 'He screwed his life up with drugs, and I screwed my life up with him. When we got busted, do you know who went down for that? I spent two years in Buckman, and the only reason why I got out is because I promised that bitch that I would never see him again.' All lies, of course (see **28**, 'The Harvest').

Valenti asks Max about Tess: 'She wanted to jump your bones?' Max: 'Something like that.' Valenti: 'Screws things up every time.'

Logic, Let Me Introduce You to This Window: When Isabel tells Grant that purple roses are her favourite, he says 'So I heard.' From Tess, as we subsequently discover. Grant then says that he was at 'the dig' all day so when did he have the chance to pick up the roses? Grant's cellphone number (555-0188) should have a completely different number scheme to the, remarkably similar, landline numbers of Max and Michael.

Quote/Unquote: Grant: 'No one's ever given me a surprise party.' Diane: 'When's your birthday?' Grant: 'December 7th.' Diane: 'And what *year* might that be?!'

Kyle, on Tess: 'She's got her underwear and her bras and her girlie things all over the bathroom. Every time I go in to shave, I feel like I'm walking into Victoria's Secret.' Michael: 'So what's not to like?'

Notes: 'Is it true? Am I a terrible person? Answer me.' A *great* episode, using the laid-back setting of a teenage birthday party to get some real horror into the series. Although she's hardly in it, this marks a major turning point in Tess's story. But it's Isabel who really shines in a delicately balanced script that keeps its major surprise for the final scene.

Tess's organiser provides addresses and telephone numbers for Max and Michael. They are 6025 Murray Lane (see **21**, 'The White Room') and (505) 555-0183, and 502 Powell Avenue (505) 555-0166 respectively (see **17**, 'Crazy'). Max is said to have planned the surprise party. The Evans family considers Isabel's birthday to be 25 October 1982 (see **8**, 'Blood Brother'). Mr Evans misses the party as he is stuck in Minneapolis. Sterling roses (purple, rare and expensive) are Isabel's favourite.

Soundtrack: Trinket's 'Boom' again (see **24**, 'Ask Not'), 'C'mon 'n' Ride It (The Train)' by Quad City DJs (what Alex is 'dancing' to at the party), Neve's 'Digital On', Fishbone's 'Psychotic Friends Nuttwerk' and Franka Potente and Thomas D's 'Wish (Komm Zu Mir)' (from the soundtrack of *Run Lola Run*).

Cast and Crew Comments: 'I wasn't really wearing a G-string,' notes Colin Hanks. Well, *that's* a relief.

Did You Know?: *Roswell* gets commented upon in the strangest of places. An article in the *Orlando Sentinel* concerning TV hairstlyes noted: 'Majandra Delfino had really cute, short hair last season. This year, she came back with ugly long hair, probably with extensions. Shiri Appleby has let her hair grow, but hers looks pretty. Punky-spiky-haired character Michael, played by one-expression actor Brendan Fehr, now has dirty lank hair. The series has been good this year so far . . .' So, to sum up, show good, hair bad? Thanks Orlando!

26
Summer of '47

US Transmission Date: 23 October 2000
UK Transmission Date: 14 March 2001 (Sky One)

Writers: Gretchen J Berg and Aaron Harberts
Director: Patrick Norris

Cast: Charles Napier (Hal Carver), Eric Saiet (Teacher),
Tom Kenny (Bar Keep), Michael Roddy (MP #1),
Finn Curtin (Patron #1), Lisa Kaseman (Patron #2),
Jeff Johnson (Bus Driver)

To raise his failing grades in history, Michael agrees to
interview a former air force pilot who served with the
509th and who is in town for a reunion. Hal Carver reveals
many secrets about the 1947 crash, the alien autopsies and
the military cover-up which followed that are key to
Michael and his friends' past, present and future.

'I've Got the Power': Michael creates a flame with his
thumb to light Hal's cigarette and fills empty beer bottles
in Maria's car.

Roswell Iconography: Michael displays a hitherto unseen
interest in aircraft, being able to identify a B-17G (the
flying fortress) from a photograph. He's been reading UFO
magazines since he was eight.

The Conspiracy Starts at Home Time: There were two sets
of alien pods, each with four fetuses inside (see **30**, 'Meet
the Dupes'). In their real (non-shape-shifted) form, adult
aliens (one was Nasedo, the other the Dupes' protector)
have brightly glowing bodies. 'They have black eyes,'
Carver notes. 'Empty. Vacant. Ageless.' In 1947 Carver
was 'a 21-year-old know-it-all.' He and his friend Richard
Dodie were sent to the crash site, where they were told to
drive the alien pods to the notorious Hanger 20. Carver
still has a piece of the alien metal that he found at the crash
site.

   Yvonne White, the military nurse who officiated at the
autopsy, tells Carver that 'there's no way those things were
even mammal. The epidermis, hands, organs. They were
nothing I'd ever seen ... Afterwards some high-ranking
general from Wright Field debriefed me. Said I couldn't
talk about it.' Later Carver sees a confidential report in
Colonel Cassidy's office, after having drafted death notices
for two privates who were supposed to have died in a Jeep

accident. 'Those kids were at the debris site when they stumbled on two sacs six feet in diameter,' he tells Betty. 'Something came upon them. One witness says it was two figures glowing white ... My brother was shot down over Manila Bay. I watched my mother open the telegram. Those privates ... families deserve the truth.'

Following the trail that Betty leaves for him, Carver discovers the location of the pods and the two glowing aliens who, he realises, only wish to protect the pods. 'They looked like human fetuses,' he tells Michael. 'There was four to a sac. Eight total. That night, I packed my things and never came back ... That's the story of Hal Carver. The only time I ever stuck my neck out to save anything, and it all went to hell.' In a defining moment for the series Michael reaches out his hand and blows up four beer bottles. 'You saved *me*,' Michael tells the old man.

High School Life: Tess thinks that the noise the granilith makes sounds like 'the fluorescent lights in Bio-Lab'. Max and Liz have a trigonometry class together. The History teacher asks Michael: 'True or false? We're not even a month into the semester and you're already failing my class. This is a new record?' Michael replies: 'To be perfectly blunt with you, sir, World War II just doesn't do it for me.'

Dudes and Babes: Two points of interest here, Emilie de Ravin as Dixie. *Phwoar!* And Katherine Heigl as Rosemary. Even *bigger phwoar*!

'You Might Remember Me from Such Films and TV Series As ...': In a career of over a hundred movies, Charles Napier played General Hawk in *Austin Powers: The Spy Who Shagged Me*, and appeared in *The Cable Guy*, *Raw Justice*, *Philadelphia*, *The Silence of the Lambs*, *3 Ninjas Knuckle Up*, *Married to the Mob*, *The Blues Brothers* and *Supervixens* (which he also produced). TV appearances include *The A-Team*, *Starsky and Hutch*, *Kojak*, *Mission: Impossible*, *Star Trek* and providing the voice for Duke Phillips on *The Critic*. He's also in the *Star Trek: Deep*

Space Nine episode 'Little Green Men' which concerns the 1947 Roswell crash. Eric Saiet is probably best known as Dalton in *Buffy the Vampire Slayer*. He has also been in *Felicity*, *Home Improvements* and the movies *Ugly Naked People*, *Godzilla*, *Groundhog Day* and *Ferris Bueller's Day Off*. Tom Kenny is the voice of Ratbert on *Dilbert*, played the mayor in *The Powderpuff Girls* and Persky in *Just Shoot Me*. Michael Roddy was Pete Price in *Speedway Junkie* and Ziggy in *Beach Babes from Beyond*. Finn Curtin appeared in *King of the Bingo Game* and Lisa Kaseman was in *Killer Tomatoes Strike Back*.

Behind the Camera: Authors Gretchen J Berg and Aaron Harberts wrote the screenplay for the recent David Boreanaz movie *Valentine*.

References: The title comes from Robert Mulligan's *The Summer of '42*. Also, *Spiderman* (the bartender, presumably Jeff Parker's dad or uncle, is called Peter Parker), Omaha Beach (site of the bloodiest fighting during the Allied invasion of Normandy in June 1944, as depicted in films as diverse as *The Longest Day* and *Saving Private Ryan*), the V-1 (a rocket-bomb, also known as the doodle-bug, devised by German scientist Werner Von Braun and used to devastating effect on numerous British cities like London and Coventry), the Yalta peace conference (1945), sexbomb actress Jane Russell (*The Outlaw*, *Gentlemen Prefer Blondes*), Microsoft guru Bill Gates, the Hoover Dam (a dam on the Colorado river at Lake Mead between Nevada and Arizona, named after US President Herbert Hoover, 1874–1964), the First Amendment to the Constitution, John Wayne, Jesse Marcel and the official 'weather balloon' explanation for the 1947 incident, 'Old Man River' (from *Showboat*) and a possible allusion to *Twin Peaks* (a coffee shop serves 'a swell cherry Danish'). One of the dead privates was called McCarthy, a possibly reference to senator Joe (see **5**, 'Missing'). Cassidy has a newspaper with a WAR ENDS! headline on his wall (presumably from 16 August 1945). The newspapers that Carver buys include the *New York Herald Tribune*, the *New York*

News (headline: SOVIET FOREIGN OFFICE PROMISES ATOMIC PEACE) and the *Los Angeles Globe*.

Teen-Speak: Michael: 'Way to prioritise, Maxwell.'

Max: 'Mean people *suck*.'

Maria: 'First off, phone protocol works like this. Messenger-leaves-message. Then messengee calls back unless messengee is deathly ill, grounded, or just *a jerk*!'

Film-Noir-Speak: Hal: 'Excitement in these parts was about as common as pink elephants, but when Jesse Marcel placed that call, the whole place was buzzing in a heartbeat.' And: 'He has a tendency to get his skivvies all up in a bunch.' And: 'Jiminy Christmas!'

Cassidy: 'Stick a cork in it, Dodie.'

Dodie: 'You always were a punk, Carver. Why couldn't you be a lazy, self-centered, *sonovabitch* this time?'

Fashion Victims: Maria asks Michael if he's using new hair gel. 'What's with that hair of yours, anyway?' asks Carver. 'The chicks dig it, grandpa,' Michael tells him.

Sex and Drugs and Rock'n'Roll: Maria wants Michael to take her to a concert by Bristol's ambient trip-hop collective Portishead. Michael and Carver share some beer whilst the old man finishes his story. The 1947 bar sequences include Carver and Dodie drinking Diamond Black. Vintage bourbon and vodka bottles are seen in Rosemary's apartment.

Logic, Let Me Introduce You to This Window: Some of the musical references are anachronistic. Frank Sinatra didn't release a version of 'Fly Me to the Moon' until 1956. 'Mack the Knife', which Sinatra also covered, whilst part of Brecht's *Threepenny Opera* (written in 1928), didn't become a popular English-language hit until versions by Ella Fitzgerald, Louis Armstrong and, most notably, Bobby Darin appeared in the mid-late 50s.

Carver is staying at the Pineview Lodge, so it seems that the Tumbleweed Inn *isn't* the only motel in town (see **13**, 'The Convention'). Carver says 'global warning' instead of

'global warming'. How can a captain order an officer of
equal rank to do *anything*? Surely orders are given by
superior officers? The frames of Cassidy and Cavitt's
sunglasses certainly don't look like they were designed in
the 1940s. The '47 crash site is said to be 30-odd miles from
Roswell Air Force base. Most estimates place it closer to
50. The phone number that Betty leaves Carver is 555-
0186. It can't be her number in Fort Worth, as that would
be a different area code. Besides, have phone numbers
changed so little in 50 years? Compare this with, for
instance, the various numbers observed in **25**, 'Surprise'
and **17**, 'Crazy'.

Quote/Unquote: Hal: 'When the going gets rough, resort to
plagiarism, huh? You kids today are softer than soap. You
ever heard of Omaha Beach or the V-1 flying bomb, Yalta,
Jane Russell?' Michael: 'Taken my teeth out to brush
them?'

Hal: 'Our senior counterintelligence agent, Captain
Sheridan Cavitt. Known around the base as Mister Brain.
So I guess when you're lacking in other assets, you've got
to trump up the one you've got.'

Hal: 'Give me another one, sweet cheeks.' Maria:
'That'll be your third banana split, sir.' Michael: 'What are
you, the dairy police? We're in the middle of a story here.'
Maria: 'I'm not the one sitting next to an ancient
gastrointestinal tract, pally.'

Notes: 'Old people creep me out.' Oh, but *this* is clever! A
mixture of satire, iconography, social comment and 50
years of Roswell conspiracy-theory mixed into a humdinger
of a script with liberal doses of smart humour. A nice
change of pace that allows the regulars to have some fun
playing other characters, a great performance from Charles
Napier, and with the huge revelation that there are another
four aliens at large. One of the series' best episodes.

Maria knew her paternal grandfather as 'Breepa'. She
never got to say goodbye to him before he died. Jim
Valenti senior, then a young deputy, was at the crash site
in 1947 (Nick Wechsler's playing his character's grand-

father). The Parker family owned a bar, Parker's, in 1947. Captain Carver's war escapades include bomber raids on Frankfurt and Duerne in Belgium and emergency-landing a B-17 in England without putting a scratch on the plane. He spent some time in Nice, France, and fondly remembers the cabaret girls there. Betty Osario worked as a reporter for the *Fort Worth Star Telegram*. She had a sister who informs Carver of her death in an, alleged, car accident.

Soundtrack: 'Free' by Vast, 'Drawing Board' by Mest, Frank Sinatra's 'Fly Me To The Moon', the Brian Setzer Orchestra's version of Glenn Miller's 'In the Mood', Jimmy Dale Gilmore's 'Mack the Knife'.

Cast and Crew Comments: As producer Ronald Moore told Jim Swallow, comparisons between his show and *Buffy the Vampire Slayer* were inevitable, given the subject matter. 'I respect *Buffy* and like it,' noted Moore. 'But they play things a little tongue-in-cheek and *Roswell* is more serious – and, I think, better. I like to play humour within the character scenes. "*Dawson's Creek*-with-aliens" is an easy box to put this show in, but [it] has really found its own particular groove. It's not what you think.'

'Basically, television writing is all about throwing an idea out there,' Aaron Harberts told the CrashDown.com website. 'For 'Summer of '47', we saw a picture of four 1940s-era army guys leaning against a jeep, and I thought, "I wonder what their story is." That's how the episode was born. We pitched it to Jason, including the idea that our actors would play the roles of the people from that time. After getting story approval, we disappeared for a few days to write a beat sheet. After that is approved, we go to outline. This goes to the rest of the staff, production folks, the studio, and the network. After they weigh in, we implement their notes, and then write the script. After you're all done, there are more notes, another rewrite, a table read, and *then* it gets shot.'

Did You Know?: As several fans have pointed out, while Highway 70 does indeed run from Roswell towards Texas, it is not the most direct route to Fort Worth. Betty Osario should have taken Highway 380 and linked up with Route 20.

27
The End of the World

US Transmission Date: 30 October 2000
UK Transmission Date: 21 March 2001 (Sky One)

Writer: Jason Katims
Director: Bill L Norton
Cast: Winnie Holzman (Madame Vivian)

A Max from fifteen years into the future travels back in time to warn Liz that their relationship may jeopardise the future of Earth. In the hope of avoiding a disastrous situation, future-Max insists that Liz betray present-Max so badly that their relationship will end, and thus prevent Tess from leaving town.

'I've Got the Power': Michael uses his full-force powers on Courtney, but she escapes and he blows up his very expensive-looking TV set in the process.

Roswell Iconography: The granilith wasn't intended to be a time machine, but it does have an enormous amount of power and future-Max was able to modify it to artificially create a tear in time-space.

On the menu at The CrashDown: 'Takeoff Tacos', 'Plutonium Platter', and the 'Greek God Salad' with feta cheese.

High School Life: Future-Max says that present-Max spent a week learning the lyrics to the 'Trez Diaz' from Mr Delgado at the hardware store. 'Wow, that's really embarrassing,' notes Liz truthfully.

Dudes and Babes: Alex says that Isabel gave him another one of those 'you're such a great friend' speeches. 'It made me want to puke.' His fight with Michael over Maria is one of the episode's finest scenes.

But, *no Isabel*! Disaster!

'You Might Remember Me from Such Films and TV Series As . . .': A former producer on *thirtysomething* and *My So-Called Life*, Winnie Holzman can also be seen in *Jerry Maguire*.

Behind the Camera: Bill Norton's previous work includes *Daughters, False Arrest, More American Graffiti* (which he also wrote) and the memorable 1972 TV movie *Gargoyles*. Film editor Peter B Ellis also worked on *Kuffs*, *Big*, *Millennium* and *NYPD Blue*.

References: The *Back to the Future* movies seem an obvious influence on this episode. And (visually) *The Terminator*. Don't know whether the producers have even seen it, but there's a 1980 BBC science fiction play called *The Flipside of Dominick Hide* that's very similar too. And the *X-Files* episode 'Synchrony'. And half-a-dozen *Doctor Who* stories (particularly 'City of Death' and 'Day of the Daleks'). Kyle mentions *Bewitched* and Tess refers to classic American novelist John Steinbeck (1902–68). Also, *The Tragedy of Romeo and Juliet* (Liz, specifically uses the play's full title), 'I Know It's Over' by the Smiths and Elvis. Michael has a poster for cult Louisiana R&B band the Residents.

Teen-Speak: Maria: 'I *have* Michael Guerin. He's mine. You should have seen his face when he apologised to me. His eyes were practically begging me to take his sorry ass back. I have so landed him for once and for all . . . I think.' And, to Michael: 'Some stupid psychic told me that the next 48 hours are critical, so could you just try not to be a bonehead? Is that, like, a possibility?'

Michael: 'I'm a germ-a-phobe. A clean girl is a sexy girl.' And: '*Dude*, it was a misunderstanding.'

Fashion Victims: Another conversation centring on Kyle's boxer shorts. In the future both Max and Liz get pairs of the production team's favourite fashion item, leather pants. Also, Liz's pink sleeveless top, and Tess's tight blue blouse.

Sex and Drugs and Rock'n'Roll: 'You are a wonderful friend. Her foundation. You will never have a carnal relationship,' Madame Vivian tells a crushed Alex about Isabel. 'There's gotta be something in those leaves,' he begs. 'A few moments of pure lust?' 'This boy. Very volatile,' she tells Maria, concerning Michael. 'That's good for sex, right?' asks an excited Maria. Courtney playfully slaps Michael's butt. Michael speculates that she might be an alien, or with the government. Maria is more concerned that 'the slut wants in your pants'. Courtney also mentions water-sports and suggests she will play any game Michael wants (indicating an intimate knowledge of, for instance, the BDSM community). There's a lot of near-nudity, Courtney stripping off her top in front of Michael and Liz getting almost-naked with Kyle. Max has tickets to a Gomez concert in Santa Fe and wants to take Liz. Future-Max tells Liz that if she doesn't break up with present-Max she will lose her virginity to him. 'Making love to you is the farthest thing from my mind,' says a horrified Liz. 'I don't even have protection.' 'I did,' says future-Max, shamefully. 'That's great,' shouts Liz, 'there you are, Max-the-Saint, walking around with a condom in his back pocket.'

Logic, Let Me Introduce You to This Window: Future-Liz looks not a day over seventeen. The granilith seems to increase the amount of stubble on future-Max's chin. Madame Vivian uses tea-leaves, palmistry *and* Tarot during her readings. All are very separate disciplines of fortune telling and it's unusual to find any practitioner who specialises in two of them, let alone all three.

Quote/Unquote: Liz: 'You're not Max. You're a shape-shifter. You're, like, some other kind of alien with the ability to look like Max with that beard and those grey hairs!'

Kyle, to Tess: 'You look really great when you're pissed!'

Courtney introduces single-entendre to the American market: 'Thanks for the ride. You handle your machine real good . . . I guess it's time for another night curled up in my sheets, fondling my remote control.'

Kyle, on Buddhism: 'It's really about approaching life through a spiritual place and becoming in tune with different planes of existence.' Future-Max: 'What a line of crap!'

Notes: 'There is no such thing as time travel . . . It's against every rule of physics, of reality, of everything.' Hmm. *Quantum Leap* anyone?! This is actually a great episode with a very clever agenda to destroy *Roswell*'s Romeo and Juliet-metaphor once-and-for-all, though the central time-travel premise is as hokey as hell. But there are a lot of nice bits and pieces and the scene of Maria finding Michael in Courtney's apartment is pure slapstick.

Maria says her mom lives her life based on Madame Vivian's advice ('and this is a recommendation?' asks Alex). Liz prefers white roses to red (see **37**, 'Viva Las Vegas'). Liz remains a virgin (see **16**, 'Sexual Healing'). Michael drives a previously unseen motorbike (licence-number HLO 175). Judging by the Halloween pumpkin not-very-subtly featured in one scene, this episode seems to take place around the date that it was broadcast.

'The Laws of Physics Don't Seem to Apply Here': According to future-Max, he cannot go near present-Max. If a person encounters himself in another time period, there could be a reaction. 'It has something to do with quantum mechanics.' Both would be destroyed if they came into contact.

Future Imperfect: In the timeline that future-Max erases, in 2014 the world will be on the verge of destruction (or, possibly conquest) by someone whom Max describes as 'our enemies' (the Skins? the Dupes? Aliens from the other four planets? Someone else? See **31**, 'Max in the City'). Max and Liz will become inseparable, but as they get closer the situation for Tess becomes intolerable and she eventually leaves Roswell. Once that has happened, the remaining Royal Three are never as strong. Max and Liz elope when they are nineteen and marry in the Elvis Chapel in Las Vegas (see **37**, 'Viva Las Vegas'). Liz then calls Maria, Michael, Isabel and Alex and they meet on the highway outside Phoenix and spend a joyous night dancing and singing (it sounds such a beautiful scene that the romantic in all of us would've loved to have seen a glimpse of it). At some future stage Liz and Max will have a friend called Serena who seems to be a scientist. Twenty minutes before future-Max time-travelled, he held the dead Michael in his arms. Isabel died two weeks before that.

Soundtrack: 'Save Me' by the Pierces (heard twice) and Sheryl Crow's 'I Shall Believe' (Max and Liz's 'wedding' song). Not forgetting an excellent 'Tres Diaz' by Jason Behr, the song that Max sings, accompanied by a mariachi band, to a startled Liz.

In an online interview with Erin Lauten, film-editor Peter Ellis notes: 'One of the really fun things about this show is that we get to use so much pop music. I spend a lot of time on every episode picking songs and planning the sound effects. When you find the right song and the right visuals, it's just the most brilliant thing in the world. One of the greatest movie moments I've seen was the end of *Magnolia* where everybody sings along with the Aimee Mann song 'Wise Up'. I love creating those kinds of moments, like Sheryl Crow's 'I Shall Believe' playing on the scene of future-Max and Liz parting, or putting the right music on an action sequence to create a lyrical, moving moment, or taking a Glen Campbell song, playing against type and putting it on a scene with a bunch of punk rockers.'

Cast and Crew Comments: According to Nick Wechsler: 'They cut *most* of my lines in my favourite scene. The one [where] Liz and I were lying in bed. They cut a crapload of that one!'

Did You Know?: If Jason Behr could be in any band, it would have to be the Beatles. 'That would have been a lot of fun,' he told an online Q&A session. That's stating the bleeding obvious somewhat, Jase.

28
The Harvest

US Transmission Date: 6 November 2000
UK Transmission Date: 28 March 2001 (Sky One)

Writer: Fred Golan
Director: Paul Shapiro
Cast: Chris Ellis (Greer),
Holmes Osborne (Walt Crawford),
Joshua Wheeler (Willy), Bella Shaw (Newscaster)

Max, Liz, Isabel and Tess travel to Arizona to find a secret organisation called the Universal Friendship League that Congresswoman Whitaker had connections with. Meanwhile, Michael and Maria hunt for the missing Courtney, whilst trying to work out if they have a relationship or not. At the end of both quests, the Skins are waiting.

'I've Got the Power': The sudden revelation that Nicholas Crawford is an alien comes when he uses his power on Isabel. Max and Greer have a *magnificent* battle in the church and Michael gives Nicholas a full-force blast as Courtney destroys the husks.

Roswell Iconography: Courtney's 'short version' of the alien back-story is that their planet was on the brink of a golden age, then it fell apart. Michael was the one who, many Skins believed, could have united the planet and pulled together the various warring factions. But he wasn't on the throne. A schism occurred amongst the rival parties but Michael would not betray his leader and brother-in-law and that loyalty cost him his life and those of everyone he loved. Courtney and her rebel faction of Skins came to Earth looking for Michael around 1950. As alluded to by

Whitaker, in **25**, 'Surprise', Earth's atmosphere is hostile to the Skins. Their husks are a parasitic lifeform technology that can be genetically manipulated to resemble human bodies. 'It's basically a shell. It protects us from the environment.'

Nicholas tells Isabel that her former-self, Vilandra, betrayed her kingdom for her lover, Kivar, the leader of the rebellion and the man who currently sits on her brother's throne (see **31**, 'Max in the City'). Nicholas claims to have killed Michael in his previous life.

The Conspiracy Starts at Home Time: A TV news report suggests that Whitaker was killed in a tragic single-car accident outside her hometown of Copper Summit, Arizona, her *real* death two weeks previously having been conveniently covered up.

The UFL is a Skin-front organisation who are growing new husks for themselves to replace their dying ones. Courtney's destruction of the husks prevents 'the harvest'.

'You Might Remember Me from Such Films and TV Series As . . .': Making his film debut at the age of three (as Gage in *Pet Sematary*), Miko Hughes played Zack in *Spawn*, Jeffrey Lovell in *Apollo 13* and can be seen in *Kindergarten Cop*, *Mercury Rising*, *Fly Boy*, *Magic Rock*, *Baywatch*, *Picket Fences* and *Beverly Hills 90210*. Chris Ellis is an instantly recognisable face as Deke Slayton in *Apollo 13*, Detective Butler in *Bean*, JL in *My Cousin Vinny* and Jim Penseyres in *Millennium*. Other appearances include *The Watcher*, *Atomic Train*, *Armageddon*, *Crimson Tide*, *Days of Thunder* and *Space: Above and Beyond*. Holmes Osborne is in *The Deep End*, *Bring It On*, *The Mod Squad*, *Nice Girls Don't Explode*, *The West Wing* and *Seven Days*. Readers may recognise him as Mr Patterson in *that thing you do!* Jenny O'Hara features in *Pumpkin Man*, *Career Opportunities* and, on TV, *CHiPS*, *Charlie's Angels*, *Remington Steele* and *The Rockford Files*. Joshua Wheeler was Michael in *The Loch*. Bella Shaw is a real-life newscaster though she also played one in *Invasion USA* and *The Larry Sanders Show*.

Holding the Camera: The non-speaking role of the TV cameraman wearing a red shirt in the funeral sequence was played by Dan Smiczek, a regular background actor on many TV series. Dan has a fascinating and humorous website, *The Adventures of Dan: Extra Extraordinaire*, at *http://www.adventuresofdan.com/* which detail his many experiences working on shows as diverse as *Buffy*, *Angel*, *The X-Files* and *The West Wing*. This gives readers an interesting look at the behind-the-scenes reality of the TV industry. Dan's account of a two-day shoot which results in about four minutes of screen-time is certainly an eye-opener. As Dan notes: 'After the day was over I went back and reread the scene. It's funny how what is filmed differs from the script. If they had done it as in the script I would have had a featured part! Specifically it says how the main characters aren't worried that anything is going to happen because the news crew is reporting live. They only realise their predicament when the cameraman rips the chord out of the wall, which differs significantly from what we see in the episode.'

References: The Who's 'I Can't Explain' and James's 'Destiny Calling' are quoted. Maria feels that she and Michael are 'like Mulder and Scully', and name-checks Culture Club, Wham! and the Backstreet Boys. Also *Bring It On*, Elvis (again) and his Memphis home Graceland and the Air and Space Museum in Washington. There are several visual links to *The X-Files* movie and to *Invasion of the Bodysnatchers* (the Philip Kaufman version). Liz has a NO WHINERS! sticker on her school locker.

The Copper Summit scenes were filmed on the backlot at Universal studios.

Teen-Speak: Maria: '*Whatever*, dude.' And: 'Oh, please! Do your lips not get chapped from all the *ass-kissing*?'

Michael: 'Are you just gonna rag on me or are you gonna help?'

Fashion Victims: Maria's hair is much tidier in this and the next episode than for much of the rest of the season. Also, check-out Michael's horrible big-collared shirt.

Sex and Drugs and Rock'n'Roll: When Michael and Maria find Courtney's 'shrine' to Michael, Maria is horrified: 'She's obsessed with you. She's, like, an alien stalker.'

'On our world,' Nicholas tells Isabel, 'I was considered to be something of a ladies' man. I even remember you giving me the eye now and again. But after spending fifty years as a teenage misfit, having all the women laugh at me, I've grown far less tolerant of the female sex.' Courtney has stolen Michael's Metallica T-shirt. She also has a poster for a concert featuring both Metallica and overrated Seattle grunge-rockers Pearl Jam in her 'stalker's lair' (Michael inherits the poster, presumably after Courtney's death. See **36**, 'How the Other Half Lives').

Logic, Let Me Introduce You to This Window: The Copper Summit postmark has no date on it, only a year. Not possible. The Crawfords don't look old enough to have had a 36-year-old daughter, but conversely too old to have a thirteen-year-old son.

Quote/Unquote: Maria, on Courtney's CD collection: 'Culture Club? Wham? Backstreet Boys? God, she really *is* an alien!'

Greer, to Max: 'You must be the once-and-future king?'

Nicholas: 'If only the people could see you now. Clueless teenagers groping for their own identities.'

Notes: 'Why are you in Roswell? Where's the rest of your evil army? And why are you obsessed with my good-looking, if badly groomed, boyfriend?' This one rattles along at a fair old pace with two separate plots that come together at the end in a convoluted, but satisfying way. The Michael/Maria plot is, again, the best thing on display. Something of an information overload in the second half, but stick with it for a peach of an ending.

Widowed six months before her politician husband John Whitaker stood for the Senate (was *he* a Skin?), Vanessa took his place and won the election by a higher margin than any Democrat in fifteen years. Her maiden name was Crawford and she was born in 1964 according to the TV report (as her family are all Skins she wasn't really 'born' at all). Isabel mentions having killed Whitaker (see **25**, 'Surprise').

Soundtrack: Cleopatra's 'U Got It' and Gene Autry's 'Back in the Saddle Again'.

Critique: Once a vocal supporter of *Roswell*, *TV Guide*'s Matt Roush noted that: '*Felicity* ought to be a keeper, especially when you consider the creative decline of WB's tiresomely self-aware *Dawson's Creek*, the stridently campy *Popular* and even *Roswell*, once a favourite of mine but now diminished into a ponderous junior-league *X-Files* with too much plot and not enough wit.' In the same magazine *Washington Post* reviewer Donna Britt gave a counter opinion: 'I'm glad TV can never return to its former naîveté. But the best teen shows downplay sensationalism in favour of illuminating kids' everyday challenges, which are harrowing enough. On *Roswell*, tough *and* tender interaction between likable parents and teens provide a realistic counterpoint to the show's sci-fi sensibilities.'

Cast and Crew Comments: '*The X-Files* didn't do well until the second year,' Majandra Delfino told WB reporter Victoria Snee. 'I think the expectations are a little too high because we're not this sellout mainstream show where we, like, just do anything to be viewed.'

Did You Know?: It's a small world in Hollywood. As Miko Hughes told Paul Simpson and Ruth Thomas: 'I worked with Majandra Delfino on a movie called *Zeus and Roxanne*, which was her very first movie. Her mom and my mom stayed friends for years. When we heard that [Maria] had got *Roswell* we tried to watch it to see her. I thought wouldn't it be really cool if I got to work with Majandra again. The first week I was [on the *Roswell* set], I counted sixteen or seventeen people that I had worked with before. The studio teacher who taught in the Bahamas on *Zeus and Roxanne* with Majandra and I, is the teacher on this show. The prop man was on that same movie. Then there was a bunch of people from *Spawn*, *Mercury Rising*, lots of different stuff. The camera guy was from *Kindergarten Cop*!'

29
Wipe-Out!

US Transmission Date: 13 November 2000
UK Transmission Date: 4 April 2001 (Sky One)

Writers: Gretchen J Berg and Aaron Harberts
Director: Michael Lange
Cast: David Batiste (James)

After turning Roswell into a ghost town by making all the humans disappear, the Skins capture Max, Isabel, Michael and Tess. Hoping to discover the location of the granilith, they torture the Royal Four in an effort to make them reveal their secrets. But they reckon without the resourcefulness of Kyle, Maria and Liz. And the *anger* of Tess.

'I've Got the Power': Tess creates the illusion of a mirror where The CrashDown bathroom door should be to confuse Nicholas. She says that she has never faced anyone with that much power before. 'It feels like someone took a sledgehammer to my head.' At the climax, like Michael and Isabel before her, she discovers that she has the power to kill. Courtney tells the others that Nicholas has all of the powers that they have, multiplied by a thousand. His most frightening ability is to 'rape you of your memories and thoughts'. When he catches Courtney, the first thing he extracts from *her* memory is that she had scrambled eggs for breakfast.

Roswell Iconography: The UFO Center is a former nuclear fallout shelter. It is situated on Central Avenue South (so, presumably, is The CrashDown across the street).

The Conspiracy Starts at Home Time: Courtney, on how to kill a Skin. 'Take the heaviest thing that you can find and smash [a point at the base of their spine] as hard as you can. It breaks the seal.' During their past lives, Isabel and Nicholas were secret lovers (alluded to in **28**, 'The Harvest'). Nicholas mentions that Courtney was a social butterfly. 'What happened to you, *guy*?' Nicholas asks when he comes face-to-face with Max who, he says, used to determine the fate of armies with the flip of a coin. Luckily for Nicholas, he says, Max always puts his faith in the wrong people. 'Rule number one of war. Keep your big mouth shut.'

High School Life: 'How does electricity work?' asks Maria. 'Why are you lookin' at me?' replies a nonplussed Kyle. 'We were both in the same remedial science class for three years!'

References: The title is from a 1963 instrumental hit by Surfaris. Diane Evans is making a frijole fritatta which, she says, home and garden guru Martha Stewart serves to her guests in the Hamptons (a popular East Coast summer resort). Also, Kathie Lee Gifford the co-host of *Live! With Regis and Kathie Lee*, the Walker Brothers' 'Make it Easy on Yourself', another (amusing) reference to Elvis and the circumstances in which he died (in his bathroom), *Apollo 13* ('That is not an option') and *Sleeping with the Enemy*.

Teen-Speak: Tess: 'Pretty quick recovery, don't you think? This "I've fallen and can't get up" routine seems a little too convenient. It's time for a Q&A.'
    Max: 'It's *our turf*.'

Fashion Victims: 'By the way, *love* the hair,' Nicholas sarcastically tells Michael. Also, Tess's fleece jacket, Nicholas's Ray-Bans.

Sex and Drugs and Rock'n'Roll: Alex's band (see **14**, 'Blind Date') have just 'burned a CD' (presumably self-produced). When Liz suggests that they need to treat Courtney with a bath of vitamins, minerals and nutrients, Maria says she has: 'Ginko, bee pollen, echinacea, C, D, E, calcium,

St John's wort, and Pamprin. *What?* I was dating Michael Guerin.'

Logic, Let Me Introduce You to This Window: The fire-escape ladder up to the roof at The CrashDown is in a different place to where it was in Season One.

Quote/Unquote: Valenti, on his son's newfound Buddhist beliefs: 'If you laid off the mumbo jumbo, you might get a date every once in awhile.'

Nicholas: 'You're shedding.' Ida: 'It's the heat. Why couldn't those brats be from Seattle?'

Liz, on Courtney: 'From what she said, the husk is starving. It's sucking at her thighs like they're two canned hams.' Courtney: 'I heard that, you bitch.'

Nicholas: 'You always were a flighty little princess. Jewels before studies, that's our Vilandra. We *have* you, you beautiful *moron*.'

Notes: 'We're the ones who destroyed their harvest. They're here to settle the score.' A classic SF situation (a small town attacked by an unstoppable exterior menace and with no escape; it's *very* John Wyndham), this is another fine episode, with Kyle and Maria getting nice meaty roles and Tess, for once, providing the solution. Miko Hughes is *superb* as Nicholas, a psychotic warrior trapped in a child's body. Beautifully directed too.

If she survives the attack, Maria intends to spend more time with her mother and write more to her grandmother. The night after Kyle's mother left home, the six-year-old boy loaned his father 'Mr Squishels' (his favourite toy) because he didn't want his dad sleeping alone. Valenti fondly remembers the first time Kyle tied his own shoes and when they removed the training wheels from Kyle's bike. The defaced billboard for the UFO Center is at the Chaparral Turnout, which can be reached from The CrashDown via Bradford Avenue. Deputy Hanson is mentioned. Jeff Parker sent Maria and Liz on an errand to Dexter, 30 miles from Roswell. This episode takes place on a Saturday.

'The Laws of Physics Don't Seem to Apply Here': According to Courtney, time exists in multiple subset dimensions on the aliens' planet. Nicholas has a technology to impose one or more of these on Earth. 'Speak English,' demands Isabel. Courtney continues that it's like being on the four US time zones (Pacific, Eastern, Central and Mountain) all at once. Human bodies can't function and are shifted to another plane of existence.

Soundtrack: Elvis Costello's 'Alison' features prominently in the scene where Liz says her mother likes to listen to the great singer/songwriter on laundry day. Also 'Next Year' by Foo Fighters, Good Charlotte's 'Complicated' and 'The Itch' by Vitamin C.

Critique: 'A suspenseful drama that blends science-fiction with the alienation of young adulthood,' noted the *Evening Chronicle*, 'this genre-bending series centres on a group of otherworldly teenagers living in the tiny, but notorious, southwestern town ... Following the disclosure of their true identities to a close-knit group of human friends, the aliens find themselves caught up in a dangerous struggle.'

Cast and Crew Comments: 'It's one of the most fun roles I've ever done,' says Miko Hughes. 'You get a feel for how to play the role from looking at the script and the lines. [The writers] give you a back-story. I do as much as I can on my own, and then if I need help, I take as much input as I'm offered.'

Did You Know?: Despite having worked with some of the biggest names in the business, Miko Hughes still finds himself awestruck occasionally. 'It's like the old McDonald's commercial,' he told Paul Simpson and Ruth Thomas. 'Can I get your picture? Yesterday I met Tony Hawk, the world skateboarding champion. I got an autograph for my nephews. Chevy Chase, Bruce Willis, Alec Baldwin, Tom Hanks. Each was a different experience.'

30
Meet the Dupes

US Transmission Date: 20 November 2000
UK Transmission Date: 11 April 2001 (Sky One)

Writer: Toni Graphia
Director: James A Contner
Cast: Sean Allen Rector (Lance), Steve Picerni (Driver)

The other four alien fetuses from the 1947 crash, duplicates of the Royal Four, are alive and well and living in New York City. After murdering their own king, Zan, they head for Roswell in search of Max to represent them at a summit with other alien leaders. The New York Dupes are streetwise, ruthless and know more about their home planet and what occurred before they were sent to Earth than their Roswell counterparts. Max is suspicious but, as usual, Michael and Isabel want to learn more. Meanwhile, as Michael takes Maria for granted, Brody Davis develops an attraction to her.

'I've Got the Power': Rath, Lonnie and Ava seem to have the same powers as Michael, Isabel and Tess, unsurprisingly. Zan uses his powers recreationally, collapsing a fruit-dealer's stall. Rath changes the number plate of the car that they steal. Rath and Lonnie have impressive shape-shifting abilities, which Michael and Isabel do not seem to have acquired yet.

Roswell Iconography: Brody's constant monitoring of alien communication (see **24**, 'Ask Not') pays dividends. He notes that a series of blips similar to those he picked up in May (see **22**, 'Destiny') appeared last week in the New York area. Brody tells Maria that he has begun to experience missing moments of time, 'bizarre dreams I can't remember in the morning. It all reminds me of the last time. So, if I suddenly disappear, it's nothing personal. I've just been abducted.' Rath says that the alien star system has five planets, each with a ruling family, and it is they who have organised the summit. On their planet there was 'some kind of revolution', and the Royal Four were all killed (see **25**, 'Surprise', **28**, 'The Harvest') and sent to Earth to be reborn. 'Ever since then, the 'hood's been a war zone.' Two sets of pods were created in case one was defective. Lonnie claims that the Royal Four are the inferior specimens. 'Too human. No offence.'

On the menu at The CrashDown: A Galaxy-Sub sandwich. Pay particular attention to the brilliantly subtle ARE THEY STILL HERE? sign in the UFO Center that Michael sits beneath.

Naming All the Stars: A black hole, notes Mr Seligman, 'is what's left after a star dies'. Last week saw 'the stellar implosion of a red giant, unheard of in the history of astronomy'. This is the first time a post-main sequence star burning in its prime has suddenly and without warning exploded in a supernova, a process that usually takes many thousands of years.

Dudes and Babes: Michael tells Brody that Rath is his twin brother, 'Bob', who lives in New York. 'That explains the hair,' notes Brody.

'You Might Remember Me from Such Films and TV Series As . . .': Steve Picerni has performed stunts on more than 60 films, including *Gone in Sixty Seconds*, *Stigmata*, *Soldier*, *Con Air*, *Jingle All the Way*, *Courage Under Fire*, *Barb Wire*, *Crimson Tide*, *Last Action Hero*, *Hook*, *Die Hard* (and its sequels) and *The Hunt for the Red October*.

References: Philip thinks Isabel (actually Lonnie) looks like rapper Queen Latifah. She says that they are doing a rock and roll version of *Romeo and Juliet* at school. Philip was Puck in his senior year production of *A Midsummer Night's Dream*. He quotes from Irving Berlin's 'There's No Business Like Show Business'. Brody gives Maria a $100 tip and they discuss American statesman Benjamin Franklin, 1706–90, and President Andrew Jackson 1767–1845 (Brody thinks the latter's hair is excellent and that he 'looks like Elvis'). Maria alludes to Oasis's 'Definitely Maybe'. Also, *Hawaii Five-0*, notorious traitor Benedict Arnold (1741–1801). Alex mentions *Halloween*, the New Orleans Mardi Gras and *The Ricki Lake Show*. Rath and Lonnie quote from 'Theme from New York New York' ('Start spreadin' the news').

The meeting of the Royal Four and their counterparts may have been inspired by the bit in *Yellow Submarine* where the Beatles meet Sergeant Pepper's Lonely Hearts Club Band. Many series have done 'evil duplicate' episodes (*Star Trek* being the most obvious example). Famous New York locations recreated for this episode include the exit of Canal Street Metro Station on Lafayette Street, and the corner of Lexington Avenue (as immortalised in the Velvet Underground's 'Waiting for the Man'). The scene where Max and Isabel almost come to blows was filmed in one of the car parks at Paramount studio. If you look closely, in the background you can see a couple of very LA-palm trees on Melrose Avenue, and a passing bus with the distinctive yellow and maroon trimmings of the LA Transit vehicles.

Noo-Yawk-Speak: Punk: 'Hey, wha's up, girl?'

Rath: 'Yo, gimme the rock.' And: 'He's already toast.' And: '*Word*!' And: 'How *whack* is that?' And: 'S'up?'

Lonnie: 'It's been a mad-long-day. Let's just *chill*.' And: 'You're the freakin' man!' And: 'Total cornball!' And: '*Totally epic*, dad!'

Fashion Victims: Rath is contemptuous of Max's wardrobe, asking if he shops at Conways ('Out here, they think that's hip,' Lonnie notes). All of the aliens have the same four-symbol tattoos. And lots of body jewellery. Brody has a Freestyle 'Tide' digital watch. Also, Ava's leather mini skirt and Max's bright orange T-shirt.

Sex and Drugs and Rock'n'Roll: Maria is singing on Saturday at the new performance space next to the museum. But Michael will have to miss this, as it's the dirt bike final. When Alex asks Isabel and Lonnie if they'd like a frosty beverage, Lonnie replies: 'No three-ways tonight, *opie*. Maybe later.'

Logic, Let Me Introduce You to This Window: Brody asks what Maria thinks of the new president. In any other election year this ambiguous question would have gone unnoticed, but the Florida-recount-saga was still ongoing when this episode was broadcast. Liz tells Max 'long before we kissed we were friends'. That's certainly not the impression of **1**, 'Pilot' where Max and Liz hardly knew each other. How did the Dupes get hold of a copy of the West Roswell High School yearbook in New York?

Quote/Unquote: Maria, after Michael has neglected to put pepperjack on Brody's sandwich: 'A person who can't even get the cheese right does not deserve to live.' Brody: 'You take your job very seriously?'

Valenti thinks Rath is Michael: 'You look like you're from another planet. For once.'

Rath, on his home: 'The Big Apple. Centre of the universe. Amazing pizza.'

Rath, on Brody: 'You want me to kill him for you?' Michael: 'I'll get back to you on that.'

Notes: 'Seems some peeps from the 'hood, they wanna hook up with us and have a sit-down.' *Sharp*! A smashing episode of bluff and counter-bluff, with Brendan, Katherine and Emilie having great fun playing punked-up New York versions of Michael, Isabel and Tess. Also includes some nice work on Brody (a potential relationship with Maria).

Liz gave Max a pocket knife last Christmas (inscribed *Max and Liz 4-Ever*). Liz owns a teddy bear (isn't she a bit old for that?) Isabel has taken up jogging to get into shape (what's the matter with the shape she's already got, one has to ask?) Max says her only exercise used to be the escalator at the mall. Max is still undergoing therapy, and it's confirmed that Isabel is too. Max's photo in the school yearbook is on the same page as, amongst others, Mark Esquivies, Geoff Franks and John Fader. He keeps a photo of Liz in his sock drawer. Brody asks Maria if she believes in God. She is undecided. He says that he used to, and maybe still does.

Soundtrack: Some real classics: Belle & Sebastian's 'Don't Leave the Light on, Baby', and Glen Campbell's 'Rhinestone Cowboy' (on the car radio). Also, Linkin Park's 'With You' (which begins and ends the episode) and 'What Am I Supposed To Do?' by Papa's Fritas.

Critique: According to *ign sci-fi*'s Susan Kuhn, 'in the grand tradition of punk-ass evil twins, this episode gives us streetwise, skankified *doppelgängers* of Max, Isabel, Michael and Tess. These kids are *mean*, man! They spit and curse. Bizarro-Michael sports even worse hair than Good-Michael, a mullet-mohawk. Bizarro-Isabel has a vague Brooklyn-toughgirl accent. Bizarro-Tess just looks extremely uncomfortable, all biting her lip and thinking, "when do I get my pretty hair back?"'

Cast and Crew Comments: 'They're putting me in a different relationship,' Majandra Delfino told *Starlog*. 'That's fine with me, I like having a relationship with somebody else because I don't think anybody could hold onto Michael for that long.'

Did You Know?: 'The physical appearance kind of sets the mood depending on what you look like,' Brendan Fehr notes concerning his portrayal of Rath. 'If you look mean, if you feel others will perceive you to be mean then it's a lot easier to play. If you're a geek in glasses and your pants hiked up to your tits you will not feel particularly mean. So the mohawk, the tattoos, the chains, the leather and the big boots that kind of sets the stage so you can walk out of the trailer just really feeling it.'

31
Max in the City

US Transmission Date: 27 November 2000
UK Transmission Date: 18 April 2001 (Sky One)

Writer: Ronald D Moore
Director: Patrick Norris
Cast: Jerry Gelb (Emissary), Faline England (Kathana),
David Reivers (Sero), Marji Martin (Hanar)

Max and Tess go to the interstellar summit in New York with Rath and Lonnie. Max meets the emissary, an alien who tests Max's claim to be king. When Max meets the peace council of representatives from the four warring planets, plus Nicholas representing Kivar, he also encounters Brody, whose body is being used as a vessel for one of the members. Lonnie and Rath are desperate to get Max to accept the agreement so they can go home. Max and Tess suspect their motives.

'I've Got the Power': Rath describes how the aliens possess humans: 'The alien emissary far away on another planet. Human *knobhead* here on this planet. Emissary reaches out with his mind, takes control of the human. Human walks around like a puppet doing whatever the emissary wants him to do.' This, presumably, explains Brody's various abduction experiences over the years (see **36**, 'How the Other Half Lives'). With Isabel's help, Liz is able to enter Max's mind and save him from Rath and Lonnie's attempt on his life by distracting him.

Roswell Iconography: Nicholas confirms that Rath and Lonnie are from the 'reject' pod and not Max, as claimed in **30**, 'Meet the Dupes' ('they were carefully hidden away in Roswell and got custody of the granilith. You were dumped in the sewer. Figure it out'). Tess suggests that the other alien with Nasedo in 1947 (see **21**, 'The White Room', **26** 'Summer of '47') became the Dupes' protector and brought them to New York.

Rath says that the representatives of the other planets hate Kivar the current ruler of the Royal Four's planet (see **28**, 'The Harvest'). Lonnie notes that their protector told them that the granilith is 'like the holy grail, some piece of junk people on our planet worship'. The representatives of the other planets also know of the granilith and were unaware that it was missing. Larek tells Max that their families used to be close. 'You and I practically grew up together. I was at your father's funeral. At your coronation, your wedding. We were friends.' It was painful, he says, to watch Max fall, and to watch him have it all taken away by a man like Kivar. 'What a shame it is to see history repeat itself.'

Rath and Lonnie still have the pods from which they emerged.

Family Life: Isabel tells Max that Thanksgiving was great. 'Mom cried all the way from the cranberry sauce to the peach cobbler. So did I.'

'You Might Remember Me from Such Films and TV Series As . . .': Voice artist Jerry Gelb worked on *Lured Innocence*, *Possums*, *Lost in Space*, *Scorpio One* and *Little Witches*. David Reivers can be seen in *Malcolm X*, *The Thirteenth Year*, *Buffy* and *Felicity*. Marji Martin played Betty in *The Last Resort* and also appears in *Shocker*, *The Man Who Saw Tomorrow* and two episodes of *The A-Team* (as 'Fat Lady').

References: Max quotes *Titanic* ('I'm king of the world'). Nicholas's opinions of New York ('stupid, rat-infested, urine-soaked, butt-ugly town') resemble Homer Simpson's. Also, *The Andy Griffiths Show* ('not quite Mayberry, is it?'), Dennis Potter's *The Beast With Two Backs*, Aldous Huxley's *Brave New World*, *My Fair Lady* ('when you get to the church on time'), *The Exorcist* ('doin' the Linda Blair, you know?'), *The Hitchhiker's Guide to the Galaxy* ('space is what we call very, very big'), *Star Trek* and Buffalo Springfield's 'For What It's Worth'. There's a huge *The Matrix* feel to the scene of Max meeting the emissary.

And a lovely view from the 86th floor of the Empire State Building.

Noo-Yawk-Speak: Lonnie: 'Yo, when he gets here we're puttin' him in his place, 'cos I'm sick of gettin' attitude from him.' And: 'Wanna use our crib?'

Rath: 'What kinda *sick mother* puts mayo on pastrami? I oughta bust your head open.'

And, just about everything else that Rath and Lonnie say.

Fashion Victims: Max's chunky leather jacket. Maria's beret and sheepskin.

Sex and Drugs and Rock'n'Roll: Rath: 'Alien sex, *baby*. Accept no imitations. *Awoo! Ooh!*' Subtle. Maria asks Liz if Kyle date-raped her and confirms that she, like Liz, is still a virgin.

Lonnie says she is sick of pizza and suggests Chinatown instead.

Logic, Let Me Introduce You to This Window: There are five planets in the system, as confirmed in **30**, 'Meet the Dupes'. We see the familiar V-shape but, **19**, 'Four Square' suggested that this referred to the four stars of the Aries system with Venus at a particular point, not to five planets orbiting a distant sun. Brody is wearing exactly the same clothes both before he left and after he returns to Roswell as he is in New York. After (at least) three days wouldn't they be a bit ripe? How did Brody get to and from New York so quickly? If he flies then surely, when he returns to normal, he would have something like a credit card slip to let him *know* where he'd been during his 'abduction'. Why, anyway, is Larek using a host body who is over a thousand miles away from the summit?

Quote/Unquote: Nicholas: 'Killed anyone today?' Tess: 'Day's not over.'

Notes: 'All you've ever done is trust me. I've never done anything to deserve that kind of loyalty.' Far too much going on here for the viewer to concentrate on everything. There's a lot of information imparted too, some of which evaporates on contact with the brain. Great locations, though, and one absolutely stunning tracking shot of the desert night sky.

Maria tells Liz that a vicious rumour is going around school that Liz and Kyle slept together (see **27**, 'The End of the World'). Who told? It was Kyle, wasn't it?!

Soundtrack: The Pharcyde's 'Passing Me By', 'Everything' by Lifehouse and Radiohead's 'How To Disappear Completely'.

Critique: *SFX* columnist Paul Cornell noted in his 'Dreams for 2001', 'that *Roswell High* goes back to being about the metaphorical alien horrors of teenage love and stops doing silly alien horror stories'.

The Pick-Up: On 6 December 2000, it was announced that: 'On the heels of a record-breaking November sweep', the WB had ordered additional episodes of resurgent drama *Felicity*, acclaimed freshman comedy *Grosse Point*, and midseason pick-ups for both *Roswell* and *The Gilmore Girls*. 'Ratings are up in Adults 18-34 on all six nights of programming,' said Susanne Daniels, the WB's Entertainment President. '*Felicity* and *Roswell* continue to exceed our expectations. It's been a great season so far.'

Did You Know?: Katherine Heigl actually auditioned for all three of the female lead roles on *Roswell* before being cast as Isabel. In interviews Katherine often jokes about how she got a big breast size, noting that when she was in her early teens she prayed a lot. Seems to have worked. Katherine stresses that she has no plans to move away from the home she shares with her mother. During a three-week visit to her father, who lives in Virginia, and her sister, who remains in Katherine's native Connecticut, she says she was anxious to get back to her home in LA's Malibu Canyon.

32
The Miracle
[AKA: 'A Roswell Christmas Carol']

US Transmission Date: 18 December 2000
UK Transmission Date: 25 April 2001 (Sky One)

Writer: Jason Katims
Director: Patrick Norris

Cast: John Littlefield (John),
Adeline Allen (Sydney Davis),
Madison McReynolds (John's Daughter),
Kelly Hill (Nurse), Biff Wiff (Security Guard),
Whitney Weston (Mother), Bill Small (Man),
Jaquita Ta'le (Caroler #1), Joshua Kranz (Caroler #2),
Jeni C Wilson (Caroler #3), Jordan Smith (Caroler #4),
Holly Gray (Caroler #5), Christine Noh (Caroler #6),
Joseph Williams (Choir Member #1),
Amye Williams (Choir Member #2),
Jason Scheff (Choir Member #3)

Max is buying a Christmas tree when he witnesses a man sacrifice himself by jumping in front of a car to save his daughter's life. Max knows he could save the man with his powers, but he fears exposure and does not intervene. Max is haunted by the dead man who says he must make amends. Discovering that Brody has a gravely ill daughter, Max takes a dangerous trip to right his mistake. Michael, meanwhile, has to find a gift for Maria, or risk losing her.

'I've Got the Power': Does this episode support the existence of life-after-death in the *Roswell* universe? Are John's appearances a genuine haunting? If so, then the message of the episode is pretty damn *mean* in this author's view. Or is it just a symptom of Max's own grief and self-criticism? Up to a point this view can be supported (Liz suggests as much), but then the ghost tells Max information that he didn't know (that Sydney had been rushed to hospital). In a hospital ward in Phoenix, Max performs a series of miracles, healing Sydney and then all of the children in the room with her. Tess uses her powers to carve the turkey.

Roswell Iconography: When Liz tells Max that if he had saved John's life it would have endangered the others, Max replies: 'I wasn't thinking about Michael and Isabel and Tess. I was thinking about myself in the white room being tortured. I didn't heal that man, because I was protecting myself.'

The Conspiracy Starts at Home Time: A TV report suggests that the children that Max heals had all been undergoing experimental treatments which may explain their miraculous simultaneous recovery.

'You Might Remember Me from Such Films and TV Series As ...': John Littlefield was Gary Sinclair in the soap opera *Another World*, and appeared in *Interstate 84*. Whitney Weston's films include *Every Minute is Goodbye* and *The Heroes of Desert Storm*, Bill Small was in *Two Room Junction*. Jordan Smith's previous work includes *Buttman's Bouncin' British Babes*, *The Pink Pussycat* and *The Back Doors*.

References: This being a Christmas episode, *It's a Wonderful Life*. Obviously. And Charles Dickens' *A Christmas Carol*. Obviously. And *Randall and Hopkirk (Deceased)*. Michael refers to Nirvana's groundbreaking (if a tad over-hyped) LP 'Nevermind'. The football game that Valenti and Kyle are watching appears to be between the Philadelphia Eagles and the Dallas Cowboys. The exterior location for the Phoenix hospital, is actually Providence St Joseph's medical centre on Buena Vista Street in Burbank, close to both Warner Brothers and the Disney studios.

Teen-Speak: Michael refers to Isabel as 'the Christmas Nazi' (which, given that she drew Max and Michael a *diagram* of the precise type of tree she wanted, isn't entirely unfair. Wonderfully, one scene later we discover that her father also calls her this).

Michael: 'I'm under a lot of pressure. She's been busting my ass for weeks about this present.'

Maria: 'Need a little wiggle room?'

Kyle: 'All I'm saying is that if the guy can't visualise his journey to the goal, he has no chance of taking the rock downtown.' And: 'Come on, look within, you putz.'

Fashion Victims: What is the matter with Isabel's hair? Looks like she's had an accident with an electrical appliance. And the woolly scarf, silly hat and *mad* earrings don't help either. Maria's brown and orange fluffy coat and yet another amusingly crap beret are further fashion crimes.

Christmas Feast: The Valentis' initial idea of Christmas food is nachos and, in an emergency, Meaty Man frozen burgers. Jim shares a glass of red wine with Amy.

Logic, Let Me Introduce You to This Window: Logic? C'mon, it's Christmas, let's ignore the fact that the episode is based on the premise that ghosts exist ...

Quote/Unquote: Michael, struggling to think of a present for Maria: 'The whole thing's a marketing scam invented to make people buy things they don't even need.' Isabel: 'You could write that on the card when you give her a dental product for Christmas.'

Amy: 'This must be the famous Tess. My daughter Maria has told me so much about you.' Tess: 'I deny everything.'

Tess: 'I have been cooking for twenty hours, while you two have been sitting on the couch like two beached whales, not even noticing or caring that I am living here. Okay. I am here. Hello?'

Kyle: 'This is really great.' Tess: 'I saw a break in the NFL schedule between the 22nd and 24th December, so I figured ...'

Notes: 'How could you let me die?' Mawkish, trite and overtly-sentimental rubbish. Or not. Because, despite its obvious (and seemingly self-imposed) limitations and an ending that's straight out of *It's a Wonderful Life*, 'The Miracle' shares with Frank Kapra's classic a (possibly naive, but fundamentally valid) faith in the basic decency of humanity. As Half Man Half Biscuit have noted, 'it's clichéd to be cynical at Christmas' and *that* is the episode's chief salvation. It's still hard to be objective about 'The Miracle', particularly when it starts snowing at the end, and many readers may despise the episode and everything that it apparently stands for. *And* it's impossible not to feel a bit (no, correction, a *lot*) manipulated when Max heals a room full of sick children and one of them asks if he's an angel. Yet for all that 'The Miracle' reassures us that some people out there still care. Plus, when it wants to be (the startling lack of domestic bliss in the Valenti household, for instance) the episode's comedy is *fantastic*.

Michael didn't get Maria a present last Christmas. Max asks Michael if he's getting her a ratchet set this year. Michael initially goes for a Braun electric toothbrush until Isabel persuades him otherwise. Then he tries a new bumper for Maria's Jetta (the old one has been 'hanging by a piece of string' for several months). Maria loves it but wants to know what her *real* present is. Fortunately Isabel has bought a pair of pearl earrings for Michael to give to Maria. Isabel is involved in a 'hunger drive', director of the 23rd annual Roswell holiday pageant, a Christmas dog show and various activities at a local nursing home. She's also helping to plan a vigil for the dead man's family. She has a Filofax.

Jim and Kyle have a plastic Christmas tree which they keep in the garage, though it hasn't been brought indoors for a few years and Kyle uses it to dry his socks! They also have a disquieting lack of chairs in their house. They usually go to The CrashDown for Christmas turkey ('$7.95, all you can eat!'). Valenti first met Amy ('before I was legal,' she notes) when he almost ran over her and Curt Pressman on his dirt-bike whilst they were doing . . . something. Their second meeting was when he arrested her (see **9**, 'Heatwave'). The third time, he rescued her from a burning attic. Tess cooks three-cheese potato gratin with bacon on the bottom (Kyle's particular favourite) for Christmas dinner. Brody's young daughter Sydney, like her father (see **24**, 'Ask Not'), had inoperable bone marrow cancer.

The episode ends with a caption directing viewers to the WB website for further information on pediatric cancer.

Soundtrack: Another eclectic bunch: Fountains Of Wayne's excellent 'I Want An Alien For Christmas' (at the start), the Wallflowers' 'Babybird', Jane Siberry's 'Calling All Angels', Angie Aparo's 'Silent Night', 'Everything's

Gonna Be Cool This Christmas' by Eels and, inevitably, 'Wonderful Christmas Time' by Paul McCartney. Plus various carols and hymns ('Jingle Bells', 'Deck the Halls', 'Amazing Grace' and 'Oh Come All Ye Faithful'. Because, like, you know, it's Christmas).

33
To Protect and Serve

US Transmission Date: 22 January 2001
UK Transmission Date: 2 May 2001 (Sky One)

Writer: Breen Frazier
Director: Jefery Levy
Cast: Breon Gorman (Judith Foster),
Woon Park (Buddha), Sage Kirkpatrick (Melissa Foster),
Sebastian Siegel (Brad)

Isabel's nocturnal voyeurism reveals that Liz is still fixated on Max and that Kyle believes he is becoming an alien. But she is horrified when she is pulled into a dream that she didn't choose to infiltrate: a girl dragged in a body bag through the woods. Valenti has problems of his own. An old friend, Dan, from the state police board is investigating the death of Hubble and the sheriff's relationship with the Evans kids. Isabel goes on a date with Grant, but her dreams continue with Grant as the kidnapper. Valenti arrests Grant, but when the 'missing' girl appears, unharmed, Valenti seems to have given his enemies an opportunity to bring him down.

Dreaming (As Blondie Once Said) is Free: In Isabel's case, free *entertainment*. Max tells her to stay away from Liz's dreams so, of course, she doesn't. In her dream, Liz and 'Brad' a hunky, yet nonexistent, guy in white passionately kiss on The CrashDown counter whilst she asks 'Would you like fries with that?' Then Max appears and it starts raining rose petals. 'Even her romantic dreams are boring,' notes Isabel. She finds Kyle's subconscious much more fun. He talks to Buddha, terrified that he is becoming an alien.

'I've Got the Power': Kyle *thinks* he's got the power to change TV channels. But it's just Tess standing behind him with a remote control. Max stops the kidnapper's bullets with his powers. When Isabel touches Laurie Dupree she has a flash and says 'it's like I know her'.

The Conspiracy Starts at Home Time: Dan demands Valenti tells him what's going on and, when Valenti refuses, Dan explodes that the government has been watching him. They know he has a relationship with certain teenagers and disappears for days on end.

Dudes and Babes: Maria's waste-of-space cousin, Sean, turns up having just got out of jail.

'You Might Remember Me from Such Films and TV Series As …': Keith Szarabajka played Harlan Williams in *Golden Years* and Mickey Kostmayer in *The Equalizer*, and has also appeared in *The X-Files*, *Miami Vice*, *Star Trek: Voyager* and *Walker, Texas Ranger*. Allison Lange was Ann in *Out of the Black*. Breon Gorman appeared as Lieutenant Curtis in *Star Trek: Insurrection*. Devon Gummersall was Zack in *Felicity*, Jake Roth in *Relativity* and Brian Krakow in *My So-Called Life* and can also be seen in *Independence Day* and *Thank You, Good Night*. Woon Park's movies include *Digital Man* and *The Shadow*. Sage Kirkpatrick was Tanya Rhodes in *Hundred Percent* and was also in *Baby Love* and *Days of Our Lives*.

Behind the Camera: Jefery Levy's previous work includes *Dark Angel*, *Harsh Realm*, *Get Real*, *Hollyweird*, *Sliders*, *Drive* and *Iggy Vile MD* (which he also produced).

References: The main visual influence for Liz's dream is a memorable moment in *American Beauty*. Kyle's is more *Apocalypse Now* and includes Polonius's quote from *Hamlet* ('to thine own self be true'). Valenti's argument with Dan contains dialogue similar to the sequence in *JFK* where Jim Garrison argues with his friend Dean Andrews.

Also, *Not of this Earth* (see **1**, 'Pilot') and an allusion to Bruce Springsteen's '57 Channels (And Nothin' On)'. Amongst the examples of TV seen when first Max, then Isabel and finally Kyle are channel surfing are the IVTV shopping network, an old western, a pop music video, World Market News (the Dow Jones Index is up), a kung-fu movie (it looks like a clip from the legendary dubbed Japanese TV series *Monkey*, though this is unlikely), a weather report and what Kyle joyously describes as 'unscrambled porn'. The title is the motto of the LAPD. Amongst the photos in the Roswell yearbook are Cheryl Cain (the writer of **7**, 'River Dog'), Laura Christie and Sabrina Potter.

Teen-Speak: Liz: 'Here I am saying his friggin' name.' Wow, Liz Parker *swore*!

Fashion Victims: We get a good look at Isabel's wardrobe. All of it.

Logic, Let Me Introduce You to This Window: What are two girls whose surnames begin with 'C' doing on the yearbook page containing Liz Parker? It's supposed to be alphabetical. Outside the sheriff's office the clock says five minutes to eight when the episode is clearly taking place during the afternoon. This is because the same stock shot used in **6**, '285 South' is duplicated. Where are her parents during Isabel's 'scream-down-the-neighbourhood' nightmare? Why does Valenti take Max and Isabel with him to a crime scene, particularly as he knows he's being watched? What is a Buddhist statue doing in the Mexican/Chinese restaurant? Dan says that the Fosters are threatening to sue Valenti as well as Sorenson. But what for? All he did was organise an (albeit massive) missing person enquiry for their, apparently missing, daughter. He and Judith Foster seem to be quite close friends, it seems unlikely, therefore, that she would wish to be party to Jim potentially losing his job for simply trying to help her family.

Quote/Unquote: Isabel: 'I just wanted what we are … What *I* am, to do something good for a change.'

Notes: 'Your daddy went down like this. Got some fool notion in his head, ignored the law and his friends and ended up handing over his badge.' Dragged out and done to death, this first of a four-part storyline feels a bit artificial, though it's emotionally very powerful and deals with strong subject matter. Kyle and Tess, bitching like nobody's business, again provide most of the highlights. Michael's in one scene and gets one line. Wasted!

Isabel says she is not good with cars, being unable to tell a Honda from a Toyota. Tess has Tabasco sauce on everything, including orange juice and strawberries and cream. Valenti takes Dan to Senor Chow's (see **9**, 'Heatwave'). Kyle had a great match for the school team recently, scoring two touchdowns; his father was also a fine footballer. Judith Foster had a huge crush on Jim, though he was wary of her boyfriend. Sorenson threatens to sue the city of Roswell for $15 million for false arrest. Laurie says she was visiting her grandparents in town (see **35**, 'Disturbing Behavior'). There is at least one other high school in Roswell, Goddard High. The WB trailed this and the following three episodes under the umbrella title 'The Hybrid Chronicles'.

Soundtrack: Two songs by seminal Canadian duo Delerium (a huge favourite of this author) accompany Isabel's dreams, 'Fallen Icon' and 'Amongst The Ruins'. Also 'Duck and Run' by Three Doors Down, 'Innocent' by Fuel, Vallejo's 'Into The New', Collective Soul's 'Turn Around' and Crystal Method's 'Busy Child'.

34
We Are Family

US Transmission Date: 29 January 2001
UK Transmission Date: 9 May 2001 (Sky One)

Writers: Gretchen J Berg and Aaron Harberts
Director: David Grossman

Cast: Rachel Winfree (Gossiping Woman in Store), Shana O'Neil (Clerk), Seema Rahmani (Nurse)

Valenti is suspended for his actions in the Laurie Dupree case. The Royal Four and their friends determine to help him, along with a newly arrived FBI agent, Duff. Laurie tells Isabel that her captor injected her with something and didn't seem human. When she sees Michael, she is terrified. Michael and Isabel go to the psychiatric hospital where Laurie was treated. There they find a photograph, seemingly of Michael, dated 1935 and labelled '*Grandpa*'.

'I've Got the Power': Tess uses her 'creepy' powers to 'save Kyle's butt' by turning a blank piece of paper into a report card. Michael smashes a window at the hospital using his powers, though he agrees with Isabel that he could have just kicked it in.

Roswell Iconography: Asteroid Pie and Chilli Orbit Rings are on The CrashDown menu.

Swedish Iconography: Alex has apparently been in Sweden for the last month (on an exchange visit) staying with a family called the Olsens in Uppsala, north of Stockholm. He seems to have landed himself a Swedish girlfriend, Leanna (he notes that they have a 'long distance-thing going', see **40**, 'It's Too Late, And It's Too Bad'). He also says he snowboarded down a mountain and took a stunning photo of the Northern Lights (*Aurora Borealis*). No opportunity is spared to slip in some culturally stereotypical references to *smörgåsbord* and furniture manufacturers Ikea (the country's flag is also visible on Liz's roof during the slide show). But, strangely, not Abba or Volvo! Big surprise.

High School Life: There's a brilliant PLEASE DON'T KICK sign on the school snack machine. It's there for Michael, right? West Roswell High's address is 2006 Meadow Brook Lane. According to the fake report card that Tess creates for Kyle, he is only getting a 'D' in Trigonometry, 'C's in Basic Science and College English, 'B's in US History and

Metal Shop and an 'A' from Coach Hernandez in Phys. Ed. who notes 'A pleasure to have in class'. Given that Tess has, presumably, seen one of Kyle's real reports, these sound like pretty accurate grades. Coach Clay (see **12**, 'Into the Woods') seems to have moved on.

'You Might Remember Me from Such Films and TV Series As . . .': Erica Gimpel was Adele Neuman in *ER*, Angela Brown in *Profiler* and, most memorably, Coco Hernandez in *Fame*. Rachel Winfree played Rose Who-Biddy in *How the Grinch Stole Christmas* and can also be seen in *Love Stinks*, *Sparkler* and *The Thirteenth Floor*. Shana O'Neil was in *Lost Angels*, *Just Pals* and *Not My Kid*.

Behind the Camera: David Grossman has worked on *Angel*, *Buffy*, *Sabrina the Teenage Witch*, *Early Edition*, *Ally McBeal*, *M.A.N.T.I.S.*, *Mad TV* and *Weird Science*.

References: The title is from Sister Sledge's 1979 disco-classic. Also, *My Favourite Martian* and *The Oprah Winfrey Show*. Posters on the door of Maria's school locker include Psycord and the Stereophonics along with a 'Trek' sticker. The neighbouring locker has a DON'T YOU YAHOO? sticker for the Internet search engine company. There's a hand-written MAKE IT REAL! poster of the corridor wall. When Tess and Kyle shop, the items they get include Skittles, Pringles and Tabasco Sauce. Valenti appears to sleep on the couch – *very* Fox Mulder. Amongst the countries Liz wants to visit are Peru, Nigeria and New Zealand.

Teen-Speak: Valenti: 'As you kids say, it *sucks big*.'
   Sean: 'You look like *road-kill*.'

Fashion Victims: Liz's 70s-style shirt and Tess's polyester nurse's uniform take all the awards here, though Michael's cord-jacket is nice. Are those Isabel's leather pants *again*?!

Logic, Let Me Introduce You to This Window: Liz's hairstyle changes between scenes. Alex gives Liz a precise little essay on the Northern Lights. Why? She's a scientist, she must surely know what causes the aurora. How does Valenti know that Isabel is at Liz's when he calls?

Quote/Unquote: Liz: '*Hur ar det*? I looked up Swedish websites whilst you were gone.' Alex: 'In that case, *tak-bra.*'

Tess: 'You're *definitely* my favourite human.' Kyle: 'Well you're my favourite Martian.'

Clerk: 'Have you seen the Evans girl? Looks like a supermodel. "Trouble" written all over her.' Amy: 'Nancy Anne, you'd be the expert on statutory rape. You must have done a ton of research when you found out your husband was sleeping with the babysitter?'

Notes: 'The Sexual Dysfunction Unit's that way.' Better. A more cohesive plot which focuses on the helplessness of Valenti, trapped by his own lies. Tess and Kyle get a nice subplot again, and Liz and Max finally talk about things that they've been avoiding all year in a quite beautiful scene in the eraser room. And it's nice to see Valenti and Amy DeLuca's relationship being allowed to naturally and believably develop through adversity. Maria's mostly missing this week, however.

Michael has a pager which he uses to contact Valenti and arrange a meeting in Frazier Woods (see **12**, 'Into the Woods'). The sheriff, according to Agent Duff, makes horrendous coffee. He likes chicken sandwiches with extra mayo. This is Agent Duff's second case. The first was an Interstate kidnapping that 'went off without a hitch'. She says she wants to make it to assistant director by 35. Walter Skinner might have something to say about *that*! Sean calls Alex 'Alice' ('that's funny. I haven't heard that since they put you away'). Laurie is said to have recently absconded from the Pinecrest Psychiatric Hospital in Brownfield, Texas, where she was diagnosed with paranoid schizophrenia. She has no parents or guardians on record. Amy DeLuca buys scratch-off lottery cards. The Roswell library closes at 8 p.m.

Soundtrack: 'King of All the World' by Old 97's, Vertical Horizon's 'Best I Ever Had (Grey Sky Morning)', the classic 'Turn' by Travis (in the gorgeous scene where Liz and Alex talk about travelling), 'Bring Your Lovin' Back

Here' by Gomez (see **27**, 'The End of the World') and
James Taylor's 'Her Town Too' (heard as Valenti and
Amy finally kiss).

Cast and Crew Comments: 'We're still relatively low on the
totem pole,' writer Gretchen Berg told *CrashDown.com* 'So
we don't assert our opinion all that much. After all, this is
Jason Katims' show. He always gets final say. Luckily, he's
always right.'

Did You Know?: According to teen magazine *J-14*, in the
section 'TV Boys: How they Found Fame', 'Nick Wexler's
[sic] tenth grade teacher Ms Tippit helped him launch his
career after seeing how much potential he possessed.' 'She
got the school to sponsor me to attend this film acting
workshop,' he explains. 'That's kind of what got me
thinking about getting into acting professionally.' Before
being bitten by the acting bug, Nick was a star on his
school's wrestling team. He loved slamming his opponents,
but could have done without the weekly weight-ins. 'I'm
really shy about being naked in front of strangers,' he
confesses. After graduating from high school in 1996, Nick
headed for LA. His first role was in a made-for-TV movie
called *Full Circle*. The article also reveals that Nick
originally auditioned for Colin Hanks' role of Alex, before
winning the part of Kyle.

35
Disturbing Behavior

US Transmission Date: 5 February 2001
UK Transmission Date: 16 May 2001 (Sky One)

Writer: Ronald D Moore
Director: James Whitmore Jnr
Cast: Wendy Speake (Reporter)

Maria and Michael help Laurie escape from the FBI and
try to gain her trust whilst Isabel and Max attempt to

understand what the blue alien blob actually does, and Liz theorises that it is some sort of parasite. At the Tucson estate of Laurie's grandfather, her aunt and uncle are shocked at the resemblance of Michael to their father, thinking he may be an illegitimate son. Bobby Dupree pays off Michael with $50,000 so he will not claim an inheritance.

'I've Got the Power': Michael uses his powers to blow up the gunman's car and to lock Laurie in Maria's Jetta. Isabel, spectacularly, uses hers to bring Larek into Brody's body.

The Conspiracy Starts at Home Time: Larek tells Max that the blue rock/slime parasite is called the Ghandarium and was a part of the alien ship which crashed in 1947. When he learns that this substance has escaped, he tells Max, Isabel and Liz that they must flee the planet immediately.

'You Might Remember Me from Such Films and TV Series As . . .': Heidi Swedberg played Brandon's Mom in *Galaxy Quest*, Mrs Mitchell in *Dennis the Menace Strikes Again*, Susan Biddle Ross in *Seinfeld* and also appeared in *75 Degrees in July*, *Breast Man*, *In Country* and *Hot Shots!* Dennis Christopher's movies include *Mind Rage*, *Skeletons*, *Bad English I: Tales of a Son of a Brit*, *Doppelganger*, *The Disco Years*, *Jake Speed*, *Chariots of Fire* (as Charles Paddock), Fellini's *Roma*, *Breaking Away* and *Alien Predator*. On TV he guest-starred in *Moonlighting*, *Hooperman* and *Star Trek: Deep Space Nine*. Wendy Speake played Shelley in *The Dead Hate the Living* and Dana in *Freshmen*.

Behind the Camera: Stunt driver Joe Cosentino's impressive CV includes *Magnolia*, *Go*, *A Murder of Crows*, *American History X*, *Boogie Nights*, *Riders of the Purple Sage*, *The Usual Suspects*, *Freaked* and *Suburban Commando*.

References: The *Austin Powers* movies ('Go, baby, go!'), *Lost Weekend*, *ET* ('I wish you guys could just phone home'), *Monty Python's Flying Circus* (there's an establishment called 'The Cheese Shop') and Oprah Winfrey. When forced to stay at Amy's awaiting Maria's call, Liz can be seen playing Whip-Ball®℠, basically a wooden table-tennis bat with a rubber ball attached to it by a piece of elastic and, according to a lengthy thread on one of the *Roswell* message boards, a favourite spanking weapon of many American moms for over three decades.

Teen-Speak: Michael: 'I finally find a family member, and she's a complete whack-job.' And: 'What kind of pyschobabble Oprah-crap do I have to tell her.'

Fashion Victims: A runaway winner: Tess's fleece jacket. Isabel's lovely fawn leather coat can't compete with that.

Sex and Drugs and Rock'n'Roll: Maria: 'We're being free spirits, mom.' Amy: 'That means you're going to Sedona to take dope and have sex in the hills.'

Michael and Maria hilariously spy on a couple having sex in Garrison's hardware store in the pre-title sequence. There's some suggestion that a vibrator is being used by the couple ('this town is *sick*!'). Bobby and Meredith Dupree drink vodka Martini cocktails.

Logic, Let Me Introduce You to This Window: When she sees Michael in **34**, 'We Are Family', and assumes him to be her grandfather, Laurie screams 'you're dead'. Here we discover that, indeed, Charles Dupree died seven years ago and Laurie was at his funeral. So what's all that nonsense about her getting Michael and Maria to drive her to her grandfather's home in Tuscon so that she can see him?

Just who did commit Laurie to the Brownfield hospital if she has no next of kin listed? Doctors have the authority to do this but, surely, the whole point is that Laurie *isn't* disturbed, it's that her family want everyone to think that she is.

Quote/Unquote: Amy: 'Do you think I wasn't seventeen once? Do you think I didn't do crazy stupid things with a *really bad boy* when I was your age?' Maria: 'Yeh, I know you did, Mom. Dad.'

Amy, to Michael: 'I want you to listen to me very carefully. On this glorious rebellious lost weekend of yours you will take care of my daughter. You will protect her and be kind to her and she will have fun. You will *not* get matching tattoos. You will not allow her to pierce any part of her body that cannot be shown in polite company. And if you have sex with my daughter, I will hunt you down and kill you like the mangy dog you are. Okay? Call me if you need bail money!'

Notes: 'Aliens are chasing our family, Mr Guerin. Don't stay too long, they might get you too.' An excellent episode with about five different storylines all battling for prominence. The Michael/Maria/Laurie one is best, but Max and Liz get a nice little subplot, and Valenti's descent into his 'dark place' is emotionally one of the high spots of the series, as this much-loved character sees his world crumbling around him. Tess appears briefly in only one scene.

Maria says that the Roadside Cafe has the world's worst chili hot-dogs in one hundred miles, but 'the best vanilla milkshakes in about five'. Pohlman Ranch is mentioned (see **21**, 'The White Room'). Grant Sorenson's previous geological work has included stays in Newcastle Wyoming, Fort Collins Colorado and Las Cruces in the San Andres mountains.

Locations used in this episode include one of the houses on Benedict Canyon Drive in Bel Air (for the Dupree home).

Soundtrack: 'Sometimes' by Nine Days, Jesse Dayton's 'The Creek Between Heaven and Hell', Palo Alto's 'Throw the Brick' and Lifehouse's 'Quasimodo'.

Cast and Crew Comments: 'Like any parent, he's happy I'm working,' Colin Hanks told *Teen People* concerning his father, though when it comes to acting, Tom 'doesn't give me too much advice'. According to Katherine Heigl: '[Colin's] not a Hollywood brat by any means.' In fact, rather than finagle his way into an advance screening of *Star Wars Episode I: The Phantom Menace*, Colin camped outside a theatre for hours to ensure himself an opening-day ticket. Ironically, months later his name would circulate as a finalist in the search for a teenage Anakin for the forthcoming *Episode II* . 'I'd be a stormtrooper, or put me in latex so I'm unrecognisable, anything!' notes fanboy-Colin.

Did You Know?: Occasionally, Nick Wechsler told the Associated Press, he does get a bit of recognition in the street. 'I'm not really looking forward to it becoming an issue,' he notes. 'I haven't gotten anybody who is crazy enough to confuse me with my character yet. I'm a little afraid of that. I try to accommodate people as much as I can. Handshake. Hug. Whatever they ask for. A couple of times, they've asked for an autograph. I don't think of myself like that.'

36
How the Other Half Lives

US Transmission Date: 19 February 2001
UK Transmission Date: 23 May 2001 (Sky One)

Writers: Gretchen J Berg, Aaron Harberts and
Breen Frazier
Director: Paul Shapiro
Cast: Antonio Vega (Clerk)

Brody, embodying the otherworldly ally Larek, tells Liz, Isabel, Tess and Max that the alien crystals infect humans with a chromosomal flaw and that the parasitic Ghandarium will wipe out humanity. Michael and Maria continue to stake out Dupree's and Maria confronts Laurie's aunt about ownership of the estate. Laurie tells Michael about her grandfather who, she says, was 'taken' by aliens. Kyle and Alex find the Ghandarium cave and, while trapped underground, discover the crystals can't live without oxygen. Grant Sorenson kidnaps Isabel and asks for her help. She realises that he is being controlled by the Ghandarium queen.

'I've Got the Power': 'You got any cool powers to take care of him?' asks Maria as she and Michael wonder how they'll get past a guard at the Dupree house. Michael just throws a rock to distract his attention. Later, he does use his power to suck the oxygen out of the room and destroy the Ghandarium queen. Eventually.

Max, Isabel and Tess try to use their powers to break the crystals that have trapped Alex and Kyle but, for once, fail utterly.

Roswell Iconography: According to Larek, the Ghandarium are a genetically-engineered lifeform designed to bridge the DNA and RNA resequencing during third-stage amino-acid synthesis. Or, more simply, they can create alien-human hybrids. Not every human, however, is a candidate for being a hybrid – their genetic structure needs a flaw (a faulty chromosome), fewer than one in 50 million people have this. Laurie does, and so did her grandfather (and possibly other members of her family – this isn't made clear). Once she has been infected by the crystals (who exist in a hive-like internal structure, including a queen), she will infect anyone she comes into contact with. Infected people will also pass on the contagion until the entire population of Earth is wiped out by the parasites.

References: Courtney's poster of a Metallica/Pearl Jam concert at the Huston Astro Arena (see **28**, 'The Harvest') appears on Michael's fridge door (when asked about the poster, Brendan Fehr notes: 'It says it was in Texas in the early 90s, which I thought would've been a kick-ass concert, but when I asked James Hetfield [Metallica's singer] if they ever played with Pearl Jam he was like, "Uhhh, NO!" So, though I've never asked, I think the prop guys just made it for me, which is *so cool*!') Also *Braveheart* (Michael and Maria prepare to watch the Mel Gibson movie on a laptop DVD by the Dupree-poolside) and *Alien* (the crystals bursting from Sorenson's chest). The discovery of the gloves in Sorenson's car and his accusation that Valenti planted them there is surely an oblique reference to the OJ Simpson trial? There's an allusion to Woody Allen's *Take the Money and Run*. Michael has a DANGER. HIGH VOLTAGE poster in his apartment.

Teen-Speak: Michael: 'If it was me, I'd tell us to get screwed and call the cops anyways.'
  Alex: 'Jackpot, baby!'

Fashion Victims: 'How do you get tree-sap out of fabric,' Maria asks Liz, concerning the black turtleneck cashmere sweater that she borrowed from her mom. Also, Tess's red jumper and Brody's grey jacket. Two horrible bits of headwear are also seen, Isabel's scarf and Tess's woolly hat. Love Michael and Maria's matching bathrobes when staying poolside at the Dupree house.

Sex and Drugs and Rock'n'Roll: Lots of alcohol. Alex and Kyle have a bottle of vodka with them in the cave (and judging by their hilariously bad version of 'American Pie', they seem to have been indulging). Meredith drinks red wine when she talks to Maria and it looks as though Michael's also been sampling the Duprees' wine cellar later. Valenti and Agent Duff share a whiskey at the end as they discuss what she will put in her report to the FBI.

Logic, Let Me Introduce You to This Window: Grant says that he was digging near the Pohlman Ranch the previous summer when he was infected by the Ghandarium parasite. Yet according to Michael in **19**, 'Four Square', the government covered up the very existence of this shortly after the crash. So why does everyone still call it the Pohlman Ranch?

Quote/Unquote: Maria, on Michael: 'Brave, handsome hero.' Michael: '*Wounded* hero.'
  Michael on Bobby and Meredith: 'Shallow, shallow people!'
  Kyle: 'What do you suppose alien crystals are going for on Ebay?'

Notes: 'My aunt and uncle need me to be crazy.' A bit too pat and anti-climactic a finale after such a good build up.

Again characters get coupled off to nice effect and often against type (Kyle and Alex is an interesting and highly watchable pairing; Maria and Michael again get the lion's share of the good lines; Isabel has a nice solo-slot with Sorenson). Lovely direction, but the story meanders far too much for comfort.

The Duprees live at 11 Osborne Road, Tuscon. Charles Dupree's wife was called Ada Jane. She is also dead. Sorenson's middle name is Ellis.

Soundtrack: 'A Taste of Honey' by Herb Alpert and the Tijuana Brass, Bebel Gilberto's 'So Nice (Summer Samba)', 'Lying in the Sun' by Stereophonics and 'Everything' by Jill Phillips. Colin Hanks and Nick Wechsler sing Don McLean's 'American Pie' (very badly) whilst trapped in the cave.

Critique: 'The WB has Fox-disease,' noted *Intergalactic Enquirer*'s Suze Campagna, 'where they build a story (in this case the "Hybrid Chronicles") and the end seems anticlimactic. They made up for it with the trip to Vegas, however.'

Did You Know?: Jason Behr seems to have the makings of a second career, playing charity basketball games, after appearing in the Suns Night Celebrity Shootout in Phoenix, Arizona. His teammates included singer Coolio, actors Joshua Morrow, Adam LaVorgna and Roger Lodge, and singer/songwriter Brian McKnight.

37
Viva Las Vegas

US Transmission Date: 26 February 2001
UK Transmission Date: 30 May 2001 (Sky One)

Writers: Gretchen J Berg and Aaron Harberts
Director: Bruce Seth Green
Cast: Samuel Ball (Dave), Linda Pine (Traci),
Howard George (Stripper Auditioner),

Eileen Galindo (Senora Villa), Gregory Saites (Glenn),
Ned Schmidtke (Pit Boss),
Michael Bailey Smith (Security Guard),
Deondray Gossett (Bellhop), Ken Cook (Dealer),
Phil Nelson (Stickman), Andrei Sterling (Bartender)

Michael wants to take a wild road-trip to Las Vegas to spend the corrupted Dupree money. The gang decide to come and help. They arrive at the Presidential Suite of their hotel, Michael giving each $3000. At the casino, Kyle wins big-style and Alex loses in the same manner. Maria tries out for what she believes is a dream singing opportunity, only to find out that the audition is as a stripper. Isabel meets an eloping couple and becomes their maid of honour, and Michael and Max end up in jail after getting in a fight. Michael surprises Maria with an invitation to sing at the hotel and her friends share a dance. When they return to their suite, a very unamused Sheriff Valenti is waiting for them.

The Story So Far: A wonderful introduction from Maria: 'The aliens, Max, Michael (or Spaceboy as I like to call him), Isabel and Tess, landed here in 1947. They gestated in these really gross pods for forty years and then, sort-of, hatched. Now there's only a few of us humans who know about them. Liz, Alex, Kyle, Kyle's dad and me ... They have special powers, of course. They eat Tabasco sauce by the crate. And trying to have a relationship with them is, like, suicide. For instance, there's this one time where future-Max told Liz that she needed to break up with present-Max or the world would end. So she did, but she ended up missing out on all this romantic stuff they would've done like eventually eloping and getting married in Las Vegas. Oh, speaking of Vegas ...'

Dreaming (As Blondie Once Said) is Free: Michael's nightmares (which he has been getting for two weeks since the events of **36**, 'How the Other Half Lives') involve him and Max being chased through a darkened school by armed men in combat gear.

Best Moment of the Series. Ever: Michael arriving in the school hallway to go on the road-trip only to find the entire gang waiting for him with cheesy grins and a big sign saying GUERIN PARTY. Brilliant.

'I've Got the Power': Michael uses his powers to change everyone's IDs. And to cheat at craps. Isabel cleans Traci's stained wedding dress with a wave of her hand. Max, prior to this episode, used his powers to heal Michael's gunshot wound from **36**, 'How the Other Half Lives'.

High School Life: Michael and Kyle share at least one class, Spanish. Kyle gets detention when caught with Michael's *Casino for Beginners* book.

'You Might Remember Me from Such Films and TV Series As . . .': Samuel Ball has been in *The Glass House*, *Chasing the Dragon* and *Sex and the City*, whilst Linda Pine features in *Ugly Naked People*, *End of Days*, *The New Woman*, *Malcolm in the Middle* and *Ally McBeal*. Howard George's lengthy CV includes *Sticks*, *Killer in the Mirror*, *My Favorite Year*, *Soap*, *Caroline in the City*, *Suddenly Susan*, *Hill Street Blues* and *Starsky and Hutch*. Deondray Gossett was in *Sister Act 2: Back in the Habit*, Eileen Galindo in *Double Parked* and Ned Schmidtke in *My Best Friend's Wedding*, *Music Box* and *Early Edition*. Michael Bailey Smith was the voice of The Thing in *The Fantastic Four* and played Belthazor in *Charmed*.

References: The title is, of course, a single by Elvis Presley (two cover versions feature in the episode). Michael has a 'Utility' sticker on his school locker. Also, *South Pacific* (the Bali Hai hotel), *Road Trip*, Play Station(TM), the Kennedy family and spring break. Michael has bought a couple of dozen DVDs, including *Braveheart* (see **36**, 'How the Other Half Lives'). He says he's trying to get an accurate body-count for the film. Kyle quotes from 'The Gambler' by Kenny Rogers, whilst Alex obliquely refers to *Kung Fu* (calling Kyle 'Grasshopper'). At school there are posters for a science fair, a band tryout and 'Rock the World!' (see **9**, 'Heatwave'). The school Vice Principal is

Mr McClure, probably named after either the late actor Doug, or *The Simpsons*' Troy. The episode, given the setting, is reminiscent of both the *Friends*' episode 'The One in Vegas', *Casino* and *Diamonds Are Forever*.

Teen-Speak: Maria: 'The only person who's going to get you there is me. So let's review, OK? Fantastic!' And: 'Alex, pop-quiz'. And: 'Come on Liz, all the cool kids are doin' it.'

Michael: 'Screw the plan, let's just go!'

Isabel: 'I must be the biggest freak on the planet.'

Fashion Victims: Tess's green velvet jacket and Maria's criminally short skirt have both been seen before.

Sex and Drugs and Rock'n'Roll: Michael has cans of beer in his fridge. The names on the IDs that Michael creates for the gang are: Harvey Wallbanger (Kyle), Pina Colada (Tess), Tom Collins (Alex), Brandy Alexander (Isabel), Magarita Salt (Maria), Shirley Temple (Liz), Rob Roy (Max) and Doctor Love (Michael, inevitably).

Logic, Let Me Introduce You to This Window: None of the gang were seen to be carrying any luggage when they arrived, yet they all wear different clothes at dinner (Isabel's gorgeous black evening dress or Michael's suit, for instance). Maria mentions that she is taking care of what everyone will wear, but this couldn't include Max – who'd already left for the airport – or Isabel, who was in a different hotel.

Quote/Unquote: Michael: 'This weekend is about fun and debauchery, you got it?'

Kyle enters the hotel room: 'Let's see about some in-house porno!'

Maria: 'Do you wanna know where I was tonight? I was auditioning to be a stripper.' Michael: 'You get the job?'

Maria: 'I gotta bail Max, and, if there's enough money, Michael, out of jail.'

Notes: 'Whoever sent us down here was smart because they sent us together. As long as we stick together, we're going to make it.' It's been a long time *Roswell* did a proper 'comedy' episode (**13**, 'The Convention' was the previous best example), and 'Viva Las Vegas' works in a similar manner, subverting both the genre it's parodying and the expectations of the audience. This is a gem of an episode that serves as a useful stepping on point for new viewers to the series.

Liz doesn't want to go to Vegas because of the events of **27**, 'The End of the World'. The cover story that Max concocts is that they are with the debate team in Santa Fe. The subject, in case anyone asks, is: 'Space Travel. Wave of the future or misbegotten dream?' Alex plays a bit of piano. Maria sings in the key of E. Kyle was sixteen hundred dollars up before giving up the money to help bail Max and Michael.

Soundtrack: Dido's epic 'Thank You', Morcheeba's 'Be Yourself', 'Chemistry' by Semisonic. Majandra Delfino sings 'I've Got The World On A String' (popularised by Frank Sinatra) when auditioning and 'I've Got It Bad (And That Ain't Good)' on-stage. Plus both ZZ Top and Shawn Colvin's versions of 'Viva Las Vegas'.

Critique: 'Although saddled with the least original title an episode about Las Vegas could have,' noted Jason Henderson of *Fandom Inc*, 'it's also a good example of the things *Roswell* can get right, mainly fantasies about how cool life can be when you're seventeen ... Interestingly, this is the first episode of *Roswell* to open with a recap of the whole series, in this case delivered by Majandra Delfino. Delfino is the best actress among the young cast and has a way of making even the most dry material breathe. It's fun to watch her singing "Viva Las Vegas" badly to entice Liz into coming on the trip and [then] singing Cole Porter *well* when the time comes to live out a dream. *Roswell* is at its best when it provides what any ensemble fantasy should – a nice escape to friends and lives we wish we had.' Exactly.

Cast and Crew Comments: The episode was originally to be a Tess and Liz episode, according to Aaron Harberts. 'Tess and Liz were supposed to switch bodies. It was going to be kind of a *Freaky Friday*. They would learn more about each other and, while that was happening, we thought of a runner where Max and Michael take his money and go off to Vegas. We pitched that episode to Jason, and he said "if we're going to go to Vegas why take two characters, let's just take all of them".'

Did You Know?: Nick Wechsler told the *Akron Beacon Journal* that as a native New Mexican, he's sometimes surprised at *Roswell's* lack of accuracy. 'I'm frustrated by how not-authentic the show is,' he noted. 'Why are there palm trees? And why are the streets always wet? Is there a cloud over Roswell?' But Wechsler said he's never actually posed some of these questions to the show's producers. 'Every TV show and movie does this stuff,' he said. 'Nothing is real.'

38
Heart of Mine

US Transmission Date: 16 April 2001
UK Transmission Date: 6 June 2001 (Sky One)

Writer: Jason Katims
Director: Lawrence Trilling
Cast: Taran Killam (Malamud), Scott Clifton (Evan),
Michelle Moretti (Allie), Mya Michaels (Juanita)

With the senior prom imminent Liz questions her future with Max and Kyle comes to a conclusion regarding Tess. Maria suspects Michael may be involved with someone else and secretly investigates him. Alex and Isabel take the first step towards rebuilding their friendship.

The Story So Far: 'Listen,' a suddenly self-aware Maria tells a baffled audience: 'Just because you haven't seen an episode in a while doesn't mean that life on *Roswell* has stopped. *Au contraire*. It's been quite busy around here.

Max and Liz, they've been in love ever since Max saved Liz's life at The CrashDown. Max is an alien from another planet and he's destined to marry Tess. She's begun helping him remember where he came from, so he's been feeling more distant from Liz. And Liz is getting closer to my lovable-but-loser cousin Sean.'

'Dear Diary . . .': Yay, it's back! 'It's April 27th. I'm Liz Parker and I think I've figured out why I haven't written on this journal for nearly a year. It's just ironic that I would figure something out really deep from like the least-deep-guy in America . . . We try to live reasonable, logical lives. But we can't tell our hearts what to feel. Sometimes our hearts lead us to places we never thought we wanted to go. And once they do, all we can do is make up for lost time . . . But at least my heart is open. And I'm writing again. I'm feeling. I'm breathing.'

'I've Got the Power': Tess and Max use their combined powers to remember fragments of their lives before they came to Earth. The water on their planet is, Tess recalls, heavier and thicker than water is here. As you swim, it reforms around you, like jelly. Max remembers that the planet has three moons and a burned orange sky with no clouds.

High School Life: Last semester, Miss Ragsdale told Isabel that she only needed to take one more class to graduate. Alex asks if she's going to college but Isabel doesn't know yet (see **39**, 'Cry Your Name').

Dudes and Babes: Liz and Maria dancing. Oh baby! Kyle finally puts his finger on the way he feels about Tess. As a sister. Tess is actually *disappointed* by this, but says she understands. Max and Tess finally kiss at the episode's climax to Liz's . . . what? Heartbreak? Relief? Combination of both? It's difficult to tell.

Max and Tess remember that, in their former lives, they first met and kissed at a party.

'You Might Remember Me from Such Films and TV Series As . . .': Taran Killam was Blake in *Undressed* and appeared in *Naked Gun 33⅓: The Final Insult*. Michelle Moretti can be seen in *Almost Famous*, whilst Mya Michaels was in *The Devil's Own*.

References: The title is from one of the greatest love songs ever, the Isley Brothers' 1966 Motown classic 'This Ol' Heart of Mine (is Weak for You)'. The theme of the prom is *2001: A Space Odyssey*. Comparisons with the *Buffy the Vampire Slayer* episode 'The Prom' are almost inevitable. Also, *Just Kill Me* and David Bowie's 'Let's Dance'. Kyle is reading Ali Bilson's *The Buddha Advises on Relationships*. Liz quotes from Primal Scream's 'Loaded' ('. . . and have a good time'), itself a sample of dialogue from the movie *The Wild Angels*. Maria uses a Mastercard to break into Michael's apartment. Michael has a sticker for the band THC on his locker. Sean refers to the Taco Bell restaurant chain.

Teen-Speak: Liz: 'It's a week night, so I probably shouldn't, you know, commit a felony.' And: 'God you are, like, ubiquitous.' And: 'I suck!'

   Maria: 'Eww, I'm gonna be sick.'

   Michael: 'The whole thing is *totally bogus*.'

   Malamud to Kyle: 'Wondering if it's gonna help you get into Tess Harding's pants? How long are you gonna let that blonde little hottie live under your roof before you make your move? Dude, you got to ask her to the prom.'

Fashion Victims: Bad: Maria's orange hippie-dress, Tess's light blue spotty pyjamas. Good: Liz's lovely purple blouse, Isabel's shorter hair, Alex's excellent black dragon shirt. The prom clothes, generally, are excellent – especially Tess and Isabel's dresses.

Sex and Drugs and Rock'n'Roll: Kyle, on his father and Amy: 'I caught them making out on the couch.' Maria: 'Dude, *I* caught them making out in the pantry closet in the kitchen. It's just so embarrassing.' Michael has been taking dancing lessons from Juanita.

Logic, Let Me Introduce You to This Window: During the scene in Alex's bedroom where Isabel asks Alex to ask her to the prom, the pair switch sides on Alex's bed twice.

Quote/Unquote: Michael: 'You actually remember our planet?' Max: 'Yes.' Michael: 'What are the chicks like?' Max: 'It's not that literal . . . In one way I have this really clear feeling. In another way it seems ephemeral.' Michael: 'Transient, fleeting, impermanent. I know what ephemeral means, Maxwell. It's my life.'

Liz: 'Do you know what? I do not need this right now. I do not want to hear any more of your stupid, inane comments. I do not want to hear any more of your little theories on life. And I do not want to write my freakin' name in mustard, okay? My life is *falling apart.*'

Notes: 'It would be my dream to take you to prom, but then we'd wake up the next morning, and you'd be onto the next thing, and I'd be right back where I was before Sweden. Obsessed, pathetic, and lovesick. So, amazingly, my answer is no. I'm not gonna take you to prom.' Fantastic. Jason Katims finally kills stone-dead the 'star-crossed-lovers' idea (and a lot of fans illusions about what *Roswell* is actually all about) with a story about the pain of teenage romance. Colin Hanks is particularly impressive in an absolutely outstanding cast performance. Has there ever been a finer moment in this series than Liz's anguished 'this is the last time we would be together' voice-over. Beautiful direction, particularly the scenes of Sean and Liz in the bowling alley.

Isabel thinks that Billy Saroyan is going to ask her to the prom, though Alex has heard Bill would be asking Amy Green. Last year Kyle went with Trudie McIntyre. Sean eats a burger and fries in The CrashDown, owns a decrepit orange, blue and green VW and used to work in the Roswell bowling alley before he went to jail. Alex has an acoustic bass guitar (which features prominently in *39*, 'Cry Your Name'). Michael has the board game Checkers in his apartment.

Soundtrack: 'Catch The Sun' by Doves, Coldplay's 'Don't Panic', '100 m Backstroke' by Josh Rouse (when Sean and Liz are at the bowling alley), Josh Joplin Group's 'Camera One'. At the prom, 'Rock DJ' by Robbie Williams, L7's 'Slide', Nelly Furtado's 'I'm Like A Bird' (see **41**, 'Baby, It's You') and Musiq's 'Girl Next Door' can be heard. Also two songs by Ivy, 'Worry about You', and 'Undertow' (when Liz finds Max and Tess kissing).

Ratings: The return of new episodes after a seven-week hiatus gave *Roswell* its best ratings since November in all of the key demographic areas, much to the WB's delight.

Trading Places: *Roswell* returned, not with the expected episode (**42**, 'Off the Menu', filmed sixteenth in the season), but with 'Heart of Mine' instead. According to an anonymous insider quoted on the *Ain't it Cool* website. '[2.16] is not lost. It's being moved to just before the finale. All logic has seemingly been tossed out the window. The memo went out on 2 April (many thought it was a joke a day late). There were rumours floating around the set on the last few days of filming that some serious re-editing was going to be done to already-finished episodes. They also did quite a few cleanup shots on earlier episodes before filming wrapped. No clue on content except that [there was] another Maria-blackboard-explanation.'

Did You Know?: While some people may hesitate to relocate to another country, it was a minor consideration for Emilie de Ravin when she left Melbourne for Los Angeles. With the support of her parents she visited LA in December 1999 to find an agent. 'I was very lucky,' she recalls. 'I'm really happy with the progression of the character, especially in the second season, it's given me a lot more to work with. I think she's trying to work out what's best for the four of them and their planet. She's a very sweet girl.' De Ravin likes to exercise, paint, shop and spend time with her new American buddies. When asked for pointers on making friends in a new city, she notes: 'You just go out and meet people. It's actually fun.'

39
Cry Your Name

US Transmission Date: 23 April 2001
UK Transmission Date: 13 June 2001 (Sky One)

Writer: Ronald D Moore
Director: Alan Kroeker
Cast: Jason Dohring (Jerry), Hawthorne James (Trucker)

An unthinkable tragedy befalls the group as Valenti breaks the news that Alex has been killed in a car accident. Max's attempts at revival fail and the group is forced to deal with the loss of their friend and the dreadful possibility that he may have taken his own life. Maria and Isabel respond emotionally, but Liz remains oddly stoic, until she discovers the odd way in which Alex signed a credit card receipt hours before he died.

The Trailer: With almost unbelievable naivety, the WB effectively sabotaged any suspense that had built in the lead-up to this episode by revealing the identity of the character who was going to die when they included Max's line 'who would possibly want to murder Alex?' as part of a trailer shown in most US states immediately prior to this episode. Nice one!

'I Haven't Got the Power': Max tries to use his powers to resurrect Alex, but fails. 'I wish I had special powers,' Diane Evans tells her distraught daughter. 'Powers don't help,' replies Isabel truthfully.

The Conspiracy Starts at Home Time: Liz believes that Alex was murdered and that his murder had something to do with Kivar and Isabel's past. The phrase 'this conspiracy' is used, by Liz, to describe the alien secret that the friends share for the first time.

The binary code that Alex 'signs' on the receipt is 11100100100111011001 (see **40**, 'It's Too Late, And It's Too Bad', **41**, 'Baby, It's You').

High School Life: Alex seems more popular around school after he dies, as Maria angrily notes, than before. Isabel is graduating early and leaving for college in San Francisco in June.

'You Might Remember Me from Such Films and TV Series As ...': Jason Dohring was Harold in *Deep Impact*. Hawthorne James played One-Eyed Sam in *I'm Gonna Git You Sucka* and also appeared in *The Color Purple*, *The Doors* and *Speed*.

References: The title is from Beth Orton's epic torch-song, 'She Cries Your Name' (heard at the end of the episode. Alex had tickets to a forthcoming concert by the singer). There are several references to poet Robert Frost (1874–1963) and to his masterpiece 'Stopping By Woods on a Snowy Evening' (a poem also heavily featured in the season three 'Faith arc' on *Buffy*). Also, *Reservoir Dogs* ('let's go to work') and The Clash's 'Cut the Crap'. Max and Michael discuss the relative merits of *Crouching Tiger: Hidden Dragon* (which Michael considers 'a chick-flick with kung-fu!') and *The Matrix*, and of these movies' respective stars Michelle Yeoh and Keanu Reeves.

Teen-Speak: Alex: 'This *blows*.'
  Max: 'You are so full of it.'
  Jerry: '*Whatever, dude.*'
  Valenti: 'Don't go there.'
  Sean: '*Later.*'

Sex and Drugs and Rock'n'Roll: Michael gives Amy rum to help her sleep. He says his foster father taught him to mix drinks before he could ride a bike. Amy is grateful to him for the kindness that he has shown her and Maria, and tells him that he will always be welcome in her house. Sleeping on the couch, of course. The food Alex orders that so upsets him when it arrives cold is from a restaurant called Malee Thai.

Quote/Unquote: Alex: 'Why does life have to be so wrong? Why does everything have to be a lie?'

A dreaming Isabel begs: 'Please don't go.' Alex: 'I'm already gone.'

Liz: 'Nothing is ever what it seems.'

Notes: 'There's been an accident. Alex is dead.' An interesting collection of fabulous images (best direction of an episode by some distance) and an emotional story that deals with the grief of loss. A pity that, for many fans, the impact was effectively derailed by the episode having to follow the (remarkable) death of Joyce Summers in *Buffy* a few weeks before, a battle for hearts and minds that *Roswell* could never hope to win. Which is a shame as wonderful stuff is on display here: Isabel's heartbreaking dreams of Alex, a gorgeous shot of dawn over the desert, the funeral sequences with Michael, Max and Kyle carrying the coffin and the roses tossed onto it after Maria's heart-tearing 'Amazing Grace'. Ultimately, the death of a major character in any series always leaves a bitter taste in the mouth, if only because of the obvious conclusion that ratings are the primary motivation and not dramatic storytelling.

Alex once electrified Mr Hoffman's desk which Liz says almost got him suspended. Max, however, notes that this would never have happened as all the teachers loved him. He also mentions Senora Villa (see **37**, 'Viva Las Vegas') and the events of the prom (see **38**, 'Heart of Mine'). Alex died the day before Kyle's birthday, the episode seemingly taking place in either late April or early May. Kyle is still sleeping on the couch, and still doing push-ups as soon as he wakes (see **24**, 'Ask Not'). Max makes Liz a meal of frozen macaroni and cheese. Sean appears only briefly as he is in court in Albuquerque (it's not stated whether this is a condition of his parole or whether he's been a naughty boy *again*). When Max rings to see how Liz is coping, Nancy Parker thinks it's Sean calling.

There are several clips from earlier episodes used when Liz looks at photographs of Alex, most (though not all) drawn from his dance in **25**, 'Surprise'.

Soundtrack: 'Storybook Life' by Blessed Union Of Souls, 'I Quit' by Meat Puppets, Emer Kenny's 'Heaven' and

'Light Of You' (during Isabel's first dream), 'Human' by Fisher, 'Nothing' by Peter Searcy and Beth Orton's 'She Cries Your Name'. Majandra Delfino sings 'Amazing Grace' during Alex's funeral.

Critique: 'Chances are if you haven't fallen under the spell of *Roswell* by now, it's too late,' noted the *New York Daily News*. 'Since its premiere a year and a half ago, WB's drama series about the teenagers of Roswell – some human, some alien – has worked through so many plot twists and so much character development that catching up would be a daunting assignment. Tonight, as it happens, is an exception. Yes, there are some details and references that will likely slip past you if you're not reasonably familiar with the show's intricate body of lore. But even if you miss those points, watching the episode still lets you experience the more fundamental quality that's responsible for the show's appeal.'

Did You Know?: May 2001's issue of *Celebrity Hairstyle* magazine featured the *Roswell* girls prominently. 'With her sarcastic humor and energetic nature, Maria DeLuca adds comic relief to the sombre mood of *Roswell*. Majandra Delfino [has] lightened her look, trading last year's sleek bob for this more ladylike, long look . . . Shiri Appleby has a star-crossed romance with an alien. But there's nothing unusual about the young star's sweet simple style. The look is longer than last season, with up-front graduation and razored ends imbuing her thick, straight strands with swing and texture.'

40
It's Too Late, And It's Too Bad

US Transmission Date: 30 April 2001
UK Transmission Date: 20 June 2001 (Sky One)

Writers: Gretchen J Berg and Aaron Harberts
Director: Patrick Norris

Cast: Michael Caldwell (Florist),
Per Bristow (Mr Stockman), Alison Ward (Deb),
Antoinette Broderick (Bank Teller),
Brendan D Pentzell (High School Security Guard),
Stephen 'Doc' Kupka (Cabbie),
David Nathan Schwartz (Crew Member).

Liz continues her investigation into Alex's death and, with Sean's help, breaks into the school guidance counsellor's office, where she photocopies Alex's personal file. Meanwhile, Isabel tells Max that she intends to leave Roswell for college in San Francisco in the fall.

'I've Got the Power': Michael uses his power to clear Amy's blocked sink. Isabel disgruntledly smashes one of the school jocks into the lockers after her argument with Max.

The Conspiracy Starts at Home Time: Liz is suspicious of the Olsens, Alex's host family, and of Leanna, his Swedish girlfriend (see **34**, 'We Are Family' and **43**, 'The Departure'). Flowers arrive from the Olsens offering condolences, though Alex's father says he did not inform them of the tragedy. There's a locked file on Alex's laptop, which holds a repetitive message *Leanna is not Leanna*. This was created on 16 January, when Alex was still in Sweden (according to school records the trip lasted from 9 December to 28 January). And though she cannot decipher the binary code that Alex signed the credit card receipt with (see **39**, 'Cry Your Name'), Liz suspects this repeats the same message. Just as Liz is ready to board a plane, she gets a call from the Swedish Embassy: the building in the photo of Alex and Leanna was demolished years previously.

Dudes and Babes: Even Maria believes that Liz's behaviour is a symptom of her grief at Alex's loss. She tells Liz that her obsession is ruining everyone's lives. After a (very) roundabout conversation with Amy, Michael reassures Maria that, although he *will* someday have to leave her to go home, he *can* give her the here and now. Beautifully, his reassurances bring them closer together.

'You Might Remember Me from Such Films and TV Series As . . .': Michael Caldwell was in *Love Stinks* and *Delirious*. Alison Ward played Miranda in *Nash Bridges*.

References: The title is a lyric from Dido's 'Don't Think of Me'. It also derives from separate classic songs by Carole King and the Jam respectively. The location for the Roswell Observatory is the Griffith Observatory, a major Los Angeles landmark which sits on the southern slope of Mount Hollywood and from where it commands a stunning view of the Los Angeles basin. Tourists can enjoy spectacular views from its balconies, especially at night. A gift to the city by philanthropist Griffith J Griffith (1850–1919), the observatory is a perennial favourite of filmmakers, best known as the location for the climax of Nicholas Ray's *Rebel Without a Cause* (a bust of that film's tragic star, James Dean, is one of the site's icons). It has featured in many other movies including, famously, *The Terminator*.

Posters briefly glimpsed in school include one for the Chess Club and another for the Beatles (reason, unclear). Liz is reading *The Lonely Planet Guide to Sweden*. Max misquotes Stevie Wonder's 'Lately'. He has a copy of the Santa Fe State University prospectus which he gives to Isabel. There are EVERYMAN and YAHOO stickers in Alex's bedroom.

Teen-Speak: Sean: 'Cool!' And, on Liz: 'She's a buzz-kill.' Hanson, to Sean: 'You're a *zero*.'

Fashion Victims: Maria's horrible stripy pants, Isabel's black sweater, Amy's 'Cowgirl' T-shirt.

Sex and Drugs and Astronomy: At the observatory, Tess points out Barnard's Star which, she says, can be seen from their home planet. In Ophiuchus, this red dwarf star was discovered by E E Barnard in 1916. It's six light years from Earth and is the closest star after Alpha Centauri. The star is reality, Tess tells Max, '*Earth* is a dream.' Max is depressed at losing those close to him. Tess assures Max that she'll be there for eternity. They kiss. Max says he is ready to wake up now. The couple then make love.

Logic, Let Me Introduce You to This Window: More telephone nonsense. Liz's cellphone is 505-555-0125, yet Victor the Florist's landline phone number is the astonishingly similar 505-555-0195. That's a very small twin propeller aeroplane for a proposed transatlantic flight, surely?

Quote/Unquote: Maria: 'I can't lose anyone else, Michael, my heart can't handle it.'
  Jock: 'Isabel Evans, you are *so hot* when you're pissed.'

Notes: 'The idea that Alex might have died because we're here ... I can't stand that.' A hard episode that tantalises fans with a major development (Max and Tess, ahem, getting some) whilst spending most of the episode in the murky depths of Liz's conspiracy and wasting the lovely Maria/Michael subplot completely. Call me a 'shipper if you like, but this is where *my* interest lies.

  Maria calls the Royal Four 'the Pod Squad' (a popular and often used fan-term) for the first time. Michael's telephone has been disconnected. Liz refers to both the shape-shifters (see **19**, 'Four Square') and the Skins (see **25**, 'Surprise'). She had $2053.78 in her bank account prior to drawing it all out to go to Sweden. Alex owned an Apple Mac laptop and at least one bass guitar that we hadn't previously seen (it looks like another Fender). His computer password was I THE STUD, which Maria knew because he once allowed her access to his e-mail. He wrote a poem about his dog having its leg amputated which, says Maria, was humorous. Folders on Alex's PC include Leanna, To Editor, Sunday Poem, Leanna Reminder, Weekday Schedule, Plan Ahead and Palindrome, along with the one file that is locked.

  Mrs Seymour from the Homeless Shelter is among several people to have given Isabel glowing references for her application to San Francisco University. The Olsens' phone number in Sweden is 011-4617-847-259. Sean used a pick that he made from a bicycle spoke when he and Liz broke into the bowling alley (in **38**, 'Heart of Mine').

Soundtrack: Paddy Casey's 'Whatever Gets You Through' (at the beginning), 'Perfect Place' by Pancho's Lament (as Michael tries to convince Isabel not to go to San Francisco), Jim White's 'Handcuffed to a Fence in Mississippi' and Fisher's 'I Will Love You' (during the climactic Max/Tess scenes and Liz at the airport).

Critique: *scifi.ign.com*'s Sarah Kuhn was worried for the series. 'Not to be pessimistic, but is that title an indication of *Roswell*'s general state? When did this show revert to such a bizarre mishmash of its former, angst-ridden, self-involved self and its newer, sci-fi edged-thing? *The Hybrid Chronicles* rocked the planet, but things have gone downhill since the prom episode. I think the key problem is that the two characters who are supposed to represent the very heart of Roswell, Liz and Max, are completely unlikable in this arc.'

Cast and Crew Comments: 'Colin never asked to leave or wanted to,' Jason Katims told Kate O'Hare. 'He was offered a pretty big movie. We decided the best thing was to let him go. For some reason Alex's character, while I love him, was very challenging for the writers to work into storylines. He always seemed to be on the periphery.' However, Katims believed that Alex's death enriched the show by 'increasing the dramatic stakes. Until this there was always a sense of safety. Alex's death sends all the characters on different journeys. We made a conscious decision in these episodes to keep them driven by our core group and not bring in outside characters, the way we did earlier with The Skins and Nicholas.'

Did You Know?: 'I've never been enough tempted to try alcohol,' Brendan Fehr told *Teen Movieline* magazine. 'On the other side I'm curious what type of drunk I would be, the horny one, the aggressive one or the funny one. But I can get horny on my own and the two others I leave to people's fantasy.'

41
Baby, It's You

US Transmission Date: 7 May 2001
UK Transmission Date: 27 June 2001 (Sky One)

Writer: Lisa Klink
Director: Rodney Charters
Cast: Jeff Wadlow (Professor), Sean Dwyer (Student),
Nelly Furtado (Herself), Jodi Ann Paterson (Herself),
Lauren Roman (Bonnie)

Max is shocked when Tess tells him that they are going to be parents. With his arm around his latest flame, the alien king strolls through the parting sea of students and onlookers. However, the extraterrestrial pregnancy yields some unexpected complications. Earth's atmosphere proves inhospitable to the unborn child.

'Dreaming (As Blondie Once Said) is Free': Kyle urges Isabel to use her powers and have some fun with them. She asks what Kyle's idea of fun is. He pulls out an issue of *Playboy* and explains that the cover girl is Jodi Ann Paterson. Isabel finally agrees and, in a dream sequence, we see Kyle and Isabel exercise with Kyle's fantasy Playmate of the Year. He approaches the girl who explains that the gym is private. Kyle spots some cake and feeds it to Ms Paterson, who licks it off his fingers. Just as she's about to follow Kyle into the showers Isabel ends the dream.

'I Got the Power': Isabel and Kyle use Isabel's powers to have some vengeful fun at Max's expense, replacing his photo in the school yearbook with an alien and sticking his feet to the floor during a fire drill. Michael uses his power to hurtle the pyramid-shaped bomb out of the window. Isabel makes it snow.

Roswell Iconography: The translation of the book, as seen on-screen states: 'You are the Royal Four. Zan, the king. Ava, the queen. Vilandra, his sister. Rath, his councilor

[sic]. You were created from the genetic material of your alien predecessors and human subjects. You were given human form so that you could live safely on the planet undetected until the time comes for your return. You have been given the granilith, a transport between this planet and Antar.' It also says that they have communication technology allowing them to access information from their original planet. Their hibernation pods and the granilith are in a chamber hidden away from human settlement and the chamber can only be accessed by the four of them. They also have a guardian to protect them and keep them hidden from their enemies.

The Conspiracy Starts at Home Time: Whilst he was supposed to be in Sweden Alex was actually at the New Mexico University in Las Cruces under the alias of 'Ray' trying to decode the language in the alien book found by Tess (see **19**, 'Four Square'). The professor explains that although the data Alex collected has been deleted, on his last day on campus he sent a huge text file (1.67 megabytes) to jcoleman@ulascruces.edu. Jennifer Coleman is the girl who appeared (as Leanna) in the photo with Alex (see **34**, 'We Are Family' and **40**, 'It's Too Late, And It's Too Bad').

'You Might Remember Me from Such Films, TV Series and Girly Magazines As . . .': Jeff Wadlow was in *Pearl Harbor*. Lauren Roman memorably played Nancy Doyle in *Buffy* and was Laura English in *All My Children*. Jodi Ann Paterson was *Playboy*'s 'Playmate of the Year 2000' and made her movie debut as 'Super Hot Giant Alien' in *Dude, Where's My Car?*

Behind the Camera: New Zealand-born director, Rodney Charters began his career as a cinematographer on movies like *The Intern*, *Brink!*, *Conundrum*, *Car 54, Where Are You?* and *Tek War*.

References: The title is a Burt Bacharach/Hal David/ Barney Williams song, first recorded by the Shirelles and probably most famous for an epic cover version by the Beatles in 1963. In the school hallway there's a poster that seems to be advertising some sort of weightlifting club with the words IS THIS YOU? prominent. Also, *The X-Files* (Maria echoes Scully's regular 'Ohmigod' catch phrase) and *Playboy*, the cover of which features references to James Bond and to *South Park* creators Trey Parker and Matt Stone. Kyle and Tess were watching *Gladiator* on video on the night that Alex died (see **43**, 'The Departure').

Teen-Speak: Michael: 'Holy crap!' And: 'Yo!' And: '*Later.*'
    Maria: 'That's totally her.' And: 'I need you to do your computer-nerd stuff.' And, on Max and Liz: 'It's beyond the worst fight they've ever had.'

Fashion Victims: Maria's tartan pants – good gracious. Also, the yellow blanket that Kyle's hiding under. Valenti's red dressing gown puts in another appearance. There's some good stuff like Maria's black negligée and Union Jack T-shirt, Liz's fawn poloneck and Isabel's Nike trainers.

Sex and Drugs and Rock'n'Roll: Love Isabel sarcastically clapping Max when he tells her that he lost his virginity to Tess. Kyle suggests that Isabel get even with Max by having him wake up one testicle short. Ouch.

Logic, Let Me Introduce You to This Window: According to one eagle-eyed fan on the *CrashDown.com* website, the New Mexico State University's colours are not yellow and brown (they're crimson and white), there is no such building as the Dona Ana dorms (Dona Ana is a separate junior college and not part of the university), and the university's e-mail addresses don't have @ulascruces.edu, rather they end @nmsu.edu. Just why is a bestselling artist like Nelly Furtado doing a free concert on the campus of New Mexico State Uni? When Isabel produces the snow shower, this is the second time in just a couple of months – see **32**, 'The Miracle' – that it's snowed in a desert town like Roswell. And nobody notices?

Quote/Unquote: Michael: 'You and Tess had . . .?' Max: 'Alien sex? Yes.' Michael, after a moment's contemplation: 'How was it?!'

Michael, on the alien baby: 'Maxwell, if this thing comes out green with four fingers and three eyes, that puts a major crimp in our "hide in plain sight" strategy.'

Notes: 'If Alex never went to Sweden and wasn't here, then where was he?' Good episode, albeit with some tough pieces at its core. The pairing of Isabel and Kyle is interesting and fun, whilst Liz, Maria and Michael get to do lots of cool detective stuff. But the Max and Tess baby-plot is just so laboured ('scuse the pun). Best scene of the episode, Max and Michael playing basketball.

Alex's e-mail address was whitsbassist@yahoo.com. He sent Maria an e-mail entitled 'The "Real" Swedish Bikini Team' which mentions a guy he met in front of Ikea (see **34**, 'We Are Family') and ends with the words 'Swedish meatballs'. No, I don't know why either. Max drinks regular Coke as opposed to diet. Kyle notes that Jodi Ann Paterson likes long walks in the rain, unicorns and funny guys. Amongst the other people whose photos are on the same page as Max in the yearbook are Sandy Dunn, Tina Eastan, Jane Edwin and John Estraphan. Max and Isabel had a guinea pig called Bigfoot. Mr Martnelli's dog savaged it to death. The day after this happened the worst snowfall in Roswell in one hundred years happened (the implication is that Max and Isabel's collective sadness caused it. They didn't seem to mind, though, spending the day building a snowman and throwing snowballs at Michael).

Soundtrack: Nelly Furtado's 'Like a Bird', 'Fade Into You' by Mazzy Star, Badly Drawn Boy's 'Another Pearl', 'I Wanna Destroy You' by the Soft Boys, 'Only One' by Lifehouse, Landing Gear's 'Atmosphere' and Emiliana Torrini's 'Wednesday's Child'. The episode's score is excellent, particularly the *Shaft*-style guitar riff in Kyle's semi-pornographic dream sequence.

Critique: 'It pains me to say this about a series that I loved so much,' noted Steve Donahue of *TV Guide online* in a review entitled 'Alien Bores Go Home'. 'The sad truth is that the once-electric WB sci-fi favourite has lost its creative juices, and worse, its focus ... In tonight's installment Max learns that a night of passion with Tess has resulted in her pregnancy. To make matters worse, Earth's atmosphere proves inhospitable to the unborn child, who may not survive. Nor may *Roswell* survive for another season, which is fairly astonishing considering the well-deserved buzz that surrounded it last year. Beyond the inferior scripts, the WB has also damaged the show with some peculiar scheduling. While the WB were spending the best part of a year wondering whether it would hold on to *Buffy*, someone at the shop should have been paying attention to what was happening to *Roswell*.'

Did You Know?: Several newspapers around this time reported the heartwarming story of Mundelein high school sophomore Jennifer Cavallero, who has juvenile rheumatoid arthritis. Whilst in hospital she met a representative from the Starlight Foundation which grants wishes to chronically ill children. 'They asked me to choose things I wanted to do,' said Jennifer. 'My first choice was to go to the set of *Roswell*.' And, sure enough Jennifer, her mother and her sister were flown to California to spend a day on set, meet the cast as well as visiting Disneyland and Universal Studio. At Covina, Jennifer noted, 'I was surprised how long it took to film ... Four hours for one minute and half a scene. There was a lot of standing around. The best part of the day was when I got a hug from Jason Behr.' Jennifer later told *CrashDown.com*, 'trust me, Jason is even cuter in person.'

42
Off the Menu

US Transmission Date: 14 May 2001
UK Transmission Date: 4 July 2001 (Sky One)

Writers: Russel Friend, Garrett Lerner
Director: Patrick Norris

Brody, using a virtual reality 'abduction simulator', receives an electric shock that gives him Larek's memories. He takes Max, Amy, Maria, Sean and Liz hostage in the UFO Center. Alien powers are useless against him, so Michael and Isabel, with the help of Sheriff Valenti, try to formulate a plan to end the siege before the local law forces can do anything drastic.

'I've Got the Power': Max uses his powers to deflect Brody's bullet into a picture but soon afterwards the effects of Larek's Trithium Amplification Generator (a pyramid-like device) blocks the Royal Four's powers. In The CrashDown, with all of the power off, Isabel heats her undercooked burger whilst complaining about the e-coli virus and 'mad cow disease' (bovine spongiform encephalopathy, BSE). Later, Max 'heals' Brody by removing Larek's memories and Tess uses her powers to make Amy forget what has happened (see **43**, 'The Departure').

Roswell Iconography: Amy has produced a (really lovely) GEORGE W IS AN ALIEN T-shirt which Sean wears to hide the fact that he has been stabbed. Brody has a number of crop-circle files which he wants Max to organise. Larek remembers that he and Zan first saw Ava at Demaras Rock (named after their planet's third moon), a beauty spot with crimson waters which is briefly glimpsed in one of Max's psychic flashes. Zan was too shy to speak to Ava so Larek made the first approach for him. Later, Zan and Ava met for the first time at the party mentioned in **38**, 'Heart of Mine'.

High School Life: On the telephone, Liz attempts to tell Maria about something 'amazing' that happened in Biology.

References: *Pulp Fiction* ('everything's pretty far from OK') and Napster, the former Internet music provider.

Teen-Speak: Maria, to Sean: 'How can you be wounded and on-the-make at the same time?'

Fashion Victims: Tess's light blue roll-neck sweater. She buys Max a black V-neck.

Logic, Let Me Introduce You to This Window: 'If you watch closely [the episode] contains the key to everything,' Maria announces. Huh? No it doesn't (see **43**, 'The Departure'). Maria's chalkboard scene features a horribly obvious bit of post-production dialogue overdubbing and a couple of nasty edits. It's confirmed for the first time since the Hybrid Chronicles finished that Valenti isn't the sheriff any more (see **33**, 'To Protect and Serve', and **34**, 'We Are Family'); Hanson has been promoted to replace him. Why? The man's clearly an idiot. Why didn't Sean bleed on the President Bush T-Shirt? If the stab wound was as serious as suggested earlier then shouldn't he have required medical attention immediately?

Quote/Unquote: Maria, on Larek taking over Brody's body: '[He] uses him as a human cell-phone. Why couldn't they invent an alien cell-phone. I mean, they're *aliens* . . .'

Liz: 'Maria just hung up on me.' Michael: 'Happens to me all the time.'

Michael, on Max: 'I think Vegas loosened him up.' Isabel: 'The guy irons his jeans.'

Amy angrily, to Sean as he tries to get them out of a locked room: 'Are you a criminal or not?'

Notes: 'You're an alien, aren't you?' This episode was filmed sixteenth during the season and was originally scheduled to broadcast before **38**, 'Heart of Mine'. And, goodness, doesn't it show? The hastily inserted Maria voice-over lines at the start to inform viewers that these events took place 'a few weeks ago' are a desperately poor attempt to explain why the story arc of the last few episodes has suddenly stopped dead. What follows is a real let down, with all of the tension that's been building up replaced by this rather false siege-scenario. Best bit: Jim encouraging Kyle to do a bit of breaking and entering at the library.

Brody drinks tea (well, he's English, what do you expect?), owns a gun, keeps a photo of himself and Sydney (see **32**, 'The Miracle') in the UFO Center and has an Apple Mac laptop that is linked to the internal security cameras and features a CD-R drive. Michael and Isabel both say that they don't take much notice of what Maria says when she's talking.

Soundtrack: Uncle Kracker's 'Follow Me', plus Joseph Stanley Williams' excellent score.

Critique: 'Fans take note,' the *Canberra Times* announced. 'Though it has a sizeable cult audience, *Roswell* is in danger of being axed by its American network. There are websites where fans can lodge support but, unfortunately, the one I visited was also in danger of being shut down. I can see why this show is in danger of disappearing; the producers seem unwilling to let a little sci-fi get in the way of a soap opera.'

43
The Departure

US Transmission Date: 21 May 2001
UK Transmission Date: 11 July 2001 (Sky One)

Writer: Jason Katims
Director: Patrick Norris

The time has come for the Royal Four to use the information in the decoded alien book and have the granilith return them home. But as the aliens say goodbye to their friends, families and lovers, Liz, Maria and Kyle make a terrible discovery about who was responsible for Alex's death.

'I've Got the Power': Max attempts to start an electrical fire in Jennifer's dorm room to punish her for what he believes to be her role in Alex's death. Liz, fortunately, stops him with the revelation (when Jennifer pricks her finger on a knitting needle) that the girl is human and had nothing to do with Alex at all, merely being a red-herring at the end of a complex trail placed by the real killer to cover their tracks.

Michael uses his powers to destroy Max's Jeep as the Royal Four prepare to leave.

Roswell Iconography: Max gives Liz the pendant from **7**, 'River Dog' as a parting gift, which angers her as she was expecting more – like, Max himself. Max says that the granilith is capable of being used to return them home only once. Thereafter it will be useless.

The Conspiracy Starts at Home Time: Kyle (with Maria and Liz's help) breaks through Tess's mind-control and remembers the events of 29 April. A frantic Alex arrived at the Valenti house to confront Tess, who had created the elaborate Swedish escapade as a cover for her use of Alex to decipher the alien book ('You mindwarped me for two months while I decoded that silly book for you and now there's nothing left for you to mindwarp. You destroyed my mind'). Tess reveals to Max that Nasedo made a deal forty years ago with Kivar that Nasedo (and Tess) would deliver the other three Royals home to Kivar once Tess became pregnant. Tess's mindwarp of Alex resulted in her accidentally killing him. To cover *this* up she used her powers on Kyle, convincing him that he was carrying luggage to the car. The sign that people who have been mindwarped by Tess are starting to remember fragments of reality is a constant drumming of the fingers, something that Kyle shares with Amy de Luca who, whilst sleepwalking, remembers the hostage events of **42**, 'Off the Menu'.

Dudes and Babes: Michael has never allowed Maria to 'see' him the way that Liz saw Max when they kissed. He says that he has spent his whole life afraid of letting others see him but rectifies this and lets Maria inside his mind. She sees flashes of his early life, including the moments immediately after he emerged from the pod (see **19**, 'Four Square'), his foster father's abuse of him (see **15**, 'Independence Day') and Maria herself, at the centre of his thoughts.

References: Michael cooks Maria dinner on plastic *Scooby Doo* plates. Ace's 'How Long'. Isabel quotes penal reformer John Bradford (1510–55) 'There but for the Grace-of-God ...' Kyle refers to Michael and Max as 'Heckle and Jekyll'. The Evanses are having Chinese food for dinner including a particular favourite of this author, shrimp toast.

Fashion Victims: Jennifer's blue blouse, Maria's leather jacket and her tight denim top.

Sex and Sex and More Sex: Maria and Michael sleep together. Although we don't actually see it, it's heavily implied that Liz also spends the night with Sean after Max breaks her heart by telling her that Tess is pregnant. Max mentions Liz apparently sleeping with Kyle in **27**, 'The End of the World'. Diane Evans has recently ordered digital cable and mentions a channel on which people discuss politics whilst naked. Wonder if Sky's got that one lined up for next year? Significantly, Michael is the only one of the Royal Four not to hug Valenti as they prepare to leave the planet. Too manly by far.

Logic, Let Me Introduce You to This Window: A real whopper: according to his grave, Alex was born 21 June 1984 and died 29 April 2001, meaning that he was just 15 when the series began and 16 when he died. How can that be, since he's in the same school year as Isabel who was born in 1982 and Max who was born in 1983? They've all been seen in class together on more than one occasion.

Quote/Unquote: Liz, to Max: 'I jumped off bridges for you.'

Max: 'How did I ever fall in love with someone like you? How could I ever marry you?' Tess: 'You were different. You were a king. Now you're just a boy.'

Notes: 'Everyone, say your goodbyes.' More evidence of last-minute production changes (Michael's sudden appearance taking over from Maria in the middle of the chalkboard scene with 'let me tell you what's *really* going on'). And the story pulls a real reset-button trick of making Tess the Big Bad enemy with no prior warning.

Was that a sop to the anti-Tess element in the series fandom, I wonder? There's some lovely stuff going on (Isabel having a final moment with Alex's 'ghost', Kyle in great form and Maria and Michael finally getting together as they were always intended to) but the sum of the parts doesn't add up to the memorable finale that this should have been.

Alex's date of death means that Kyle's birthday is 30 April (see **39**, 'Cry Your Name'). The epitaph on Alex's grave reads MAY YOUR SONG ALWAYS BE SUNG.

Soundtrack: The gorgeous cover of Lennon and McCartney's 'Blackbird' by doves, David Gray's 'My Oh My', Remy Zero's 'Perfect Memory', 'Trouble' by Coldplay and U2's 'Walk On' plays at the end of the episode, when Max tells Liz that he loves her.

Cast and Crew Comments: Brendan Fehr told the *NY Vue* that the relationship between Michael and Maria comes to a head in the season finale. 'We've been riding the fence and we finally choose one way to go with it. The fans will enjoy it, or they won't, depending on what they want,' he added, noting that the season will end with another cliff-hanger. However, whilst giving nothing away ('''cos I'm obligated not to') he was quick to acknowledge that plotlines keep leaking on to the Internet. 'These shows always have a mole. If we knew [who it was] it wouldn't happen, but it's not like the movies where George Lucas can keep *Star Wars* a secret. It's harder on a TV show, you've got extras mulling around. You have to send the scripts to the network and studio. Someone probably got a couple hundred bucks to sell the story to buy his wife a new ring.' Cynical, much?

Did You Know?: Among the popular fan rumours that *didn't* happen in 'The Departure' are the following: Tess mindwarped Max into just thinking they had sex and that she's pregnant; Tess craves salt as a symptom of alien PMS; Tess is revealed in the finale to be a pawn of Rath and Lonnie; Tess dies at the end; the Royal Four stage their own deaths; Liz tells Max about FutureMax; Liz and Kyle exhibit superpowers; Rath, Lonnie, Ava, or Nicholas (or all four) appear and Leanna is revealed to have killed Alex.

Kevin Kelly Brown told *popgurls.com*, 'We constantly throw fake spoilers out. Ninety per cent of what's on the spoiler board is wrong. Fans will put out spoilers that are not really spoilers at all but are their wishful thinking, their fantasising, their speculating. That stuff, we look at and go, "Huh? There's no way that came from our camp."'

The Future . . .?: 'It leaves a bunch of things wide open,' Brendan Fehr noted. 'But that doesn't guarantee that we have a third season. That's not up to us. I think the writers assumed that there will be one, but wrote it with the attitude, "If we don't, we don't. Too bad."'

The Roswell High Novels

*'At a time when most kids are trying to figure out who
they are, they're trying to figure out WHAT they are.'*

Book series advertisement

It may come as a surprise to many fans of the series, but
before there was a TV show, there were the books.

Written by Melinda Metz, a series of ten *Roswell High*
novels have appeared to date. The first, *The Outsider*, was
published, to some industry fanfare, by Archway in 1998.
The novels themselves are well-written teenage pulp-SF,
quick-moving with good characterisation and are worthy
of considerable attention. However, a word of warning,
although the pilot episode of *Roswell* was quite closely
based on the book series (and specifically the first novel),
subsequent episodes have had far less in common. The
characters of Liz and Alex have different surnames in the
books (Ortecho and Manes, respectively) and Liz is
described in the novels as a Hispanic girl.

Other significant differences: certain characters only exist
in one or the other medium (there's no Tess in the novels, for
instance). Certain relationships differ significantly, and what
we know so far about the TV aliens' powers and origins
suggests even more divergence to come. In the book series,
the main characters are all seniors (meaning that the novels
take place in a compressed time span of months rather than
years). Rachel Hyland of *The 11th Hour* web-magazine
believes that the novels 'walk all over the TV series in the
quality, plot, characterisation, wit, thoughtfulness, pop-
culture-aware and idealism departments.' What follows is a
very basic description of the novels published so far:

The Outsider, as noted, is very close to **1**, 'Pilot' except
for some minor details (Liz had a older sister, Rosa, who

died five years ago from a drug overdose). Max's explanation of where the aliens come from is dissimilar to the TV show. Valenti tells Liz he works for 'Project Clean Slate', a secret government organisation which exists to track down aliens. Maria and Alex learn of Max, Michael and Isabel's origins at the same time as Liz, and they all share a 'connection' in which they see each other's auras and hear a unique musical note. The next book, *The Wild One*, concerns another alien, Nikolas, who turns up on his motorcycle and with whom Isabel becomes involved, leading her into an orgy of petty crime. This makes Alex jealous and worries all of Izzy's friends. During a break-in at the mall, Nikolas is shot by Valenti. Whilst attempting to help straighten-out Isabel, Maria finds a mysterious ring. And Max's boss at the local museum, Ray Iburg, turns out to be another alien. This is probably the only novel (SF or otherwise) to include references to Elvis Presley *and* Carl Sagan in the same sentence.

In *The Seeker*, book three, Maria finds that by using the ring she gains telepathic powers. However, using it is very bad for her (or anyone else's) health. The ring is actually a homing device for alien bounty hunters, who are seeking a renegade alien who crashed on the ship that Max, Michael and Isabel were on in 1947. Michael, meanwhile, is having problems with his foster parents, the Pascals, whilst Alex's father (a major in the military) is also giving his son a hard time. Following on from this, *The Watcher* concerns Max suffering from his race's form of puberty and he has to link with the 'collective' or die. The only way that this can be done is to find where their ship is being held by the government. They discover the location, in a base just outside Roswell, and get some communication crystals, but Michael is captured.

This leads directly into *The Intruder*, in which Michael (held in a compound) meets another alien, Adam, who has been a prisoner at the base all his life. Valenti has told Adam that he is Adam's father. Isabel and Michael share a link, enabling her to know what he is feeling and making her wonder if they are meant to be together. Michael and

Adam are rescued and Valenti kills Ray before, himself, being killed by Adam. *The Stowaway* sees Michael getting involved with Cameron, a human girl from the compound, which upsets both Maria and Isabel. Both Adam and Isabel are possessed by another sinister alien, and the ring is used to force the possessor to emerge. An alien bounty hunter is called to open a wormhole to their planet to send the alien back for trial. However, Alex is sent by mistake and the wormhole closes, leaving him trapped on a strange planet with aliens who fear the unknown.

The Vanished has Max looking for a power-stone to get Alex back. Liz and Adam become close and discover that Alex's father is also a member of Clean Slate. But Major Manes assures them that he means them no harm. He tries to help them get Alex back but the plan fails. *The Rebel* sees Ray having left the museum to Michael in his will, enabling Michael to leave his tricky foster home situation and live independently (with Adam) in a flat above the museum. Alex returns out of the blue and, on the same night, Michael's previously unknown brother, Trevor, appears in town. But Trevor is not what he seems. Maria has a younger brother who is kidnapped by a deranged Kyle, in an attempt to uncover the truth about his father's death.

After this, *The Dark One* sees Isabel run away from home and Max, knowing that her life is in danger, trying to find her. Alex, meanwhile, is a changed man. He looks better, feels fitter and is ready to live life to the fullest – without Isabel. Little does he know, however, that he is the only person that can help to save her life. Book ten in the series, *The Salvation*, has recently been published in the US. From next season Melinda Metz will be joining the writing team on the TV series itself.

Roswell and the Internet

These days it seems unlikely there will ever be a TV series (particularly one dealing with the kind of subjects that *Roswell* does) that, if it's any good, fails to gain a vocal and passionate following on the Internet. We've seen this template before with *The X-Files*, *Stargate SG-1*, *Buffy* and *Angel*, *The Simpsons*, *Friends* and dozens of other series. Just as, once upon a time, *Star Trek*, *Doctor Who* and *Red Dwarf* fans communicated their love for their shows through fanzines, now a new generation of fans have usenet newsgroups, posting boards, mailing lists and websites to convey what they like (and dislike) about the series they watch. As Joan Giglione noted in the *Los Angeles Times*, 'Message boards are a way that Internet users can share a burning need to talk about their relationships with characters from *Roswell*, *The X-Files* and *Buffy*.'

Within weeks of *Roswell* beginning, a flourishing Net-fan-community had spawned numerous websites. As with most fandoms there is a lot of good stuff and a little bad in what has emerged. This is a rough guide to get you started.

Newsgroups: alt.tv.roswell is an unmoderated usenet group, discussing the merits of new and old episodes and including speculation on likely developments, rumours and other topics of general interest. It's an interesting forum with debate encouraged amongst participants though, as with most newsgroups, it does occasionally feature that curse of usenet, 'trolling' (people who deliberately send offensive messages to see what reaction they get). There is a fine FAQ (a list of Frequently Asked Questions) that is regularly posted, which will help acquaint new arrivals with what *not* to ask. According to this 'as of November 2000, it is common to see as many as 150 messages per day'. Encouraged topics of discussion include 'the premise of the series, plots, characters and the actors who play them, production staff, writing and the social impact of the show'.

Websites: There are literally hundreds of websites relating to *Roswell*. What follows is a (by no means definitive) list of some of this author's favourites, which should give readers an idea of where to start. Many of these are also part of webrings with links to other related sites. An hour's surfing can get you to some interesting places.

Disclaimer: Websites are transitory things at the best of times and this information, though accurate when it was written, may be woefully out of date by publication.

www.crashdown.com (CrashDown: The Roswell Experience) is one of the most impressive fan websites you will see for *any* series. Very active in the 'Save Roswell' campaign, it's a mighty collection of episode reviews, transcripts, a *huge* archive of interviews, cast biographies and press releases. The site also contains a message-board (which was actually up and running about a month before the series was first broadcast), a chat-room and sections for fan-fiction and artwork. Plus, the links page is *phenomenal*, with hypertext links to just about every other fan site worth mentioning. As Suze Campagna noted in *Intergalactic Enquirer* magazine: 'The CrashDown is maintained by several creative people and they accept submissions from other fans as well giving it a nice variety of content. This is a site for everyone, whether you are a new viewer or a long-term fan.' Hugely recommended. An affiliate site, roswell-high.com (*www.roswell-high.com/*), features a discussion board, interviews, spoilers and excellent picture galleries and wav-files.

www.danbbs.dk/ ~ smaalipz/roswell/actors.htm (Roswell: Meet the Stars) is a simple and well laid-out site featuring lots of information on the actors and thorough episode details. Another fine general site is *www.e-fansource.com/ roswellrevealed/* (Roswell Revealed) which also has a variety of interesting info sections, galleries, and a superb 'spoilers' page.

http://roswell.na.nu/ (Roswell MP3s) features excellent coverage of the music used in the series (a vital part of *Roswell*'s popularity), with sections dedicated to the bands featured and their lyrics. The Cutting Room Floor (*www.roswellscripts.com/*) is a macromedia site that contains downloads of first season scripts and deleted scenes for a fully interactive experience.

www.agalaxyfaraway.xrs.net/ (A Galaxy Far Away) has been recently reactivated. It takes a long time to load but is worth sticking with for some excellent fan-fiction, artwork, a message-board, a spoilers section and cast biographies. *Love* the little floaty alien-heads that follow you around the page! The Roswell Café (*www.angelfire.com/hi4/roswellgyrl/index2.html*) is yet another little gem of a site with some great photos.

http://anightonthetown.tripod.com/index4.html (A Night on the Town) strikes a good balance between humour and facts, featuring parodies, poetry and the self-explanatory 'Babes of Roswell' section. *www.angelfire.com/nm/ThreePodsFromHeaven* (1947: Three Pods From Heaven) has worthy episode reviews, a page on The CrashDown Café menu and lots of quotes. Similar features can also be found at Chocolate Cake and Hot Sauce (*www.tvsroswell.com/*) whose thorough episode coverage is complemented by such unique features as a birth chart of the stars, the amusing 'De Luca Shop' page and a message-board called 'The Eraser Room Wall' plus lots of interviews.

www.angelfire.com/scifi/leavingnormal/ (Leaving Normal) is an excellent site with the usual features on the cast and the episodes, but also extensive coverage of the Roswell High novels, the 'real story' of the 1947 crash and lots of multimedia extracts. Roswell Communicators (*http://roswellcommunicators.tripod.com/*) has detailed behind-the-scenes trivia, a 'story so far' section, a 'True Believers' archive and much fan fiction (all with PG ratings).

www.roswellian.org/main.htm (Roswellian.Org) features a news section, breathlessly excited coverage of several set visits by fans and lots of bare-torso photos of Brendan Fehr. Nice. Fans of the actor may like to supplement this impressive domain with BRENDAN-FEHR.COM (*www.brendan-fehr.com*) a well laid-out unofficial fan-site which has an 'Ask Brendan' section and loads of links to interviews and articles.

There are numerous unofficial websites dedicated to the main cast, some of the best include Jason Behr@Crash-Down Café (*http://Sonya7599.tripod.com/home.htm*), Colin Hanks Online (*http://funny.as/ColinHanks*), Majandra-Delfino.Com (*majandra-delfino.com*), Shiri Appleby Ultimate (*http://clubs.yahoo.com/clubs/shiriapplebyultimatefanclub*), Emilie: A Shimmering Star (*www.angelfire.com/celeb/Emilie/Main.html*) and the wonderful Katherine-Heigl.Com (*katherine-heigl.com*) which is every bit as good-looking as the actress it's dedicated to. Outcasts (*www.wearenow.com/outcasts*) is a charming, and proudly unique, 'Kyle and Tess' site with fan-fiction, pictures and biogs of Nick and Emilie, whilst Kyle-fans will also need to get registered with the Kyle Valenti Estrogen Brigade otherwise known as 'Fans Understand Cranky Kyle' (*www.fortunecity.com/lavender/hoskins/263/*). Tess-fans might like to give The Alienist (*www.geocities.com/puppy_got_out/*) a miss, however. This is the home of 'R.A.G.E' an anti-Tess group of some bile and spite. There's much related fan-fiction included. William Sadler's many admirers are directed to the actor's fabulous official site Wild on the Web (*www.williamsadler.com*).

Readers wishing to sample more *Roswell* fan-fiction need look no further than the excellent Roswell Fan-Fiction Museum (*http://members/nbci.com/ff_museum/*) which features the full range of 'Shipper' fiction, plus more diverse material, much of it of a very high standard. Also worthy of your attention are Czechoslovakians Can't Resist Temptation (*www.geocities.com/LizParker8/Czech.html*) which has a fan-fiction section, though it's been stuck in limbo recently due to its editor being 'grounded'. Other worthy fan-fiction can be found on the multi-character Candy

Dream Gazers (*http://candydreamgazers.homestead.com/
enter.html*) and the excellent Dreamweavers (*http://dream-
weavers.myqth.com/*) hosted by Laura, Nicole and Courtney,
which has some top quality fiction and a very useful 'lingo'
section. This explains lots of the terminology in fan-fic
circles. 'Candy Clan' are Maria/Michael 'shippers, 'Star-
gazers' are Alex/Isabel 'shippers, etc. Lastly, Ender's
Unconventional Couples Roswell Fiction (*www.geoci-
ties.com/enderguerin/index.html*) is just the site for those
adult readers interested in both Slash and Het-erotica.

http://ozwellian.cjb.net/ (Ozwellian: The Australian Roswell
Embassy) is a smashing site with an extensive bloopers
section and impressive episode and books reviews. Another
Aussie domain, Oz Crash Festival (*www.users.bigpond.com/
eleen/*) prides itself on being 'a site jam packed with all you
ever needed to know about the show', and has many
unique features like 'The Style Files' (where you virtually
dress your favourite character), floor plans of the sets, alien
information, brilliant episode summaries and lots of
behind-the-scenes tidbits.

Roswell is also popular in many other countries, amongst
the most interesting unofficial non-English-language sites
are: Sweden's Roswell: En Annan Planet (*www.envy.nu/
roswellian/*), Germany's Die Inoffizielle Roswell Homepage
(*www.roswell-planet.de*), Finland's FIRoswell (*www.geoci-
ties.com/firoswell*), Brazil's RoswellBR (*http://orbita.star-
media.com/* ∼max_evans/*), France's Roswell's World
(*http://sev.cid.free.fr/roswellsworld.html*), Italy's Roswell-
italia (*www.roswellitalia.com*) and Denmark's RoswellDK
(*www.roswelldk.homestead.com/*).

Finally, two UK sites, Roswell-1947-Centre (*www.ros-
well1947centre.homestead.com/*), a little treasure-trove of
photos, episode reviews and coverage of the books, and
Funki Alien (*www.e-fansource.com/funkialien/*) a general
site featuring a bit of everything.

Bibliography

The following books, articles, interviews and reviews were consulted in the preparation of this text:

Alexander, Starr, '*Roswell* Star from Albuquerque', *Daily Lobo*, 5 October 1999.

Antonucci, Mike, 'Here's Hoping That . . .', *San Jose Mercury News*, 29 September 2000.

Atherton, Tony, 'Fantasy TV: The New Reality', *Ottawa Citizen*, 27 January 2000.

Atkinson, Richard, 'Men Are From Mars: My boyfriend is an alien! Teenagers have it hard nowadays, especially at Roswell High', *Starburst*, Special #43, Summer 2000.

Ault, Suzanne, ' "Hollow" Carves Most Saturn Awards Nominations', Associated Press, 15 March 2000.

Baxter, Greg, 'Frakes to Guide *Roswell* Towards Older Generation', *Los Angeles Times*, 10 April 2000.

Behr, Jason, 'Behr Essentials', interview by Paul Simpson and Ruth Thomas, *DreamWatch*, issue 68, April 2000.

Berliner, Don, and Friedman, Stanton T, *Crash at Corona: The US Military Retrieval and Cover-Up of a UFO*, Marlowe & Co, 1997.

Berlitz, Charles and Moore, William L, *The Roswell Incident*, Berkley Publishing, 1991.

Brady, James, 'In Step With . . . Jason Behr', *Parade*, 15 October, 2000.

Britt, Donna, 'The Truth About Teen TV', *TV Guide*, 28 October 2000.

Brown, Lars-Erik, 'See It Before It Vanishes', *Canberra Times*, 14 May 2001.

Bryson, Jodi, 'Heavenly Creatures', *Teen*, November 2000.

Bundy, Kim, 'Skin and Bones' review, *Cinescape*, October 2000.

Calderone, Samantha, *Meet the Stars of Roswell: An Unauthorized Biography*, Scholastic Inc., 2000.

Campagna, Suzanne, 'CrashDown: The *Roswell* Experience', *Intergalactic Enquirer*, May 2000.

Campagna, Suzanne, 'TV Tidbits', *Intergalactic Enquirer*, March 2001.

Cardy, Tom, 'Aliens Show-Off the Planet', *Evening Post* (Wellington, New Zealand), 23 February 2000.

Carter, Bill, '*Dawson's* Clones: Tapping into the Youth Market for All it is, or isn't, Worth', *New York Times*, 19 September 1999.

Carter, Chelsea J, 'Five Questions with Colin Hanks', *Bergan Record*, 17 March 2000.

'Celebrity Shame', *Dolly*, October 2000.

'Close Encounters of the Teen Kind', *New York Daily News*, 23 April 2001.

Cornell, Paul, Day, Martin and Topping, Keith, *X-Treme Possibilities: A Comprehensively Expanded Rummage Through the X-Files*, Virgin Publishing, 1998.

Cornell, Paul, 'Dreams for 2001', *SFX*, issue 74, February 2001.

'Crash for *Roswell*', *Dreamwatch*, issue 69, May 2000.

Day, Martin, and Topping, Keith, *Shut It! A Fan's Guide to 70s Cops on the Box*, Virgin Publishing, 1999.

de Ravin, Emilie, 'Rising Star', *Cosmogirl*, 1 January 2001.

de Ravin, Emilie, 'Going Ravin Mad!', interview by Ian Spelling, *Xposé*, issue 52, January 2001.

'Death Warmed Up', *DreamWatch*, issue 63, November 1999.

Delfino, Majandra, 'Woman on the Verge', interview by Rob Hill, *Playboy*, October 2000.

Delfino, Majandra, 'Earthy Girl', interview by Ian Spelling, *Starlog* issue 12, April 2001.

Dougherty, Diana, '*Roswell* Episode Guide', *Intergalactic Enquirer*, June 2000.

Durham, Rena, 'CreepySexyCool Brendan Fehr', *Popstar!*, December 2000.

Fehr, Brendan, '10 Things You Never Knew About . . .', *Xposé*, issue 52, January 2001.

Fehr, Brendan, 'All the Fun of the Fehr', interview by Ian Spelling, *Xposé*, Special 15, May 2001.

Freedman, Linda, 'What's Next for Colin Hanks?', *Teen People*, December 2000.

Friedman, Stanton T, and Striber, Whitley, *Top Secret/Majic*, Marlowe & Co, 1997.

Giglione, Joan, 'Some Shows Aren't Big on TV', *Los Angeles Times*, 25 November 2000.

Goodman, Tim, '*Roswell* Mixes Noirish Sci-Fi with *Dawson's Creek*', *San Francisco Examiner*, 6 October 1999.

Green, Michelle Erica, 'Darla and Topolsky Are More Than Bad Girls', *Fandom Inc*, September 2000.

Hamilton, Kendall, 'All of Life's Little Mysteries', *Newsweek*, 2 October 1999.

Havens, Candace, pilot episode review, *Talkin' TV*, September 1999.

Huff, Richard. 'WB Net Returns to Gender-Build on Initial Appeal Among Young Women', *New York Daily News*, 14 September 1999.

Huff, Richard, 'Future is Rosier for *Roswell*', *New York Daily News*, 27 April 2000.

Hyland, Rachel, 'From Whence They Came', *The 11th Hour*, 2000.

'The IT Girl – Shiri Appleby', *Dolly*, December 2000.

Jackson, Terry, 'WB Matches Teens/Aliens in *Roswell*', *Miami Herald*, 24 July 1999.

Kaplan, Don, '*Roswell* Hopes for Same Fate as *Buffy*', *New York Post*, 14 May 2001.

'Katherine Heigl: LA Life', *Los Angeles Daily News*, 27 June 2000.

Keveney, Bill, 'When it's Quality Vs. Ratings, Casualties Abound', *The Charlotte Observer*, 31 August 2000.

Klass, Philip J, *The Real Roswell Crashed-Saucer Cover Up*, Prometheus Books, 1997.

Kronke, David, 'Alienation Permeates Teen-Themed *Roswell*', *Los Angeles Daily News*, 5 October 1999.

Lane, Andy, *The Babylon File*, Virgin Publishing, 1997.

Lane, Andy and Simpson, Paul, *The Bond Files: The Unofficial Guide to the World's Greatest Secret Agent* [revised edition], Virgin Publishing, 2000.

Levy, David, *Skywatching: The Ultimate Guide to the Universe*, Harper Collins, 1995.

Lowry, Brian, 'Graybeards Trip Up Youth Movement', *Los Angeles Times*, 9 November 1999.

McIntee, David, *Delta Quadrant: The Unofficial Guide to Voyager*, Virgin Publishing, 2000.

McLeod, Tyler, 'Surprise *Roswell* Finale', *Calgary Sun*, 15 May 2000.

Marsh, Tanya D, '*X-Files* Meets *Felicity*', *TV Guide Online*, October 1999.

Mason, David, 'Fates To Be Revealed on *X-Files*, *Roswell*', *Ventura County Star*, May 2000.

Mendoza, Manuel, 'The caring teens on WB's *Roswell* really *are* from a different planet', *Dallas Morning News*, 29 January 2000.

Moore, Richard, 'Leaving Normal', *Xposé*, issue 42, January 2000.

Moore, Ronald D, 'Moore the Merrier', interview by Jim Swallow, *SFX*, issue 74, February 2001.

O'Hare, Kate, 'OtherWorlds', *Ultimate TV*, 13 March 2000.

O'Leary, Devin, The Idiot Box: 'Alien Angst', *Weekly Wire*, 25 October 1999.

Patton, Philip, *Dreamland: Travels Inside the Secret World of Roswell and Area 51*, Villard Books, 1999.

Pennington, Gail, 'Get up to speed on TV favourites', *St Louis Post*, 21 June 2000.

'Readers Say *Roswell* Should Stay', *USA Today*, 1 May 2001.

'Returning Favourites', *TV Guide*, 9 September 2000.

Robins, J Max, 'The Robins Report: How *Roswell* was Saved', *TV Guide*, 29 July 2000.

Rosenthal, Phil, 'Will Your Show Go On', *Chicago Sun-Times*, 12 April 2001.

'*Roswell* Ends Season on High', *DreamWatch*, issue 68, April 2000.

'*Roswell* Episode Review' ['Blind Date'], *Cinescape*, February 2000.

'Roswell Girls', *Celebrity Hairstyle*, May 2001.

'*Roswell* Revelations', *Science Fiction World*, issue 3, August 2000.

'*Roswell* Second Season Preview', *Sci Fi Magazine*, October 2000.

Roush, Matt, 'The Roush Review. Midterm Crisis – Frothy *Felicity* Deserved Seniority', *TV Guide*, 18 November 2000.

Saler, Benson, Zieglar, Charles A, and Moore, Charles B, *UFO Crash at Roswell: The Genesis of a Modern Myth*, Smithsonian Institute Press, 1997.

Salomaa, Janne, 'Emilie de Ravin: "I was teased and rejected"', *Suosikki*, March 2001.

Sangster, Jim and Bailey, David, *Friends Like Us: The Unofficial Guide to Friends* [revised edition], Virgin Publishing, 2000.

Schneider, Michael, '*Roswell* Joins *Buffy* for UPN Fall Lineup', *Variety*, 16 May 2001.

Simpson, Paul and Thomas, Ruth, 'Miko Hughes', *Cable Guide Online*, February 2001.

Simpson, Paul and Thomas, Ruth, 'Shiri Appleby interview', *Xena Magazine*, March 2001.

Spelling, Ian, 'Desert Hearts', *Xposé*, issue 39, October 1999.

Spelling, Ian, 'The Kids are E.T.', *Cult Times*, January 2000.

Spelling, Ian, 'The Law in Roswell', *Starlog*, issue 272, March 2000.

Starr, Michael, 'Can Hot Sauce Save This Show?', *New York Post*, 7 April 2000.

'Starstruck', *Daily Herald*, 19 April 2001.

St Germain, Pat, 'All's Fehr in Hollywood', *Winnipeg Sun*, 2 March 2001.

Streisand, Betsy, 'Young, Hip and No-Longer-Watching-Fox', *US News & World Report*, 15 Nov 1999.

Strobe, Clement K, 'Leaving Normal', 'Missing', '285 South' and 'River Dog' reviews, *Xposé*, issue 42, January 2000.

Strobe, Clement K, 'The End of the World', 'The Harvest', 'Wipe-Out!' and 'Meet the Dupes' reviews, *Xposé*, issue 52, January 2001.

Swallow, Jim, 'The Spoof is Out There: The *Roswell* Incident and Other Fairy Stories', *Trash City*, issue 22, August 1999.

'This Babel-ing Business is Confusing', *Orlando Sentinel*, 13 April 2001.

'Tonight's Satellite Choice', *Evening Chronicle*, 11 April 2001.

Topping, Keith, *Slayer: The Revised and Updated Unofficial Guide to Buffy the Vampire Slayer*, Virgin Publishing, 2001.

Topping, Keith, *Hollywood Vampire: The Unofficial Guide to Angel*, Virgin Publishing, 2000.

Topping, Keith, 'Hot Spot', *DreamWatch*, issue 66, February 2000.

Topping, Keith, 'Highs & Lows', *DreamWatch*, issue 70, June 2000.

Topping, Keith, 'Teenage Kicks – How the Kids of *Roswell* Changed', *Intergalactic Enquirer*, April 2001.

Tucker, Ken, '*Roswell* Review', *Entertainment Weekly*, October 2000.

'TV Boys: How They Found Fame', *J-14*, May 2001.

Weeks, Janet, 'John Doe Finds New Beat on *Roswell*', *TV Guide Ultimate Cable*, 5 February 2000.

Weinstein, Farrah, 'Katherine Heigl Interview', *New York Post*, 6 February 2000.

Wright, Matthew, 'Endings and New Beginnings', *Science Fiction World*, issue 2, July 2000.

Think About The Future

During early 2001 things looked relatively healthy in the *Roswell* camp. Having survived a slight slip in ratings the show was, seemingly, back-in-the-black as far as the WB was concerned (although it has a loyal and vocal following, *Roswell*'s ratings have always been 'average' at around four million viewers per episode). Then something completely out of the production's control changed all the rules.

A season-long fight between Fox, the company that produces *Roswell*, and the WB, the network that broadcasts it, over the future of another of the WB's Fox-produced shows, *Buffy the Vampire Slayer*, culminated in the sale of that series to the UPN network. This, effectively, killed *Roswell*'s future at the WB along with that of another Fox show, *Popular*. As early as 24 April, just days after the *Buffy* decision had been made public, industry magazines were reporting that *Roswell* had another, greater, cancellation fight on its hands. And Brendan Fehr, for one, couldn't see them winning it, famously telling a reporter, 'We're outta here!' ('I think I'd be ignorant to say whether or not we'll be back,' Brendan told Ian Spelling of *Xposé*. 'Right now, with all the political stuff that's happening with *Buffy*, Fox, the WB and contracts, we're a pawn.') 'Taking us off the air for six weeks was definitely not a good sign,' Ronald Moore told Kate O'Hare around the same time. 'There was no way to spin that as a positive thing, so we knew that was a bad omen.' It seemed, for several days that Max saying 'This isn't over, Tess' in **43**, 'The Departure' was to be a hollow lie.

However, a crumb of encouragement arrived in the shape of *Variety* magazine which confidently announced that, if the WB dropped *Roswell*, UPN was likely to pick it up. This view was substantiated by a radio interview given by Jonathan Frakes in Boston a week later. The *Buffy* situation made renewal 'more of a challenge', Jason Katims told *USA Today*, but he hoped that level heads would prevail. 'There might be heated feelings, but it's stories you have to look at, not the politics or business involved.' The *Ain't it Cool* website reported on 1 May that, although *Roswell* was the threatened show most *USA Today* readers wanted to save, 'media buyers have been e-mailing us all day suggesting that Fox has already gotten unofficial word that, despite the fan outcry, the WB would definitely not be renewing *Roswell*'. Finally on 14 May, the expected news arrived that *Roswell* had been dropped by the WB without further comment or, seemingly, any regret. Don Kaplan in the *New York Post* noted that 'The series has been axed by the WB, but it may hook up with *Buffy* at UPN and air right after the super-popular vampire show.' 'I know that UPN has been seriously interested in *Roswell* for several weeks,' executive producer Kevin Kelly Brown was quoted as saying. 'We very much appreciate that UPN is interested. I don't think anyone can imagine a more killer night than putting *Buffy* and *Roswell* together. To me that's got "homerun" written all over it.'

The fans, of course, had already swung into action, bombarding UPN with Tabasco sauce bottles. Additionally, the production was able to deliver an online petition to save the show signed by about 30,000 fans (including this author, incidentally). 'Aren't these the kind of fans that networks pray for?' Jason Katims asked. 'But we could not have been happier with these past two years at the WB,' Brown was careful to remind the *Post*. 'People tend to forget that the WB rescued us when Fox Broadcasting passed us up. Were it not for them, we wouldn't exist.'

Finally, after an agonising wait of two more days, on 16 May, Michael Schneider in *Variety* announced that 'the alien teens of *Roswell* will join *Buffy* on the trans-network express from the WB to UPN next fall. UPN sealed an 11th-hour deal [for] 22 episodes of *Roswell* from Fox and Regency TV. Both sides had been hammering out an agreement all week.' 'We were fortunate that a show that had been growing on the WB became available,' said UPN's Dean Valentine. 'It's a terrific show and it's got a fanatical audience.' 'I think our fans would go anywhere to see the show,' Jason Katims, told Kate O'Hare. 'They get on a plane and fly to Los Angeles to go to a party, so they'll definitely be able to change the channel!' 'UPN is owned by Paramount which is owned by Viacom,' Brown told *Popgurls.com*. 'Viacom also owns MTV which last year shared *Celebrity Deathmatch* with UPN. I think it would be ideal to use the same plan to promote *Roswell* which is ideal for the MTV audience.'[18]

Interviewed by *E Daily News* the next day, Shiri Appleby spoke of the relief felt by everyone connected with the show: 'It's just wonderful to be at a network that's supportive. Two days ago, we weren't on television at all. Now we have a full season ahead of us.' In today's cut-throat ratings and demographics-driven world of television as the business of compromise, and of business itself, that's often as much as fans of *any* series can dare to dream. But *Roswell* has been to the brink of the precipice twice and been hauled back each time almost entirely because of the support that it has received from its dedicated, loyal and vocal fanbase. And even in today's TV world, that really *does* seem to count for something.

---

[18] At the time of writing, it appears that the third season of *Roswell* will begin on Tuesday 9 October 2001 at 9 p.m. on the UPN. Many celebration parties are planned by fans around the world. One thing about your average *Roswell* fan, they like a party!